EDITORIAL CORRECTION COPY
Do Not Remove From Library

THE RV/TRUCK/VAN CONVERSION GUIDE

THE RV/TRUCK/VAN CONVERSION GUIDE

BY THE EDITORS OF 4X4'S AND OFF-ROAD VEHICLES AND TRAVELIN' VANS

MODERN AUTOMOTIVE SERIES

BLUE RIDGE SUMMIT, PA. 17214

FIRST EDITION

FIRST PRINTING

Copyright © 1982 by TAB BOOKS Inc.

Printed in the United States of America

Reproduction or publication of the content in any manner, without express permission of the publisher, is prohibited. No liability is assumed with respect to the use of the information herein.

Library of Congress Cataloging in Publication Data

Main entry under title:

The RV/truck/van conversion guide.

    Includes index.
    1. All terrain vehicles—Design and construction. I. 4 × 4's and off-road vehicles. II. Title: R.V./truck/van conversion guide. III. Title: Recreation vehicles/truck/van conversion guide.
TL235.6.R86   629.2'2042   81-18368
ISBN 0-8306-2109-1 (pbk.)   AACR2

Contents

	Introduction	ix
1	**Ford Courier Conversion** V-8 Engine—More Modifications	1
2	**Rebuilding a Small-Block Chevy Engine** Torque Output—Compression Ratio—Intake Manifolds and Camshafts—Engine Preparation and Assembly	5
3	**Quadravan Transformation** Seats and Seat Belts—Other Features	16
4	**Kal Kustom Kit**	23
5	**Four-Wheel-Drive Mini-Truck Conversions** Baja Conversion Kit—Results	30
6	**Camshafts** Getting the Shaft—Dictionary Diversions—Selecting an Off-Road Cam—How Valve Train Affects Cam Performance—How to Swap Your Own Cam the Right Way	38
7	**Installing Electric Windows** Installation Procedure—Kit Instructions	67
8	**Installing Headers on a 4×4** Removing Exhaust Pipes and Exhaust Manifolds—Exhaust Pipe Installation	78

9	**Engine Oil Coolers** Function of an Oil Cooler—Oil Cooler Installation—Oil Heating Facts	88
10	**Grille Guard for a Blazer**	100
11	**Keeping the Kinks Out of Your Hood** Installing Hood Stiff'Ners—Realigning the Hood	102
12	**Performance Shocks for Your 4×4** High-Performance Shocks—Definition of a Shock Absorber—Twin-Tube Shocks—Monotube Shocks	107
13	**CompuSensor Ignition System** Breaker-Point and LED-Type Distributors—Capacitive Discharge (CD) Units—Facts on the CompuSensor System	115
14	**Security Systems** Vehicle Theft—Jacobs Stop Action—Gora Fuel Lock—Clifford Computerized Preprogrammed Locks—Ungo Box—Unistop Stop Hit	123
15	**Trans-Go Kit** Gil Younger's Work—Research Company	143
16	**Facelifting the Chevy Blazer** Ruff Rider Grille—Headlights	152
17	**Installing Superior Running Boards**	157
18	**Building a Swinging Step** Construction Tips—Mounting the Step	165
19	**GMC Sierra Truck** Suspension—Cab Protection	168
20	**Removing and Replacing Locking Hubs**	171
21	**Liquid Petroleum Gas Conversion** Sonny Bono's Jeep Wagoneer—Propane—Conversion Advantages—Conversion Disadvantages	174
22	**Installing Rigid Racks**	185
23	**Improving Basic Suspension on Vans** Rear Suspension—Front Suspension—Shock Absorbers—Stabilizer Bars	188
24	**Installing Dual Batteries**	193

25	**Installing an Auxiliary Fuel Tank**	**201**
26	**Installing a Door Extender**	**209**
27	**Changing a Roof Vent to a Roof Scoop**	**217**
28	**Installing Flooring** Particle Board and Screws—Procedure	**221**
29	**Installing Headers for a Van** Function of Headers—Installation Steps	**230**
30	**Hooking Up Sidepipes** Hooker's Universal Sidemount Exhaust System—Procedure	**238**
31	**Insulating a Van's Interior** Foam Rubber—Fiberglass	**246**
32	**Installing a Sunroof**	**253**
33	**Installing Flares and Spoiler**	**266**
34	**Installing Maserati Air Horns** Mounting the Horns—Plastic Air Hoses and Relay	**274**
35	**Installing a Roof Rack and Ladder** Mounting the Ladder—Roof Rack	**279**
	Index	**289**

Introduction

Van and 4×4 owners are always looking for ways to improve the appearance and performance of their vehicles. This book offers plenty of suggestions.

Among the projects are a conversion/modification/customizing job on a Ford Courier, the transformation of a Quadravan, a four-wheel-drive conversion for a mini-truck, and the installation of a Trans-Go kit to increase the durability of a truck's automatic transmission.

There is a chapter on vans' suspension systems. Other van projects are the installation of a dual battery setup, an auxiliary fuel tank, and a door extender; replacement of a roof vent with a roof scoop; and the addition of a sunroof, flares, air horns, roof rack, and ladder.

Chapters on camshafts, engine oil coolers, performance shocks, and security systems are included. The installation of electric windows, headers, and running boards is explained. You can save plenty of money by doing the work yourself.

The editors of *4×4's & Off-Road Vehicles* and *Travelin' Vans* have supplied the material for this book. Without their efforts and cooperation, the book would not be possible.

Chapter 1

Ford Courier Conversion

The new Courier was purchased in the latter part of 1976. It had a deluxe interior, tinted glass, rear step bumper, and chrome side molding options. After driving the vehicle a few hundred miles to determine if any factory warranty was needed, the transition was begun.

The front end (all that could be unbolted) was removed. This included the hood, radiator, bumper, engine and transmission, and related parts. The axle assembly and suspension system was cut away leaving only the bare frame rails. A new front cross member was added and longer than usual leaf springs were installed, using an outrigger rear spring perch of special design. This setup would ultimately give a much improved ride and a lower front end.

A Spicer 30 front-axle assembly was installed intact (spring pads remained in original position). A special boxed front spring shackle was made and used. A Bronco power-steering unit was set in, attached to the outside of the left frame rail. A special Pitman arm was made, which had a broader arc and was extended 3 inches lower. This was done to give the vehicle a lock-to-lock turning radius of under four revolutions of the steering wheel. Special shock mounts were installed to the frame, and Gabriel shocks were mounted.

V-8 ENGINE

Next came the hard part—installation of the V-8 engine (Fig. 1-1). A Ford specially prepared 302 V-8 and four-speed Ford top-loader trans assembly was set in and out of the normal space occupied by the engine so many times that we lost count. Each time, some other unforeseen modification was made until finally everything fit. (Five cubic feet were reprogrammed to fit into 3 cubic feet.)

Fig. 1-1. The 302 V-8 was modified from start to finish. The building and installation was all done by the owner (photo by Blaine Lentz).

A Hurst shift kit was attached to the trans, and a Dana 20 transfer case was attached via an Advance Adapter kit to the four-speed. A new boxed cross member was made and installed (Fig. 1-2). The rear-axle assembly was replaced with a Spicer limited-slip model 44 assembly. This rear end was subsequently made full-floating with the installation of special axles and hubs. The original spring pads were removed and placed on the top of the axle housing. New lower shock mounts were made, and gas-adjust shocks were installed. To get back to the front section of the vehicle, the location of the original Courier radiator was now gone. The entire panel to which this attached was removed and modified to make way for the much longer V-8 engine. Now a new location for the new radiator (Bronco cross-flow) was fabricated ahead of the original location. The radiator sits in two rubber cradles on the bottom and is held in place by two similar cradles on the top, making it very easy to remove or install the radiator.

The engine is endowed with the following: Edelbrock Torker manifold, Holly 600 cfm, Igniter ignition, Crower Baja cam, and lifters—which makes for a pretty healthy "little sleeper."

An air-conditioning condenser was added to the front of the radiator, and then the grille was reattached. After the front bumper was reinstalled, as Superwinch and front push-bar assembly was installed. A slight modification was made to the bottom portion of the push-bar to attach to the new front cross member, and a frame-mounted tow bar (removable) was made integral with the push-bar and bumper.

Back in the engine compartment for a minute, the full-flow oil filter was rerouted and relocated to a spot up high in the engine compartment for much better access.

To finish up in the engine compartment, special headers were fabricated by Stan's Headers in South Gate and, after a bracket was fabricated for

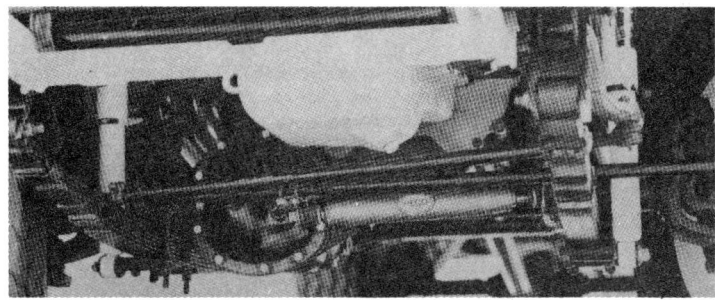

Fig. 1-2. Special front end incorporates a new cross member, extra-long leaf springs, Spicer 30 axle assembly, a Bronco power-steering unit, Gabriel shocks on relocated mounts, and a hydraulic steering stabilizer for total performance off-road (photo by Blaine Lentz).

it, the compressor and remaining air-conditioning components were installed. With all parts attached, including air filter, the hood closed with no modifications.

MORE MODIFICATIONS

Next the front fender wells were modified to accept the Firestone 10×15 All Terrain tires and 15×8 Appliance white spoke wheels. No modification was needed for the rear wheels which, incidentally, are All

Fig. 1-3. Interior features thick plush carpet with matching high-back buckets, plus an AM-FM 8-track stereo and Hurst shift linkage throughout (photo by Blaine Lentz).

Fig. 1-4. The only thing we could find left stock on this truck was the letters across the hood that say F O R D (photo by Blaine Lentz).

Terrain 11×15 on 10-inch rims for a little wider rear traction (the diameter is the same). Fiberglass fenders were then installed on all four fenders.

After a new floorboard was fabricated to cover the new trans and transfer case, the vehicle was sent to Jeff's Place in Fullerton for its beautiful paint job.

New thicker carpeting and matching-color bucket seats were installed (Fig. 1-3). A booted rear sliding window was installed for access to the fiberglass sleeper over bed. The bed is heavily carpeted and protected by a double, specially made, roll bar by "Smittybilt." Two KC Daylighters attach to the top of the sleeper.

After completing all the aforementioned modifications, it was decided to go a little farther. The Ford toploader was pulled, and a Ford C-4 auto trans was installed in its place. This turned out to be quite an undertaking, as it necessitated a new cross member location, longer front drive shaft, shorter rear drive shaft—and the floorboard was redesigned, eliminating most of the hump in the floor. This latest conversion of trans has made the vehicle much more effortless to drive in the city and doesn't hurt its performance off-road.

It took approximately four months to complete the entire conversion and *much* money, considering that the truck and all the component parts used in the conversion were new (Fig. 1-4). The truck is very strong, comfortable, easy to drive, and absolutely quiet. With the windows up, the air on, the 8-track stereo playing—and by ignoring a lot of stares from other motorists—you are in whatever type vehicle you want to imagine: a sports car, a hot rod, a luxury coupe, a "Travelin' 4×4," or a Ford Courier.

Chapter 2

Rebuilding a Small-Block Chevy Engine

When engine rebuilding time rolls around, it is wise to consider what can be done to improve the performance of your 4×4 under driving conditions that *you* expect it to encounter. Typically, and with few exceptions, your 4×4 is probably powered by a basic passenger-car engine. Though this practice has only become popular over the last six or seven years, economics (from Detroit's point of view) makes it necessary.

Prior to 1970, Chevrolet's truck engines were *really* heavy-duty. Though detuned for truck use, their basic specifications were very similar to the formidable super-car engines of the era. This not only provided closer to bulletproof dependability, but gave them longevity under severe operating conditions.

You might think that you pamper your engine because you drive relatively slowly when off the road. Low-speed lugging, though, particularly with high (numerically) axle ratios, can be more detrimental to engine performance and durability than can constant-speed conditions found on streets and highways.

Admittedly, a 4×4 is equipped with special gearing to help a passenger-car engine cope with its new environment, but this is not always the case. A good case in point is to take a Blazer, equip it with full-time four-wheel drive (4WD), automatic transmission, and a mountain of optional equipment, then fit it with 2.76 or 3.07 axle ratio as standard equipment.

They're striving for improved gas mileage with those high ratios, but the truth is that they are really limiting the efficiency of the vehicle as a whole. Generally, these *economy* measures backfire. And the proof is that the same Blazer, equipped with tall tires (10-15 or larger), can get similar, if not better, mileage utilizing *4.11 gears*. If you've ever driven a Blazer equipped with these low cogs, *you know* what the factory is giving up in the way of driveability.

Full-time 4WD and an automatic transmission used in combination will give up some 15 to 20 percent of its power just turning the transfer case and front axle gears, and pumping oil through the transmission.

What to do about this factory mismatch is another thing. There have been numerous articles expounding surefire ways to improve performance as well as economy, or both in combination, but the only realistic approach to the problem is to rebuild your engine from scratch, and match it to *your* driving needs. We are going to try to outline some of the points worth your attention, but again, we can't recommend a cure-all for improper gearing, low-octane fuel, or a vehicle that weighs 10,000 pounds. Many deficiencies are built-in and can't be reworked without spending huge amounts of money that would eventually offset any actual rewards in improved economy and/or dependability.

How does an engine suitable for off-roading differ from a conventional passenger-car engine, or a racing engine? It must operate in an entirely different rpm range in most cases. A pasenger-car engine that has the automatic transmission to multiply its torque output at low speeds usually operates, in the 1700 to 3000-rpm range—the latter usually being exceeded only by kickdown during passing.

A race engine operates in a much higher range, usually between 4000 and 8000 rpm, since it produces very little torque at low engine speeds. Thus, it needs the high revs to produce power, which is a product of torque.

TORQUE OUTPUT

This leads us to believe that all we must do is redesign the little Chevy engine to produce as much low-speed torque as possible. Theoretically, that's the case in a nutshell, but it's easier said than done. Torque output for the most part is a product of engine displacement, and to a lesser degree, crankshaft stroke. Generally, you can assume that a typical engine will produce about one pound-foot of torque at the flywheel for every cubic inch of displacement, while the engine speed at which it will attain that value depends on camshaft timing and induction/exhaust tuning (Fig. 2-1).

Since the maximum displacement we have to work with is 350 or 400 cubic inches, we aren't going to exceed similar values of torque output, unless the engine is built to exotic racing specs, and subsequently made marginal as an off-road performer. The more logical approach is to match the point where peak torque is attained to the requirements of the vehicle. This brings us back to the subject of gear ratio. If you're running 3.07 cogs, you'll undoubtedly want to reach the peak at a lower engine speed than when running 4.11's, so this must be taken into consideration when selecting new components for your engine.

Fig. 2-1. If your rig is equipped with a four-speed transmission, you might want to opt for a heavy flywheel of 40 pounds or more. More torque can thus be stored, which in turn will allow you to creep more readily without stalling the engine (photo by Fred Freel).

Before we can determine just what modifications will be suitable for a specific chassis combination, we must first decide where the peak torque speed will be most effective. Typically, if your engine's torque curve peaks at or near the truck's *cruise* speed, it should be pretty closely matched for both economical highway travel, as well as off-roading in the lower transfer-case gears.

Let's compare this thinking to the speeds attained at the production torque peak of 2800 rpm with the 350-CID engine:

MPH and GEAR RATIO

TIRES	2.76	3.07	3.73	4.11
H78-15	82	74	*61*	55
10-15	90	80	*66*	*60*
12-15	98	88	72	*65*

Now, let's assume that we've modified the engine to reach its point of maximum torque at 2200 rpm:

H78-15	65	*58*	48	43
10-15	70	*63*	52	47
12-15	76	*69*	57	51

The 2.00-to-one transfer-case ratio will halve these speeds when driving in low range and top gear. We've shown the combinations that would be most practical for a cruise speed of 60 to 65 mph in italics, and you can see that reducing the peak torque speed is really only practical when high (numerically) gear ratios are utilized. Otherwise, the factory peak is quite acceptable, as long as the tires used are of suitable proportion.

COMPRESSION RATIO

Compression is one of the most important factors in attaining good driveability and mileage. For every point of compression increase from a base of 8.0 to one, you can expect about 1.5-mpg improvement. There will be proportionate increases in both horsepower and torque.

About the easiest method of increasing compression ratio is to apply a set of cylinder heads from an earlier Chevy engine that incorporates small combustion chambers (Fig. 2-2). When searching these castings out in the wrecking yard though, be certain that they incorporate all the necessary mounting holes for your engine's accessories. These bolt holes are normally located in the ends of the castings, but there may be exceptions (Fig. 2-3).

You should also shun cylinderhead castings that utilize large valves. Optimum would be those that incorporate 1.94-inch intake and 1.50-inch exhausts. Small valves and ports promote high-mixture velocities at low engine speeds, which in turn means more low-speed torque (Fig. 2-4). If you're looking for a real grunt motor, castings with a 1.72-inch intake could even be tried, though they may be difficult to locate with late-model attachment features. Don't try them, however, if your engine will be called upon to exceed 4000 rpm, as power will fall off rapidly above this speed from pumping losses.

Tuning the intake and exhaust system to match your engine's torque *speed* is important, too. Generally, long, skinny headers are the order of the day when searching for low-speed torque. Large-tube types will give less

Fig. 2-2. Here are the two types of combustion chambers used in Chevy small-block cylinder heads. The smaller one (left) is preferred, since it will not only increase compression, but is a more efficient shape. Large-valve performance castings are not recommended for good low-speed power output (photo by Fred Freel).

Fig. 2-3. Most truck engines produced before 1976 incorporate cylinder blocks with four-bolt main bearing caps. This type is preferred over the two-bolt, since the block is much sturdier in the main bearing webs. Two-bolt blocks will, however, withstand the punishment of off-roading with proper blueprinting (photo by Fred Freel).

back pressure, and subsequently better mileage, but they are tuned for an engine speed closer to 6000 rpm, so they will have little effect on driveability at lower speeds.

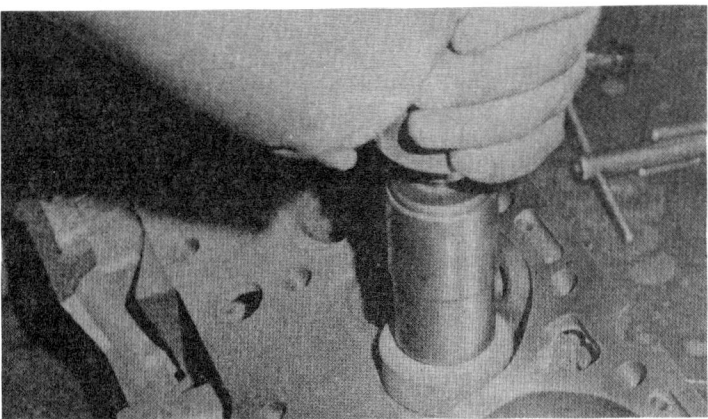

Fig. 2-4. Grinding the valve progressively can improve mixture flow at low valve lifts, which in turn will enhance low-speed performance. Don't, however, employ narrow valve seats common to racing engines. The wider the seats, within reason, the longer they will last before a regrind is necessary (photo by Fred Freel).

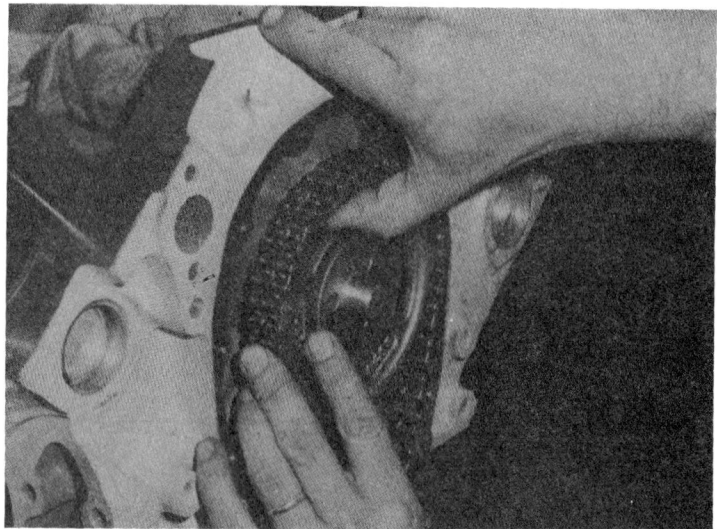

Fig. 2-5. A chain-drive conversion is recommended to drive the camshaft. Not only is it more durable than the nylon and steel production type, but the chain is prestretched, so there is less likely to be any change in timing after a long period of time (photo by Fred Freel).

INTAKE MANIFOLDS AND CAMSHAFTS

Induction systems must also be matched, in terms of carb size and intake manifold design. A carburetor with a flow rating of 650 cfm should be considered maximum for *any* small-block Chevy engine, and smaller types will usually perform more effectively with the higher gear ratio combinations. The latest 450- and 500-cfm carbs will probably prove to be the best suited to both highway and off-road use. They may sound awfully small

Fig. 2-6. It's not mandatory, but double checking the timing of a new cam is a guarantee that it is the grind specified, and that all associated components are compatible and properly installed. A dial guage is handy for this check, but it can be done with a degree wheel alone (photo by Fred Freel).

compared to GM's 725-cfm Q-Jet, but they will flow more than their rating; there'll just be a greater pressure drop across them and in the intake manifold.

Intake manifolds are an ongoing controversy, but we feel that the latest "X" types are most effective—such as the *Holley Street Dominator* and *Edelbrock Streetmaster*. Again, these designs are most effective with the higher axle ratios. They are designed to enhance low-speed power output. They do tend to give up at speeds above 4000 rpm though.

The *camshaft* is probably the most misunderstood component in the engine (Fig. 2-5). Virtually all late-model Chevy engines are equipped with

Fig. 2-7. Cleanliness is a must during engine assembly if you want your engine to have lasting durability. It's also a good practice to coat all bearing surfaces, particularly those that will be stressed during break in with a moly-disulfide lubricant (photo by Fred Freel).

11

low-speed cams. They are designed to give the maximum possible torque at low speeds, without losing high-speed flexibility. There are aftermarket camshafts that claim to provide more torque at even lower speeds, and they are worth trying if you are attempting to get maximum torque near the 2000-rpm range. If, however, you select the wrong grind for your particular application, you may be in for a disappointment. With this in mind, let the camshaft grinder select the one best suited for your needs (Fig. 2-6). If you send him all the necessary data pertaining to your truck, and the use you'll be putting it to, he'll be more than happy to select the proper grind from his various profiles.

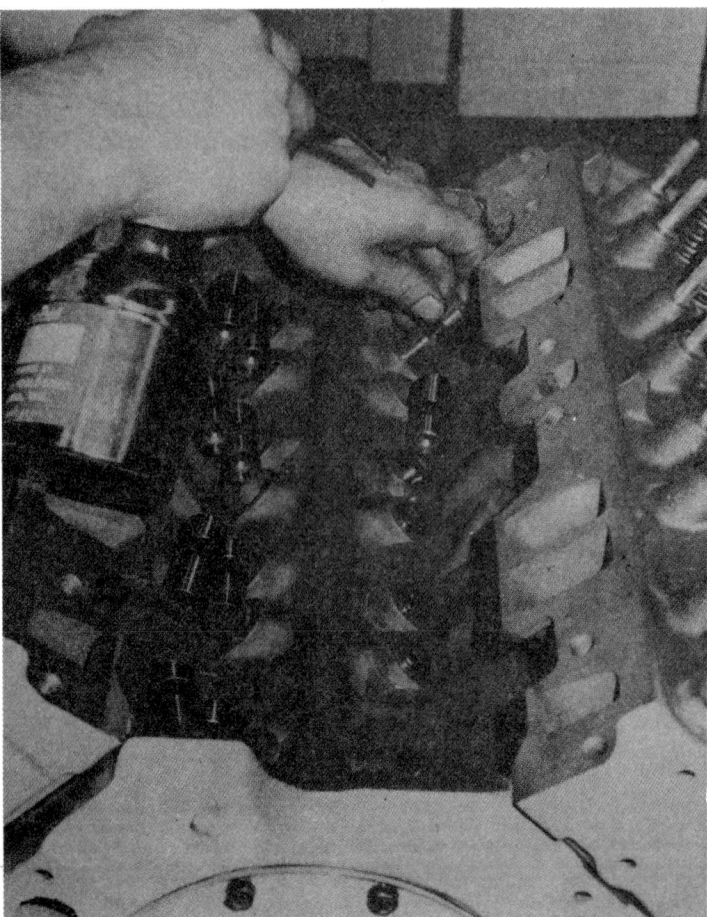

Fig. 2-8. Coat every part with oil during assembly to make certain that no rust can form from condensation, and to assure proper oiling during the initial startup. New camshafts also require special attention, so adhere to the manufacturer's recommendations during installation (photo by Fred Freel).

Fig. 2-9. You're undoubtedly going to spend money bringing your engine up to off-road specs, so it's very important that you protect your investment. Dirt is an engine's worst enemy, so apply an oil-soak air cleaner like this K&N cloth mesh type (or the foam type such as that made by Filtron). Don't rely on a paper filter to keep desert dust out (photo by Fred Freel).

ENGINE PREPARATION AND ASSEMBLY

Last but not least, preparation and assembly of the engine during the rebuilding is also very important. The components you select will depend on how serious you are about improving your engine's durability, but in any case, cleanliness and close adherence to the recommended clearances and tolerances is of utmost importance (Figs. 2-7 through 2-9).

Employing special components that are no longer used in Chevy truck engines is also a good idea. Some of the more important items are: a forged crankshaft, forged aluminum pistons, connecting rods with ⅜-inch bolts, and a heavy-duty vibration damper (Fig. 2-10). There are others that were originally used on Camaro Z-28 engines, but most pertain to mechanical lifter combinations that really aren't necessary in a low-speed, off-road engine.

A cast-iron crankshaft, or cast pistons for that matter, are suitable for an off-road engine. The forged items will give you just that much of an edge

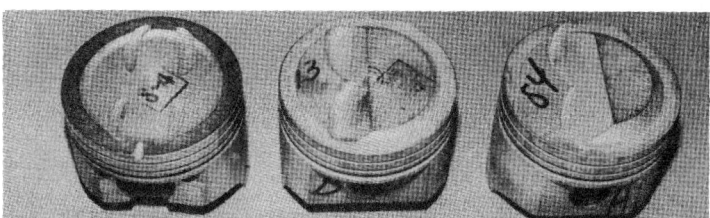

Fig. 2-10. Another approach to increased compression is pop-up forged pistons. A variety is available from Chevy, TRW, or Speed-Pro, but compression should be limited to about 10 to one maximum, unless the octane rating of fuel available in your area exceptionally high (photo by Fred Freel).

13

toward dependability. We've listed some specifications you can go by when assembling your engine with the forged parts, but don't attempt to use them with production pieces (Table 2-1). The standard components should be assembled in accordance with the specs outlined in Chevy's shop manual for best results.

The *service* clearances we've listed are nominal (with forged components), while the heavy-duty specs are those that you should strive for when blueprinting the engine. All of these specs are Chevrolet's, so they should be adhered to for optimum durability (Fig. 2-11). If you've run across a point that can't be adjusted to the recommended spec, replace that component, or have it rebuilt to the next undersize before proceeding with the rebuild.

Giving your engine project a bit of forethought will, in the long run, result in more enjoyment from your rig under just about any driving condition. There's no reason to go overboard seeking maximum torque at a super-low engine speed. That would just be overkill. Decide how and where

Table 2-1. Heavy-Duty Versus Factory Service Specifications.

	service or production	heavy-duty
Piston to Bore Clearance:		
cast pistons	.0007 - .0017"	—
	.0027" maximum	
forged pistons (Chevy)	.0046 - .0056"	.0050 - .0055"
Cylinder Bore Preparation:	Hone with medium grit stone to establish crosshatch pattern, then finish hone with #400-500 stone for smooth bore.	
Piston Ring Gap:		
top ring	.0100 - .0200"	.0220" minimum
	.0350" maximum	—
second ring	.0100 - .0250"	.0160" minimum
	.0350" maximum	—
oil ring	.0150 - .0550"	.0160" minimum
	.0650" maximum	—
Piston Pin Clearance:		
pressed—in piston	.00025 - .00035"	.0004 - .0008"
	.0010" maximum	—
—in rod	-.0008 - .0016"	-.0010 - .0012"
floating—in piston	—	.0004 - .0008"
—in rod	—	.0005 - .0007"
—end play	—	.0050"
Rod Bearing Clearance:	.0013 - .0035"	.0020 - .0025"
	.0035" maximum	—
side play	.0080 - .0140"	.0100 - .0200"
Main Bearing Clearance:		
journal #1	.0008 - .0020"	.0020 - .0030"
	.0020" maximum	.0020" preferred
journals #2-4	.0011 - .0023"	.0020 - .0030"
	.0035" maximum	.0020" preferred
journal #5	.0017 - .0032"	.0020 - .0030"
	.0035" maximum	.0020" preferred
end play	.0020 - .0060"	.0050 - .0070"

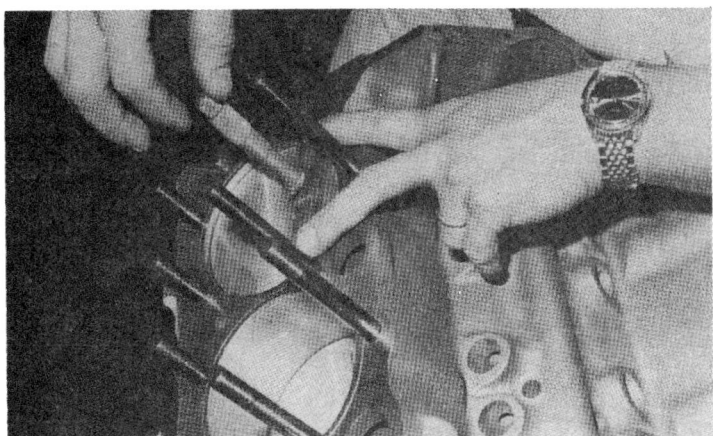

Fig. 2-11. Adhering to Chevy's assembly specs is important, not only in terms of performance, to keep a minimum of variation from cropping up from cylinder to cylinder. Also, temperature of both the oil and cooling liquid will be more uniform, and oil pressure will be greater with given clearance (photo by Fred Freel).

you'll be driving your machine, and match the existing or new components to those requirements. The overall cost might be just a bit more, but the rewards should prove to be worth the effort.

Chapter 3

Quadravan Transformation

It's a great day for any businessman when a customer walks in knowing exactly what he wants and has all the money in the world to buy it cash in hand. Ed Pearlman, proprietor of the Baja 500 Off Road Mart in Pasadena, California, had just such a customer. Ed is the founder of the National Off-Road Racing Association (NORRA), along with his good friend and still partner, Don Francisco. NORRA pioneered those early Ensenada to La Paz races that were the beginning of off-road competition as we know it today.

What this customer had was a 1977 Econoline, long wheelbase Quadravan outfitted underneath by Pathfinder. He also had some excellent ideas and plenty of money. The customer was planning a trip to Guatemala, and he wanted his Quadravan to be able to cope with any possible driving hazard he might encounter. Ed Pearlman was given a rough idea of what was desired and a virtual blank check.

Because we've known Ed since the early, organizational days of NORRA, he gave us a call when the project was about to begin. As a result we were able to photograph the stock Quadravan before its transformation, during and after (Figs. 3-1 and 3-2).

The Heco steering stabilizer was already installed when the Baja 500 crew went to work. They had to start somewhere, so the first things installed were the wire mesh headlight protectors from Dick Cepek. Next came the Desert Dynamics side-door extender, necessary to clear the wide wheels and tires which would be installed later (Figs. 3-3 and 3-4).

SEATS AND SEAT BELTS

The customer expected to be encountering some pretty rugged going. The Baja 500 staff figured that only the best would do when it came to seats.

Fig. 3-1. The Quadravan before transformation (photo by Jim Matthews).

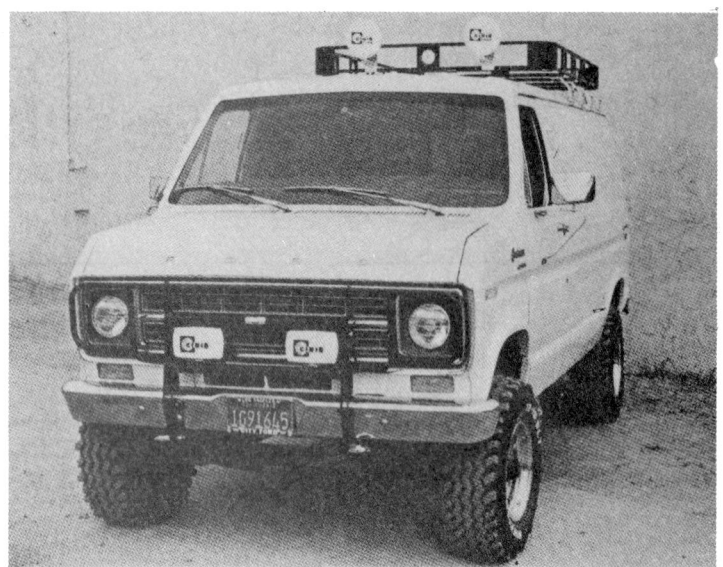

Fig. 3-2. It hardly looks like the same truck (photo by Jim Matthews).

For any kind of racing or rugged work, the ultimate in seating is Recaro (few of us can afford them), giving magnificent lateral and thigh support with the maximum in comfort (Fig. 3-5).

Continuing in the theme of safety with comfort, Ed and Don next installed 3-inch Superior Industries competition seat belts complete with

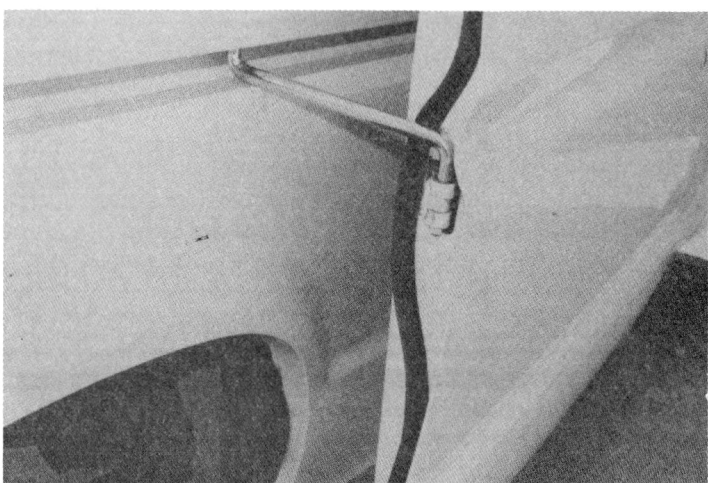

Fig. 3-3. A door extender from Desert Dynamics was necessary to clear big wheels and tires (photo by Jim Matthews).

Fig. 3-4. The OEM wheels and tires are woefully inadequate and look it (photo by Jim Matthews).

racing-style shoulder harness for both driver and passenger (Fig. 3-6). Behind the seats, on each side, there's a quick release La France fire extinguisher (Fig. 3-7).

OTHER FEATURES

To the tender under-parts Hickey skid plates were added for off-road protection along with KYB shocks (Fig. 3-8). For protection of the occupants in case of a rollover, the experts at Smittybilt fabricated a custom roll cage (Fig. 3-9).

Up front, on the Hickey brush guard, there are Cibie driving lights with another pair topside on the roof rack mounting bars. Around to the rear is a Fay step bumper with trailer ball, and hidden out of sight is an equalizing hitch from Ez-lift of Sun Valley, California. Also at the rear is a Dick Cepek spare tire carrier and cover.

The chrome spoke wheels are Applicance, wearing true off-road Ruffian tires, 12-16.5, with very aggressive tread also from Cepek. Just under the front doors there's an assist step on each side from C-P Auto Products. Under the *dog house* there's a Filtron air filter for those Central American dust storms.

Fig. 3-5. Recaro seats, the finest in the industry, offer comfort and superb support (photo by Jim Matthews).

19

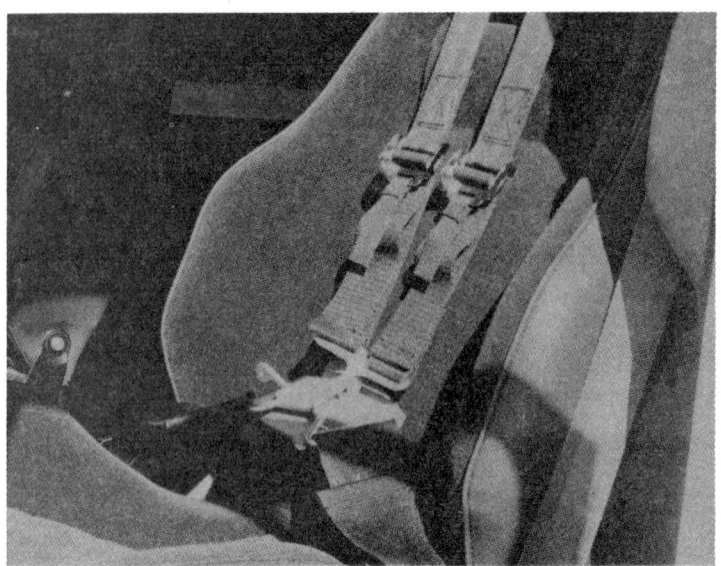

Fig. 3-6. Three-inch competition seat belts and shoulder harness were added (photo by Jim Matthews).

Back in the luxurious cockpit, the custom steering wheel, racing size and type, is from Vic Hickey. The digital clock is Cepek, and the illuminated rocker switches for the driving lights are KC (Fig. 3-10).

Almost everything about this modified, transformed, customized truck has been a bolt-on. It's the sort of thing you can do to your four-by, whether it's an F-250, a Quadravan, a Jeep, Blazer, Bronco, Scout, or Land Cruiser.

Fig. 3-7. La France fire extinguishers behind each seat (photo by Jim Matthews).

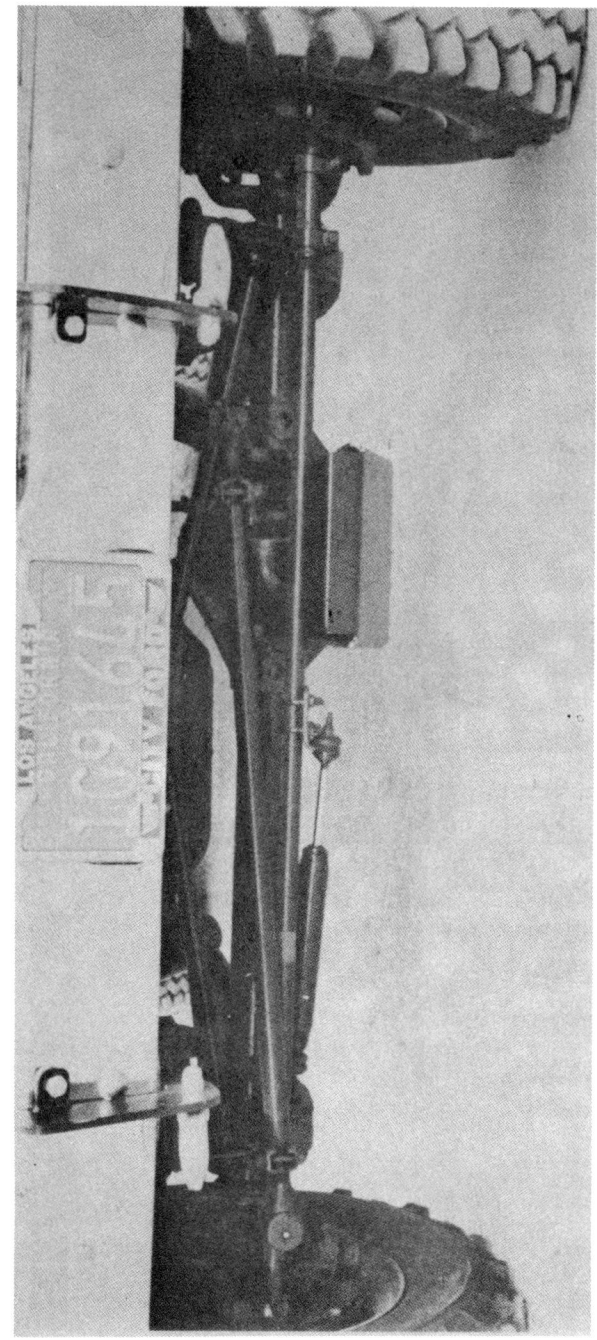

Fig. 3-8. Underpinnings include Heco steering stabilizer, Hickey skid plats, and KYB shocks (photo by Jim Matthews).

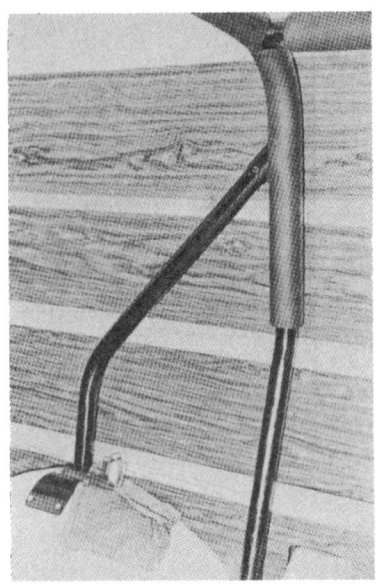

Fig. 3-9. Smittybilt fabricated the custom roll cage for the interior (photo by Jim Matthews).

Fig. 3-10. Illuminated K-C rocker switches on the left and a Cepek digital clock on the right (photo by Jim Matthews).

Chapter 4

Kal Kustom Kit

Bouncing through Baja recently, we had occasion more than once to thank our lucky stars that our heads didn't go through our headliners. Some headliners last for years, and some seem to disintegrate at the first rifle, fishing rod, or head or hand poked through them.

Headliners, carpeting, and upholstery—those are the wonderful semiluxuries we like to have in our trucks that give us a part of the overall thrill of owning and operating an off-road rig (Fig. 4-1). They also take the brunt of our activity—as much as any other part of the machine.

That's why we were glad to run into Greg Nelis of Kal Kustom. Greg has developed an outstanding interior kit that makes the whole job of repair or replacement as easy as it will ever be.

Those of us who drive trucks, from minis through full-size jobs, can most likely find a kit at Kal Kustom. Since truckers are more garage than show oriented, Kal Kustom's kit should be doubly appreciated. With a minimum of time, anybody can install a headliner, carpeting, or seat covers anywhere.

Greg's made an art of supplying truckers with the good-looking, long-lasting interiors they need, interiors that add to the pride we take in our machines. He got his start by working at Pacific Vinyls making kits for minis. When he got the opportunity to buy Kal Kustom, an outfit with a solid 23 years of good reputation behind it, he took it. The results have been good for both.

The word was that Greg's kit was very simple to install. Being the skeptics that we are, we decided to try one out. Though Kal Kustom supplies kits for most early and late-model trucks and minis, we took one of our favorite project trucks along: a 1956 Ford F-100.

Fig. 4-1. A Kal Kustom interior kit will make your truck look great (photo by David Miller).

Did Greg have a kit for it? You bet he did. Was it easy to install, or would we have to have an expert (and a lot of money) to get it done?

We'll let you decide. Figures 4-2 through 4-13 outline the major steps in replacing our old headliner with Greg's sweet custom job. Our own answer is a resounding, "Yes, it's easy to install."

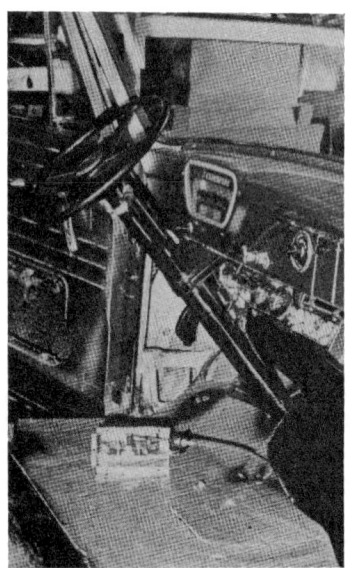

Fig. 4-2. Strip out the old to get ready for the new. That's step one in the Kal Kustom kit installation (photo by David Miller).

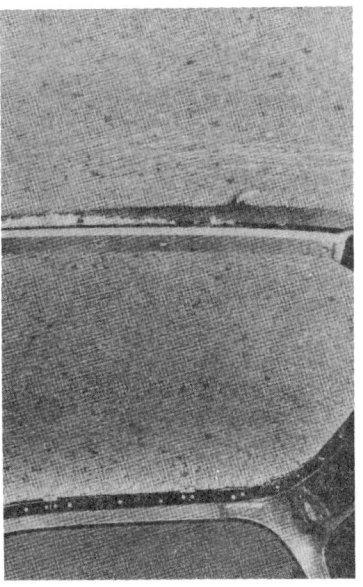

Fig. 4-3. Installation of the headliner, the most commonly replaced interior item (photo by David Miller).

Tools needed include a screwdriver, stapler or staple gun, and a razor knife. You also need a can of contact cement (Scotch 3M aerosol, or order through Kal Kustom. A pint can with brush will serve).

If you'd like to try it yourself, or if you'd just like to get in touch with Greg and find out what he's got to offer, contact him at Kal Kustom, Dept. T4, 1558 South Anaheim Blvd., Suite D, Anaheim, CA, 92805. For a catalog, be sure to send a dollar—and tell them we suggested it.

Fig. 4-4. Bows, which will stiffen the headliner and hold it in shape, are first tested at their chosen locations. The OEM brackets are fine and save time and much trouble (photo by David Miller).

25

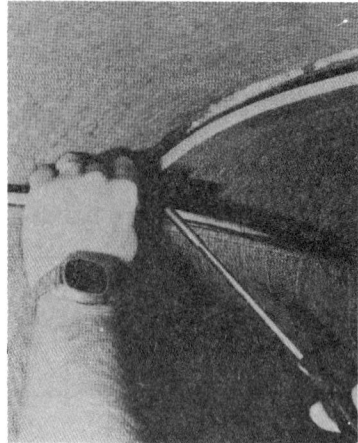

Fig. 4-5. Pushed through the hangers on the backside of vinyl, bows are then attached in the center to the cab ceiling (photo by David Miller).

Fig. 4-6. With bow ends inserted in brackets, the vinyl headliner begins to take shape (photo by David Miller).

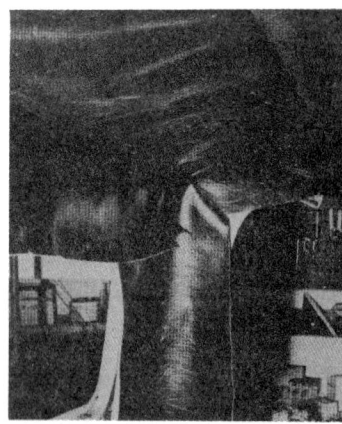

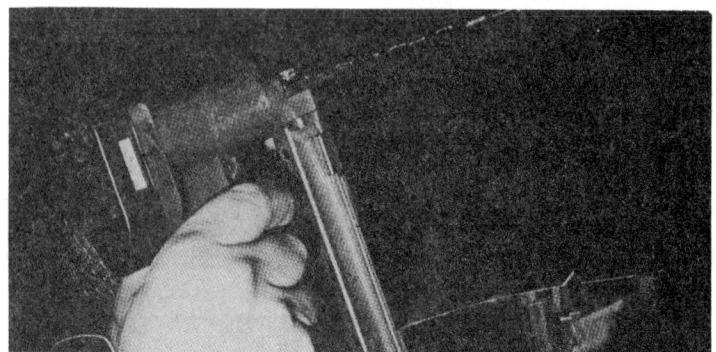

Fig. 4-7. Edges are stapled to the tacking board. Start from the center and work outward to keep vinyl in shape (photo by David Miller).

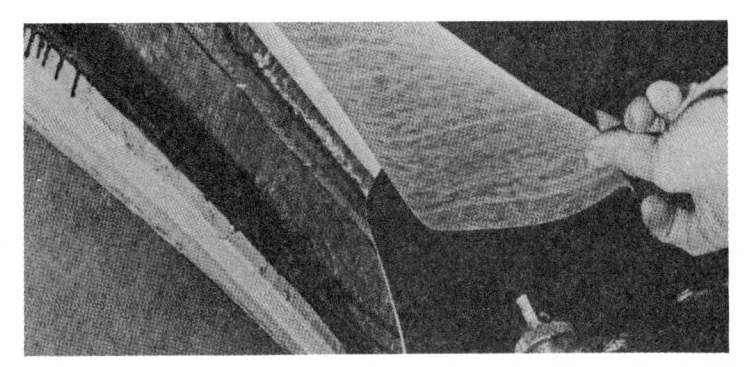

Fig. 4-8. Contact cement holds the vinyl around the window. Enough trim should be left so that when the window glass is popped in, it will help hold the vinyl (photo by David Miller).

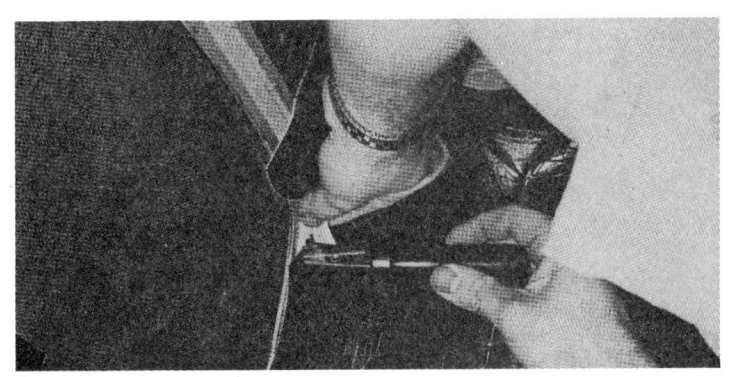

Fig. 4-9. Excess is trimmed away. Cut corners with two-on-a-slant nicks to help preserve the shape of vinyl and prevent creases (photo by David Miller).

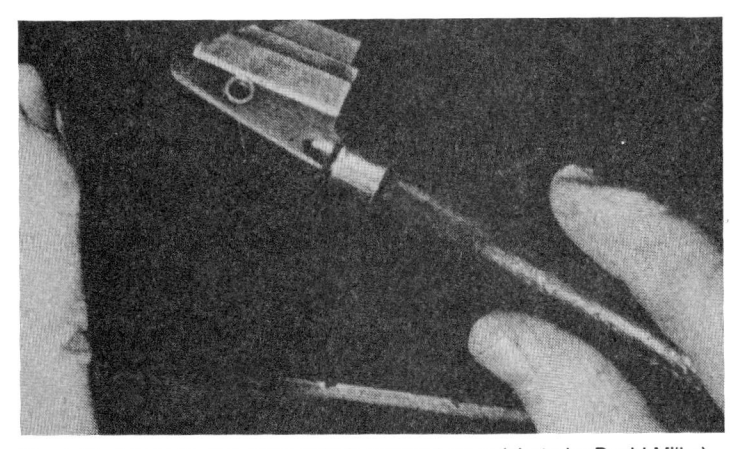

Fig. 4-10. A hole for the dome light is next cut open (photo by David Miller).

27

Fig. 4-11. The dome light is then bolted in place, pinning headliner around it (photo by David Miller).

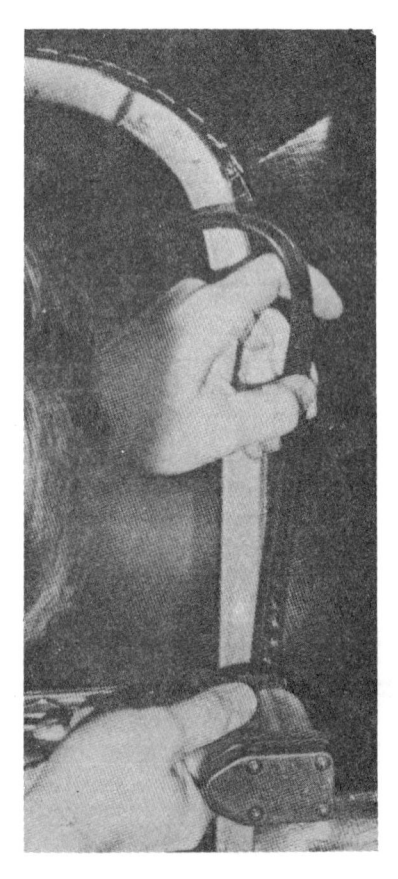

Fig. 4-12. Molding strip is stapled down. Edges of molding fold over, and all staples are hidden (photo by David Miller).

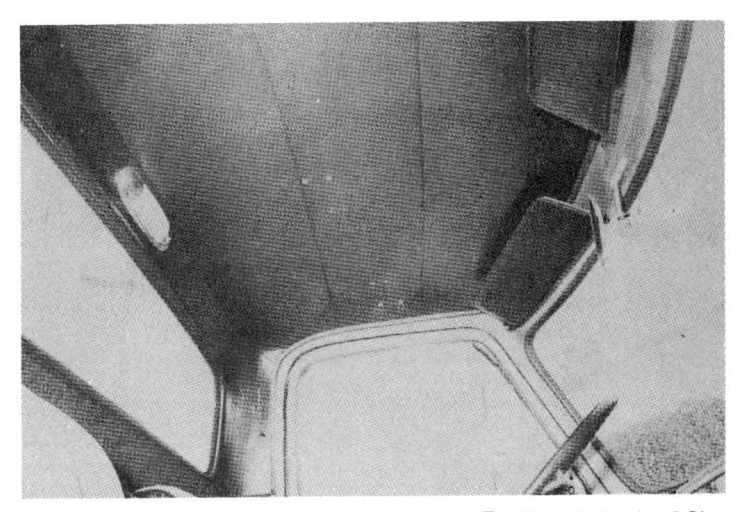

Fig. 4-13. Your finished headliner should be smooth. Total installation time? Give yourself an afternoon, you could be done in two hours.

Chapter 5

Four-Wheel-Drive
Mini-Truck Conversions

Four-wheel-drive conversions for mini-trucks have been available for several years now. Most of the conversions were done only in large cities where there were shops that had the experience to do the job. So someone with a hankering to own a 4WD mini had to either live in such a city (which isn't exactly the best place for four wheeling) or make a long trek to pick one up.

BAJA CONVERSION KIT

Such is no longer the case. There is now a complete conversion kit for all mini-trucks—Datsun, Toyota, Mazda, Chevy LUV, and Ford Courier—that is available for delivery anywhere in the country. The kit was put together by South Bay Four-Wheel-Drive, a firm that has had many years of experience building 4WD minis. The kit is one of the most complete you will find and includes everything needed, down to the last nut, bolt, and washer (Fig. 5-1).

The kit is available from Baja 4WD Conversions, Inc. (3818 W. Imperial Highway, Inglewood, CA 90303), and costs $1995. The cost is the same, no matter which make of vehicle is being converted.

While the kit does include all parts and one of the most detailed sets of instructions we have ever seen, it is not just a bolt-on unit (Fig. 5-2). To assure a top-quality conversion, there are a number of items that must be welded in place. With more than four years of experience building mini-pickup four-wheel-drive conversions, the engineers at South Bay decided that only by welding could sufficient strength for off-road be achieved in a mini.

While the Baja Conversion is truly a kit, it does require a good bit of mechanical skill and know-how to put together properly. Those with the

Fig. 5-1. The kit provides everything needed for the conversion, down to the last nut and bolt. However, you may want to add aftermarket goodies like lights, push-bar, and winch to suit your own taste (photo by Lin Ford).

ability and access to an arc welder (which will do the job, though South Bay recommends a MIG welder) should be able to put the kit on the vehicle in approximately 20 hours. In addition to the welding, the rear drive shaft must be shortened (Fig. 5-3). If the home mechanic lacks the tools for that job, a good machine shop can handle the chore.

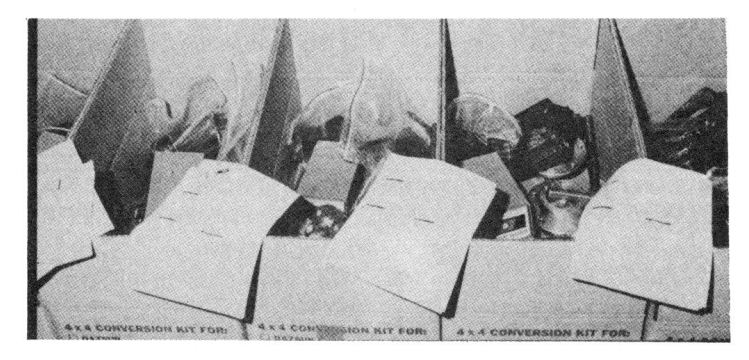

Fig. 5-2. Boxes contain smaller parts of the kit and are being packed for shipment. Large items, such as front axle, front subframe, springs, and transfer case are naturally shipped separately (photo by Lin Ford).

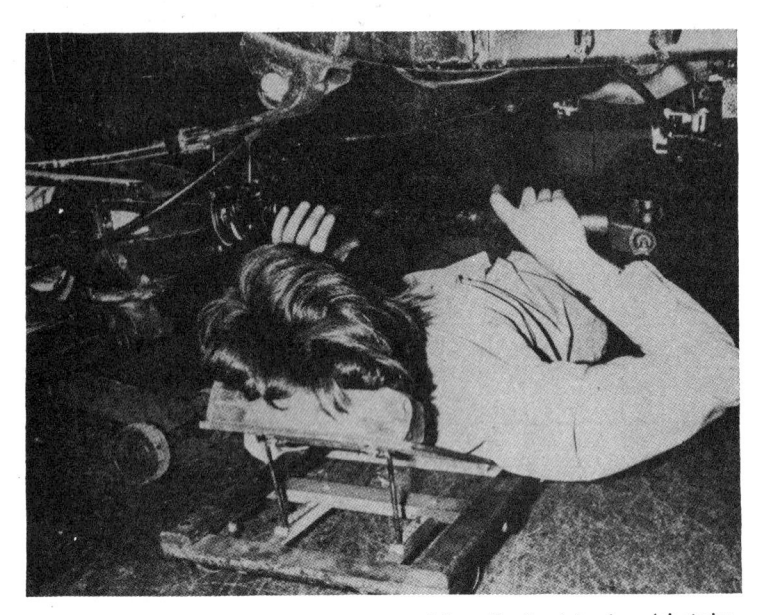

Fig. 5-3. Once the rear driveshaft is shortened, it easily slips into place (photo by Lin Ford).

Those who lack the required skills will find that any good four-wheel-drive repair shop should be able to do the installation in a couple of days. With the shop doing all the work, the installation cost should be no more than $500. For someone who owns a mini-pickup in good shape, the conversion kit certainly looks a lot cheaper than the $7000 or so that most dealers want for a new four-wheel-drive mini.

We stopped at South Bay Four-Wheel-Drive's shop in Long Beach, California, to take a look at all the pieces in the kit and to see how one went together. Watching the conversion process on a Datsun and later having an opportunity to ride in it convinced us that this kit can indeed turn any mini into a very sturdy vehicle, capable of handling just about any type of off-road terrain.

The major mechanical pieces supplied with the kit are a model 30 Spicer front drive axle, Dana 20 two-speed transfer case, Warn locking hubs, heavy-duty seven-leaf springs for the front axle, Dana/Spicer front driveshaft and KYB gas shocks for the front (Figs 5-4 through 5-7). The Dana transfer case comes already mounted in a special cradle which serves both as a skid plate and to make mounting of the transfer case much easier (Fig. 5-8). The kit also includes a heavy-duty front subframe which is welded into place on the stock frame to strengthen the frame and prevent flexing (Fig. 5-9). All necessary hardware and brackets are supplied.

One nice aspect to the kit is that the original brakes are retained in all cases, which helps keep the cost of the kit down. All minis except the

Fig. 5-4. Transfer case and front axle are shipped dry and must be filled with gear lube before vehicle can be run (photo by Lin Ford).

Toyota retain the original wheel-bolt pattern and metric studs, so that factory wheels and lug wrench still fit. With the Toyota, the stock bolt pattern is changed to a five-bolt on a 5½-inch circle. The original metric studs and lug nuts are retained.

Fig. 5-5. Special front spring mounts must be welded on to take the kit's specially stiffened seven leaf springs (photo by Lin Ford).

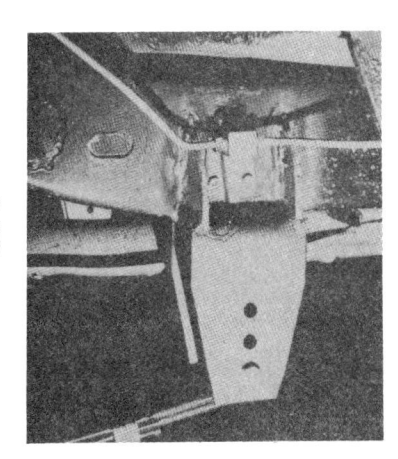

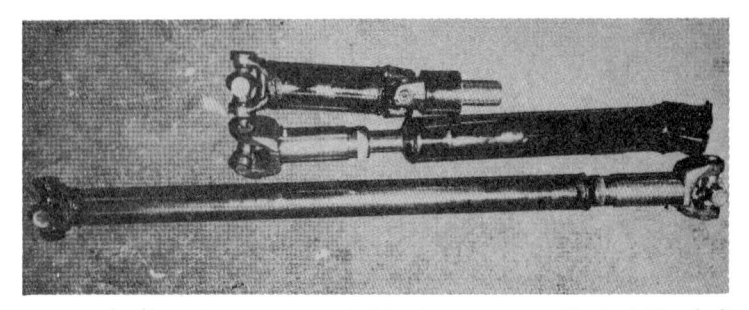

Fig. 5-6. Three driveshafts are needed for the conversion. Shortest driveshaft connects transmission to transfer case. Second driveshaft connects transfer case to front axle. The longest driveshaft is taken from the vehicle being converted. It must be shortened to fit (photo by Lin Ford).

Fig. 5-7. Mounts for front shocks must be welded onto frame. Kit includes two KYB shocks for the front suspension (photo by Lin Ford).

Fig. 5-8. The Dana 20 transfer case is premounted in a cradle which serves as a skid plate and makes mounting the case to the frame an easy job (photo by Lin Ford).

Fig. 5-9. Subframe must be welded onto the front for strength and to prevent flexing (photo by Lin Ford).

The Dana transfer case has both high and low four-wheel-drive settings, as well as two-wheel-drive high and neutral gear positions. In low range the Dana case has a 2.01:1 ratio for rock crawling and stump pulling.

RESULTS

The addition of all the goodies give the mini an increase of some 7 inches in height and a ground clearance of about 7½ inches, depending on the type of tires used. At the front the installation of new springs and axle gives the truck its additional height. In the rear, to match the front's increased height, the springs are remounted to the top of the axle (Figs. 5-10 through 5-13).

Fig. 5-10. Here's a shot of the front end with everything in place, including the front axle, before the driveline is connected (photo by Lin Ford).

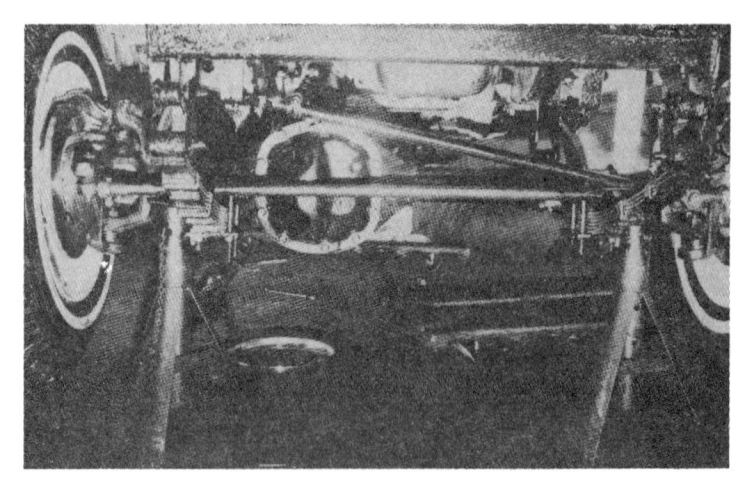

Fig. 5-11. Here is the fully assembled front end, with just one step to go before vehicle is ready to drive (photo by Lin Ford).

Fig. 5-12. At the rear, kit supplies parts to move springs above the axle for increased height to match increased height at front (photo by Lin Ford).

Fig. 5-13. After conversion is completed, toe-in must be set to factory specifications (photo by Lin Ford).

Fig. 5-14. Baja 4WD Conversions can take it, as this test in the rugged oil fields of Signal Hill, California, proved (photo by Lin Ford).

The end result of all this work is a little pickup that will go just about anywhere. The ride is stiffer than stock on the street, but once the back country is reached, it feels just right. The steering is a bit heavy at very low speeds, but at anything over 10 mph it is not noticeable.

If you plan to do much slow-speed off roading, keep the stock steering wheel, or use a custom wheel of the same diameter. There is a trend among mini-pickup customizers to go to small-diameter steering wheels. The larger-diameter stock wheel will give you more leverage thereby increasing mechanical advantage when turning the wheel, a real plus during slow-speed maneuvers.

With all the new suspension components, the truck seems quite happy taking on terrain any other four-wheel-drive vehicle can handle (Fig. 5-14). Up hills, over rocks, through sand washes and over cross grain, the converted mini we rode in could do it all.

The Baja 4WD Conversion kit is the best engineered mini-truck outfit we have seen. The instructions are excellent both in terms of completeness and case of understanding. Should there be any problems with the instructions, there is even a phone number included so the purchaser can call for help.

So all you mini-owners with off-road desires, what are you waiting for? This kit will give you one tough truck, no matter whether it's a Ford, Chevy, Datsun, Toyota, or Mazda.

Chapter 6

Camshafts

The average owner of an off-road vehicle is often willing to make a number of changes to his 4×4 in an effort to improve its off and on-road performance. Different tires and wheels, a bigger carburetor, and a more efficient manifold are often items one can add to extract that something extra from his stock vehicle. Yet in the search for better performance, one area many off-roaders ignore is the *camshaft* and *valve train* (Fig. 6-1).

The backyard mechanic may feel that while he can handle changing a carb or manifold, a camshaft swap is beyond him. The owner who has a competent off-road shop do his alterations for him may feel that changing the cam is a bit too exotic for his four-wheeler.

People with attitudes like that are missing the opportunity to change a piece of hardware which has a vast effect on engine performance. A well-designed and properly installed off-road type, aftermarket cam can provide significant boosts in both horsepower and torque in the low rpm range which is so important to the off-road driver. In addition, swapping such a cam for the stock cam is not as difficult a task as many seem to believe.

GETTING THE SHAFT

The camshaft itself is the basic mechanism in the engine for timing the operation of the valves (Fig. 6-2). It sees to the job of opening and closing the intake and exhaust valves at the proper times, so that the flow of gases, both fuel and exhaust, can occur freely and efficiently.

The shaft is usually made from an alloy iron casting, but it may also be made from a steel forging or even a solid steel bar. The lobes of the camshaft (one lobe for each valve) are located radially around the shaft and are designed to provide the proper valve timing and firing order in the engine for which it is designed (Fig 6-3).

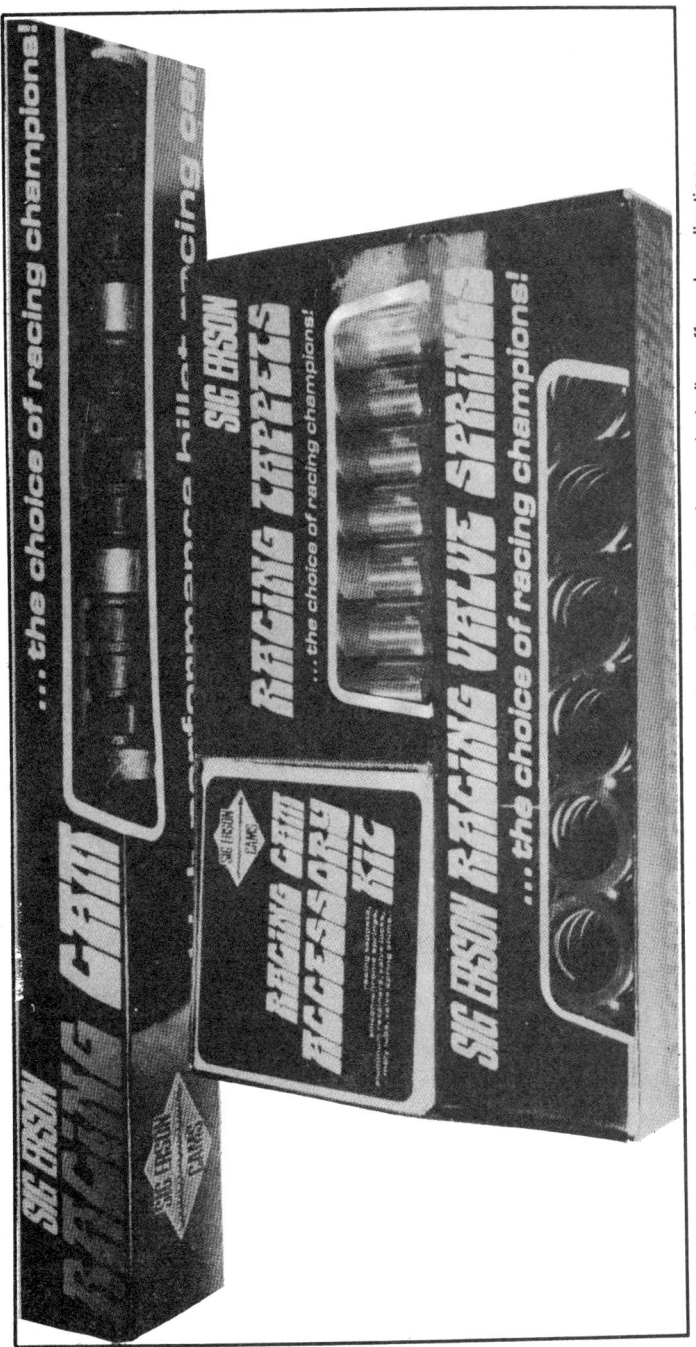

Fig. 6-1. Cams and valve train parts are available neatly packaged for a wide variety of uses, including off-road applications.

Fig. 6-2. The camshaft itself is the basic mechanism which times the operation of the valves in an engine.

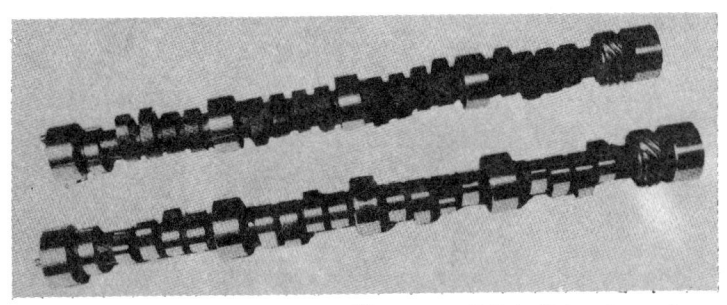

Fig. 6-3. Most off-road type cams start life as a cast billet with bearing surfaces and distributor drive gear already cut (top shaft). Cam maker then grinds lobes for specific application (bottom shaft).

Although in some engines the camshaft operates from above the valve, in all common 4×4 engines now in use in this country, the camshaft operates within the block, with the lobes pushing up on *tappets* (also known as lifters) which lift *push rods*. The push rods activate *rocker arms*, which rotate on a rocker shaft. The rocker arm pushes down on the valve stem, opening the valve. A spring attached to the valve stem by a retainer, washer, and split collar closes the valve when the lobe is not pushing upwards through the valve train.

The cam is driven by a timing chain from a gear on the end of the *crankshaft*. The gear on the end of the camshaft is half the size of the gear on the end of the crank. The cam revolves at twice the speed of the engine. The crankshaft gear, cam gear, and chain are all neatly covered by the timing cover at the front of the engine.

The camshaft is carried on three or five bearings mounted in the block. These bearings rarely go bad. Unless the engine has many miles on it (over 100,000) or there has been a failure in the oiling system, the cam bearings do not need to be replaced when an aftermarket cam is installed.

DICTIONARY DIVERSIONS

Many are already familiar with the various terms that concern camshafts. Because a clear understanding of what the terms mean is vital to understanding a cam and how it works, let's review some important ones.

First, consider the basic construction of the cam lobe. See Fig. 6-4.

Nose. That's the pointy looking part of the lobe. It gives the peak lift of the cam.

Base Circle. A theoretical circle, which is the no-lift portion of the cam. The base circle opposite the nose is the area the tappet rides on when the valve is closed.

Heel. The portion of the lobe 180 degrees opposite the nose.

Clearance Ramps. Those portions of the lobe designed to take up the clearance (valve lash) in the valve train where the tappet begins to accelerate upwards and where the tappet finished dropping back down. The

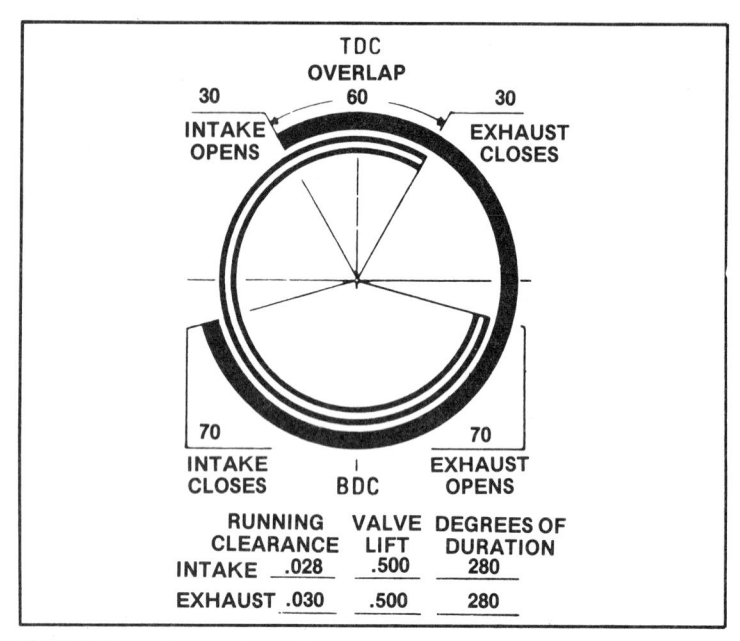

Fig. 6-4. The various portions of a cam lobe are illustrated here (courtesy of Sig Erson Racing Cams).

ramps help slow the valve train as it opens and closes the valve, thus minimizing opening and closing shock. Correctly designed ramps insure long valve train life and help in quiet valve train operation.

Flanks. The portion of the lobe between the ramp and the nose. The flank is the portion of the lobe that actually opens and closes the valve. The shape of the flank gives the cam its rate of lift.

Here are words used when discussing cams.

Cam Lift. The height in inches the lifter is raised from the bottom to the top of its travel by cam.

Valve Lift. This may vary from cam lift depending on the rocker arm ratio. If the cam lift is .450-inches and the rocker arm ratio is 1.2, then the valve lift is (.450 × 1.2) .540 inches.

Timing Figures. Data indicating when the valves open and close, always given in reference to TDC (top dead center) and BDC (bottom dead center) of piston travel. Intake valves open before TDC and close after BDC. Exhaust valves open before BDC and close after TDC. For example, timing figures for the Sig Erson RV-10-H cam for Ford small-block V-8s are as follows: IO 22, IC 54, EO 62, EC 14. This means the intake valve opens at 22 degrees before TDC and closes 54 degrees after BDC. The exhaust valve opens at 62 degrees before BDC and closes at 14 degrees after TDC.

Duration. The number of crank degrees during which the cam keeps the valve open. The longer the valve remains open, the more gas can flow past it. Some people mistakenly believe the more duration, the better. This is true only up to a point, for if the intake valve remains open too long after the piston begins its upward travel, it may wind up pushing the fuel mixture out of the combustion chamber. Especially when choosing an off-road type cam, be careful of overly large duration figures. Duration of a cam can be figured by adding both timing figures for one valve to 180. In the example above, if the intake valve opens 22 degrees before TDC and closes at 54 degrees after BDC, the duration is 22 plus 54 plus the rotation of the crankshaft from TDC to BDC (180 degrees) for a duration of 256 degrees (Fig. 6-5).

Overlap. The number of degrees when both intake and exhaust valve are open at the same time. Some overlap is helpful. When the engine is operating at high rpm, overlap can help vent the combustion chamber and cool the exhaust valve. Since most four-wheeling is done at low rpm, it is not necessary to have a great deal of overlap in an off-road cam.

SELECTING AN OFF-ROAD CAM

What the off-roader should be looking for in a cam is one which will fatten up horsepower a torque in the low rpm ranges (Fig. 6-6). It is in the low rpm band that most off-roading is done, and it is here that the engine and vehicle can use the most help. Cams which may be great on the drag strip with their ability to increase horsepower at the top end will only cause

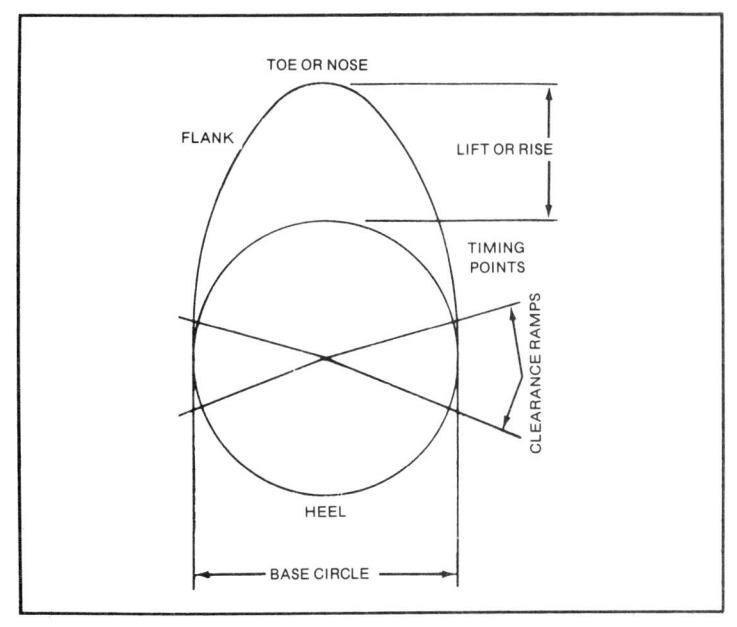

Fig. 6-5. Most cam grinders include a tag similar to this listing lift, duration, and valve timing figures (courtesy of Sig Erson Racing Cams).

43

Fig. 6-6. Pakerization treatment, seen here at the Sig Erson factory, is designed to assist in proper break-in of cam.

problems for the four-wheeler. Not only is the power in the wrong place in a drag cam, but at low rpm an engine with such a cam will run quite rough.

To obtain power in the important low rpm range, a cam should provide added lift over a stock cam, short duration, and relatively little overlap. Cam grinding experts recommend a duration of 255 to 270 degrees and lift in the area of .450 inches (Fig. 6-7). This will serve to increase torque and horsepower at the bottom and mid-range, without sacrificing too much top-end performance.

There are a number of good cam manufacturers who make cams which have these characteristics. Before selecting any one specific cam, it would be a good idea to consult with friends and off-road shop salesmen before buying. Their experience and knowledge about what works well under local conditions can be invaluable. If you can't find anyone in your local area with knowledge about cams, take a good look at several manufacturers' catalogs. Many of the catalogs contain extensive information on cams, their choice, and installation procedures.

While the camshaft may be the most important part of the valve train, it's not the only part. There are a lot of other funny little pieces that affect how efficiently those valves are opened and closed.

HOW VALUE TRAIN AFFECTS CAM PERFORMANCE

Fortunately for the recreational off-roader, most of the valve train other than the cam is well suited to providing good performance in off-road applications. Since the off-roader is interested in low and mid-range rpm performance, the demands on the valve train are not excessive (Fig. 6-8).

Exotic parts used in racing engines, such as roller tappets, roller rocker arms, and chrome moly steel seamless tube push rods, are simply not necessary for a recreational vehicle's engine. These parts are needed only in high rpm applications and would be overkill for the just-for-fun off-roader.

There are two parts of the valve train that the off-roader should consider if the stock cam is being replaced by a more efficient aftermarket cam designed to increase low and mid-range torque. First on the list is *lifters*.

To begin with, lifters must *always* be replaced when the camshaft is changed (Fig. 6-9). The reason is that the base of the lifters will take a set from the old camshaft and can quickly cause lobe failure on a new camshaft. No matter how good the old lifters may look, new lifters must be installed with a new cam.

Hydraulic lifters are perfectly sufficient for all recreational off-road uses, and a replacement set should be available from the same manufacturer who supplies your cam. A hydraulic lifter is made of two parts, one of which slides within the other. Oil, supplied under pressure, causes the lifter to lengthen and take up any clearance when the engine is running.

Fig. 6-7. Camshafts are ground on a special machine with a master cam used as a guide to obtain the exacting tolerances necessary.

45

Fig. 6-8. Unlike this off-road race truck, most off-road vehicles don't need high revving engines, which means there are only a couple of valve train areas to worry about when swapping cams.

This type of lifter is perfect for nonracing applications because it is quiet and needs no adjustment after the initial adjustment when lifters and cam are installed. Indeed, today some hydraulic lifters can rev to 7500 rpm, well past an off-roader's needs.

In engines with movable pivot arms, such as those made by Chevrolet, there is an initial valve train adjustment which must be made after the cam is installed. While this procedure can be done with the engine shut off, most experts, and Chevrolet, recommend you get a bit dirty and do the job with the engine running.

First, all tappets must be adjusted to the point where there is no engine noise. Then, with the engine idling, the rocker stud nut is backed off to the point where the lifter just starts to click. The nut is tightened slowly until the click disappears, then tightened three-quarters of a turn more. The exact procedure will vary according to manufacturer and engine model, so check for specs on your specific engine.

For engines that use mechanical lifters, replace them with lifters recommended by the cam manufacturer. In most cases there will also be mechanical. Mechanical lifters must be set with a specific valve clearance. Check with the manufacturer and set according to his specifications.

Before final installation of lifters, it is a good idea to check the lifters for proper fit. After lubricating the lifters and lifter bores with light engine oil, the lifters should be operated up and down by hand over their full range of travel. A mechanic's magnet on a long handle helps here.

If there is any sticking of the lifter, the cause must be found before the new cam goes in (Fig. 6-10). The sticking may be caused by just a small scratch or burr in the lifter bore or on one of the lifters, but the problem must be solved before the new cam goes in.

Once the new cam and lifters are in place, again check the lifters before push rods are installed and rocker arms are tightened down (Fig. 6-11). Check to see that the lifters are all easily following the cam contour as the engine crank is turned by hand. The lifter's own weight and gravity will be enough for them to follow the cam if everything is working correctly. If everything looks good, the installation can be finished.

Aside from lifters, there is only one other area of major concern in the valve train when installing an RV-type cam, and that is the *springs*. Racers often worry about the proper springs because they fear valve float. This is where the spring tension is not sufficient for the lifter to follow the cam contour, and the spring will not close the valve fast enough to follow the cam.

Valve float happens at high rpm and is not a cause of worry to the recreational off-roader. His one worry is with valve coil bind (Fig. 6-12). This is where the coils in the spring stack up together and all compressibility is lost (Fig. 6-13). This can cause severe strain and lead to destruction of the entire valve train.

Valve coil bind can occur with RV cams because they provide more lift (and thus more compression of the spring) than stock cams. One solution is

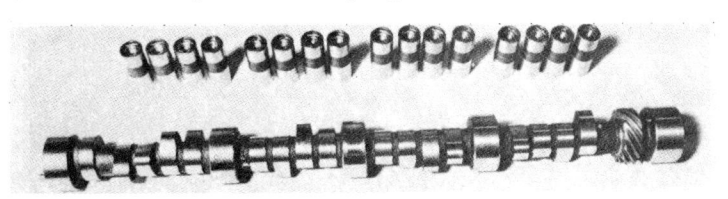

Fig. 6-9. These two parts always go together. Anytime a new cam is installed, new lifters must go in at the same time.

Fig. 6-10. Lifters should always be checked to be sure they move smoothly in lifter bores. It's easy to do with the engine on a stand, as seen here, but not much harder with the motor in the vehicle.

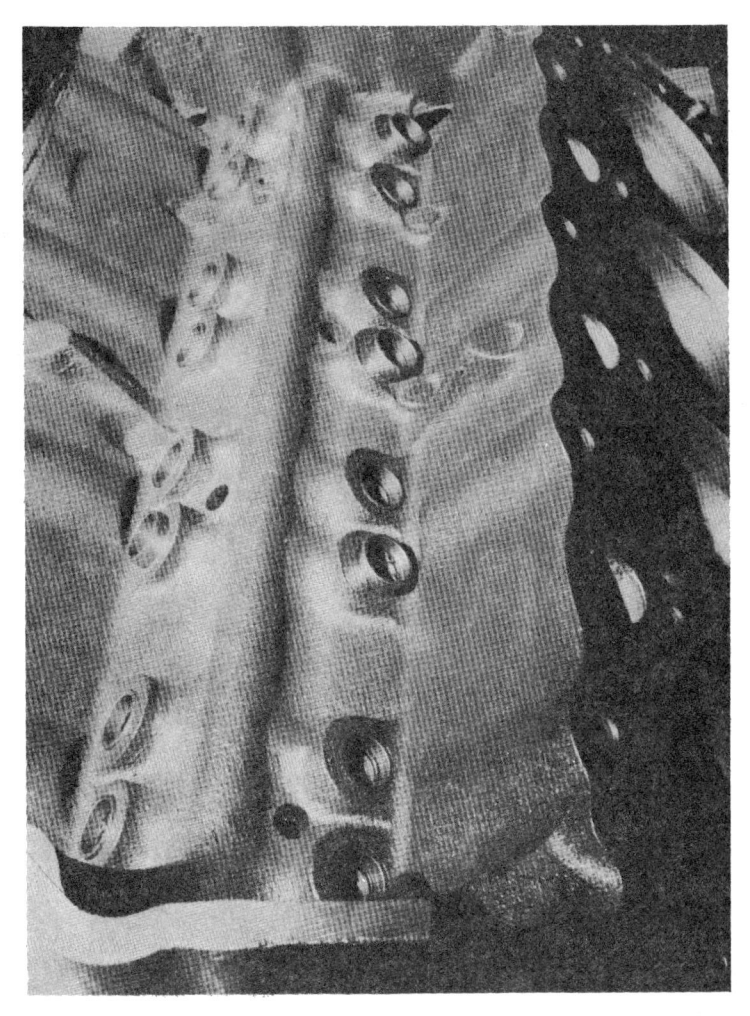

Fig. 6-11. With all new lifters in place, check to see they all follow the cam smoothly before push rods are installed.

to simply replace your springs when installing the cam. All cam manufacturers have spring sets suitable to use with their RV cam grinds (Fig. 6-14).

If you don't want to go to the trouble and expense of installing the new springs, be sure to check for coil bind before starting the engine. Rotate the engine until the intake valve is fully open (spring fully compressed). You should be able to place a .010-inch feeler gauge between every coil in the spring (Fig. 6-15). If you can't, the springs will have to be replaced.

Now rotate the engine until the exhaust valve is fully open. Again, the .010-inch feeler gauge must fit between each coil spring to assure proper

Fig. 6-12. Upper part of valve train can remain stock when swapping cams in a recreational vehicle, but be sure to check for coil bind.

operation. Since springs may differ even on the same engine, it would be a good idea to check all the springs. If coil bind is present, don't run the engine until proper springs are fitted, or valve train failure could result.

The rest of the valve train should present no problems to the average off-roader, if all the parts are in good condition. If in doubt, check with a reputable mechanic. A new RV-type cam won't be placing much in the way of extra stress on the valve train, but worn parts could prevent you from getting all the benefit of the new cam.

HOW TO SWAP YOUR CAM THE RIGHT WAY

At last we're ready to show the steps in exchanging a stock cam for a better performing aftermarket camshaft (Fig. 6-16). The cam swap shown here was done on a GMC four-wheel-drive pickup equipped with the 400 cubic-inch V-8. This is the large displacement version of the standard General Motors small-block V-8, and the procedure will vary little for any Chevy or GMC 350 or 400 cubic-inch V-8. The biggest differences will be in the accessories that are hung off the front of the engine (air conditioning pump, power steering pump, smog pump). Since these must all be removed to gain access to the camshaft, jot down on a piece of paper how the items come off, so you'll be able to put them all back on correctly.

Actually, the basic method for a cam change doesn't vary greatly on any of the U.S. V-8s. For other than GM blocks, it would be a great idea to read through a good engine manual before diving in.

Since the manifold must be removed for a cam swap, the time you decide to change cams is also a perfect time to swap manifolds, so that's what we did with the GMC. For this project, we added an Edlebrock SP2P

Fig. 6-13. Here is what coil bind looks like. There is no room between coils of the spring which means the valve cannot open fully.

Fig. 6-14. New lifers always go with a new cam, but while new springs aren't always necessary, buying matched springs from the cam maker eliminates any potential coil bind problems.

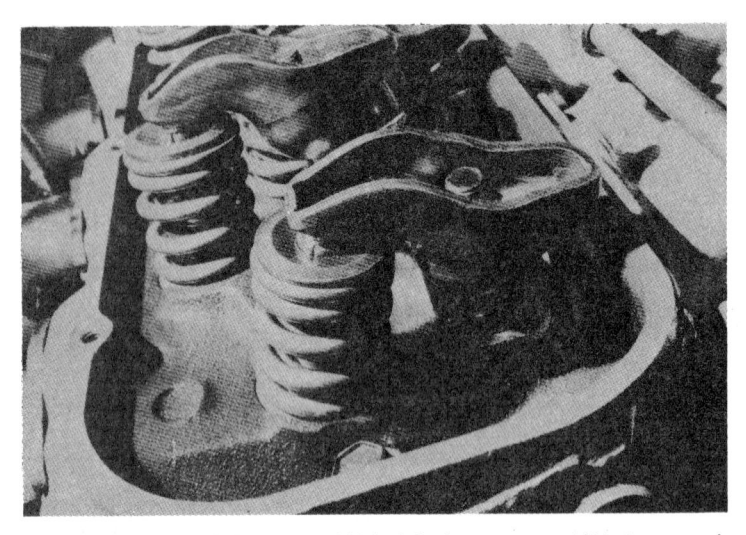

Fig. 6-15. With valve fully open, a .010-inch feeler gauge must fit between each coil to be sure the coils are not binding.

manifold. This is designed for off-road needs, providing better midrange torque and hopefully some help in the mileage department as well.

Figures 6-17 through 6-44 show the step-by-step details of the swap, but there are a few points that should be stressed. First, distributor

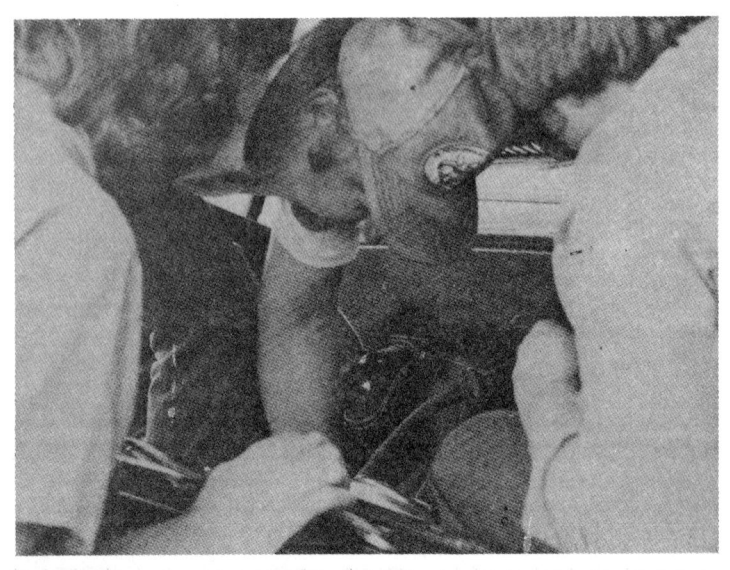

Fig. 6-16. A cam swap isn't all that hard, but it's nice to have a few friends to help (and fill up your engine compartment).

52

Fig. 6-17. Here's the GMC 400 cubic-inch V-8, just waiting for the addition of a Sig Erson cam and Edlebrock SP2P manifold.

Fig. 6-18. First drain the radiator, then remove hoses and pull it out. You'll need the extra room when you pull out the camshaft.

53

Fig. 6-19. All belts must be removed, then the fan is unbolted. After that the water pump bolts come out, and the water pump comes off.

removal is critical if you want that engine to start when everything is bolted back together.

Begin by removing the spark plug in the number one cylinder. Have someone crank the engine over while you hold a finger over the hole. You will feel the compression against your finger as the piston rises toward top

Fig. 6-20. Distributor is removed. Then all lines and linkage to the carb are marked before the carb is removed.

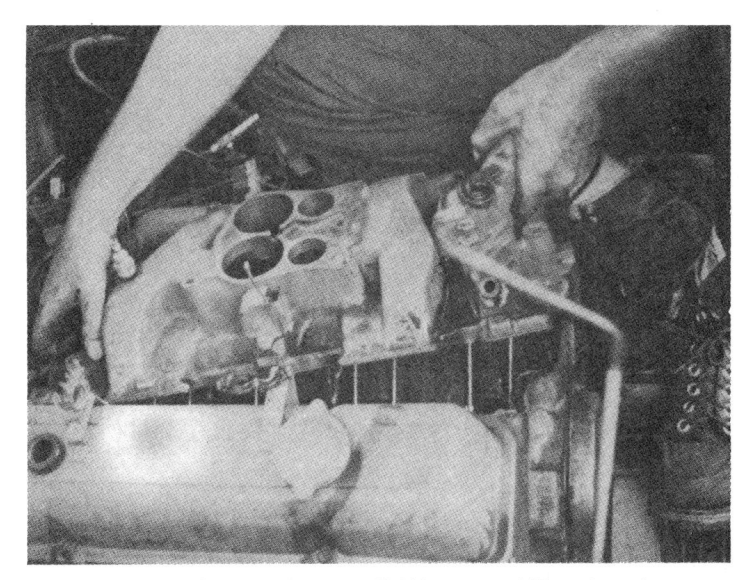

Fig. 6-21. After the carb is off, the manifold is removed. Then the valve covers can be unbolted so you're ready for the next step.

dead center (TDC). Now remove your finger and have the engine turned by hand until the mark on the harmonic damper aligns with the "0" mark on the timing tab on the timing chain cover. The number one piston is exactly at TDC.

Fig. 6-22. Rocker arms are unbolted and push rods are removed. Rocker arms and push rods should go back to the same valve they came from.

Fig. 6-23. Lifters are removed from lifter bores. A long-handled mechanic's magnet may help remove any that can't be grasped by hand.

The distributor cap is now taken off, and the position of the rotor is marked on the distributor body. The distributor can now be removed from the engine, as it must be to replace the cam. As long as the crankshaft isn't moved (or if it is, as in the valve adjustment procedure explained later, it can be cranked back so the number one cylinder is at TDC) the distributor can be replaced so that the timing will be correct. Just make sure the rotor is pointing at the mark on the distributor body when it is reinstalled.

It's a good idea to replace the timing chain if your engine has many miles on it, as they tend to stretch. We took off the old GM chain and

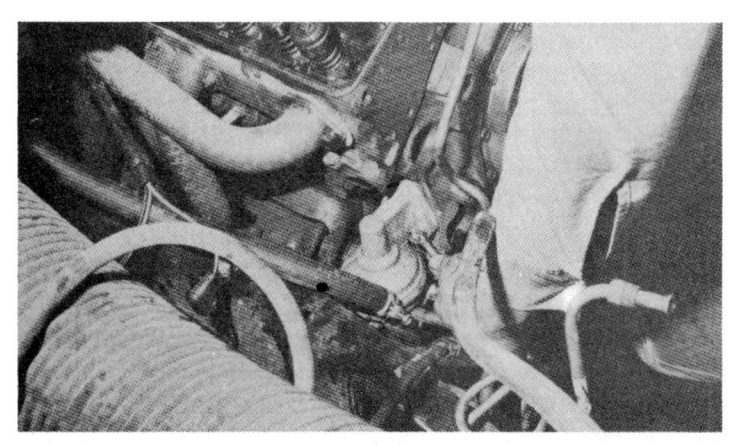

Fig. 6-24. As the fuel pump is driven by the cam, pump must be unbolted and pulled away from the block. Fuel lines can be left in place.

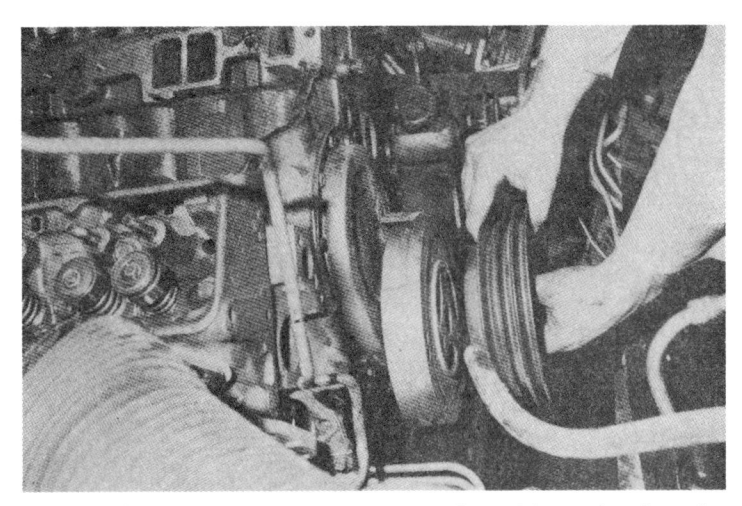

Fig. 6-25. With all other items removed from in front of the engine, the pulley assembly is unbolted and removed from the harmonic damper.

replaced it with one of the best on the market, a Cloyes roller chain, which was matched to new Cloyes camshaft and crankshaft gears. When installing the new chain (and new gears if you chose to replace yours), it is vitally important that everything go on in perfect alignment, or you'll never get the timing right. Figure 6-27 shows how the dot on the cam gear is matched so that it is exactly above the crank gear. Remember, if either gear moves just a tooth out of position as you install the chain, you will have greatly altered

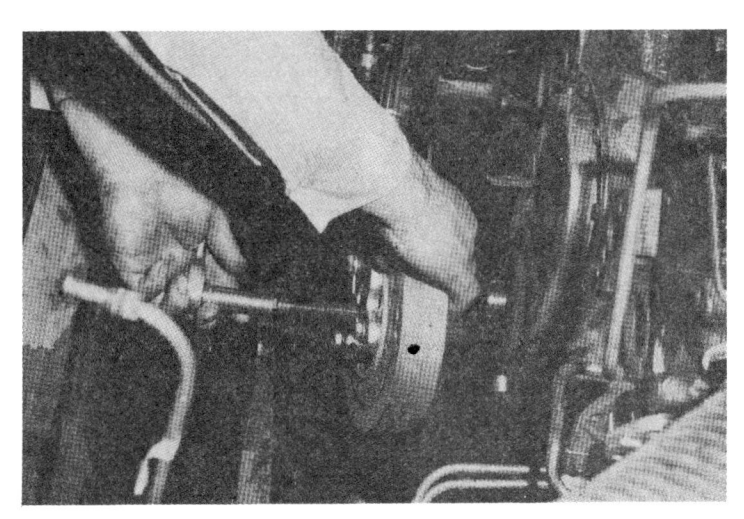

Fig. 6-26. You will need a puller to remove that harmonic damper from the nose of the crankshaft, as that's a very tight fit.

Fig. 6-27. With the timing cover removed, timing dots on crank and cam gears line up perfectly. When new gears are installed, dots must line up.

Fig. 6-28. Bolts which hold the camshaft gear in place are removed. Then the cam gear and the timing chain can be pulled off.

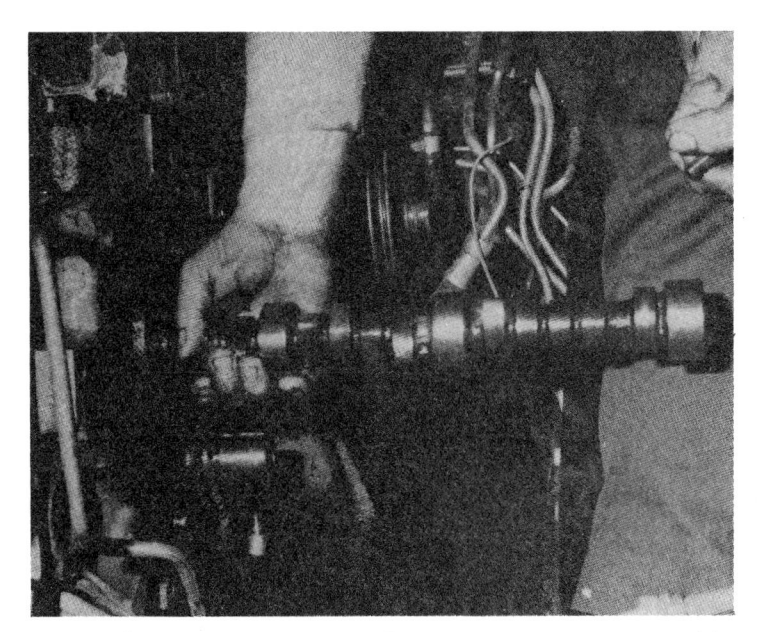

Fig. 6-29. Cam can now be pulled out. Take it easy, as the sharp edges of the lobes can damage the cam bearings if you're not careful.

the cam timing. After the chain is on, double check to be sure the two dots are lined up.

Sometimes installing a new crank gear can cause problems, as the fit is very tight. If you are unable to get the gear on the crank by pounding on the

Fig. 6-30. The new pieces going in include Sig Erson cam, lifters and push rods (new springs weren't needed), and Cloyes chain and gears.

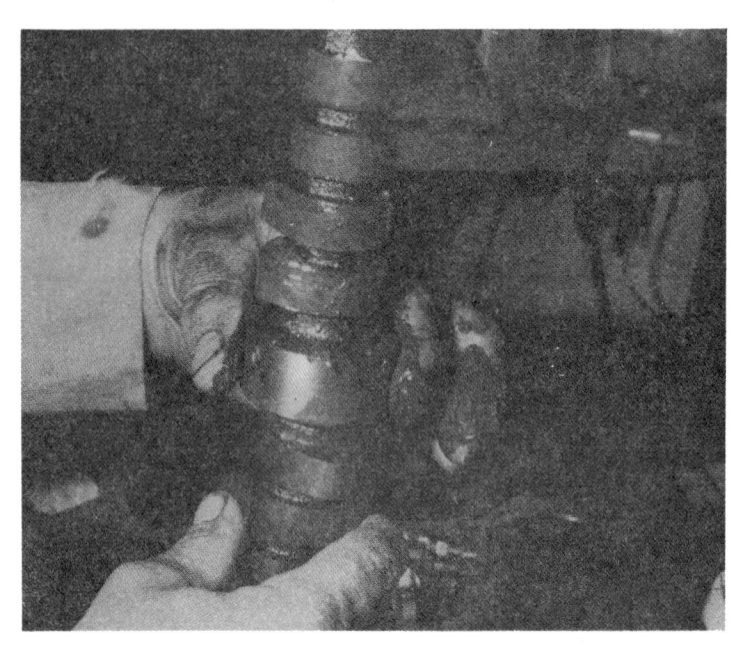

Fig. 6-31. New cam is washed with solvent to remove oil and dust, then coated with cam lube. Sig Erson cams come complete with lube.

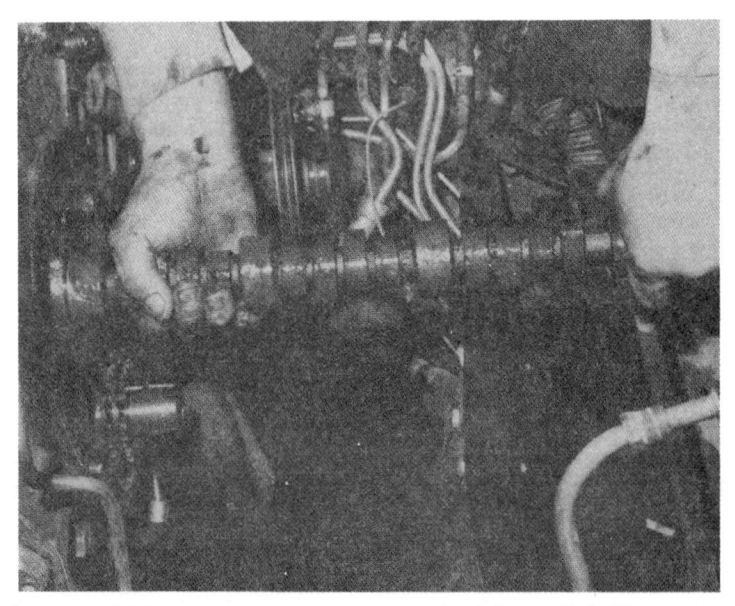

Fig. 6-32. After cam is lubricated, it is slipped into place carefully, with both hands, so that no cam bearings are damaged.

Fig. 6-33. With cam in place and gears properly lined up by timing dots, the Sig Erson cam button is put into place.

gear with a wood block and hammer, try heating the gear to approximately 250 degrees in an oven, while cooling the nose of the crank with ice. Place the gear on the crank. It should slip on with a bit of pounding. Some people

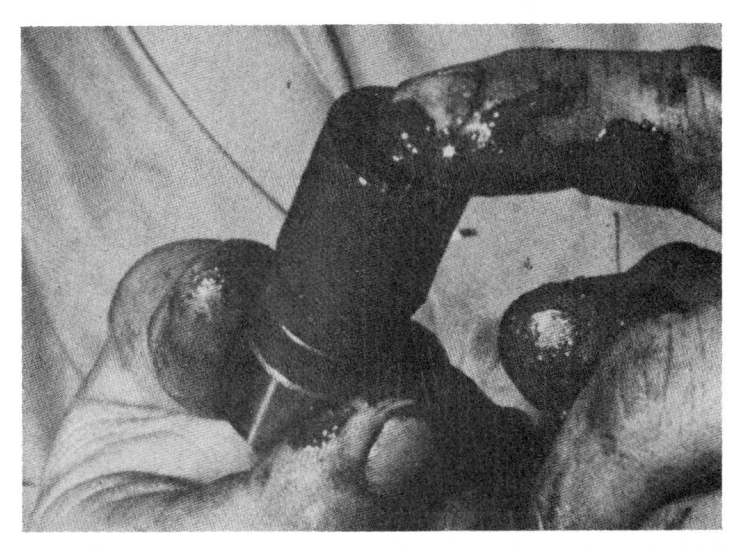

Fig. 6-34. Lifters, as well as tips of push rods and tops of valve stems, should all get a coating of cam lube before installation.

61

Fig. 6-35. Reinstall lifters, push rods, and pivot arms. Then adjust all the valves using the procedure outlined.

report the same problem when installing the harmonic balancer, and the same procedure should be used here. With our late model GMC we experienced no problems.

Fig. 6-36. Timing cover, harmonic damper, pulley assembly, and water pump can all go back in place now that the new cam is installed.

Fig. 6-37. Since the manifold had to be removed, now is a good time for a new one, such as the Edelbrock SP2P, for better midrange torque.

Fig. 6-38. Before installing the new manifold, all old gasket material must be scrapped from heads to prevent leaks.

Fig. 6-39. Gasket cement is brushed on the heads, and then new gaskets supplied with the Edlebrock SP2P are put into place.

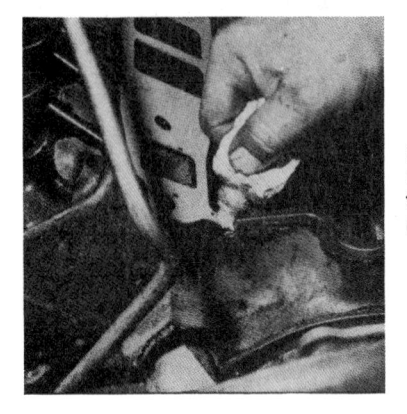

Fig. 6-40. Spot where the head meets the block is prone to leaks, so fill this with some silicone gasket material to prevent any problems.

Because the engine must be started and run immediately at 2500 rpm to break in the cam after it is installed, on engines with hydraulic lifters and movable rocker pivot arms, such as the GMC and Chevy engines, the valve train should be adjusted before the engine is started.

The easiest way to do this is with the manifold still off the motor. Looking down into the valley between the cylinder heads, turn the crank until both lifters in cylinder number one are at the low point. Then run the rocker arm down until it just touches the push rod, and give the adjusting nut another half turn. Follow this procedure for each cylinder, being sure at one end the number one cylinder is at TDC so the distributor will go in properly.

Proper breaking in of a new cam is vital to its long life. Research shows that the vast majority of cams that fail do so because of improper break-in. Follow these simple rules to prevent camshaft damage or failure.

●Be sure that the cam lobes, cam, and push rod faces of the lifters are coated with a moly disulfide-based assembly lubricant. Most cam kits, like the Sig Erson we installed, come with the proper lube. Use it.

●Install the camshaft using the manufacturer's recommended component parts kit. Be sure all parts are installed to manufacturer's specs.

Fig. 6-41. With all gaskets properly in their places, the manifold is put down and the bolts are tightened up in a crisscross pattern.

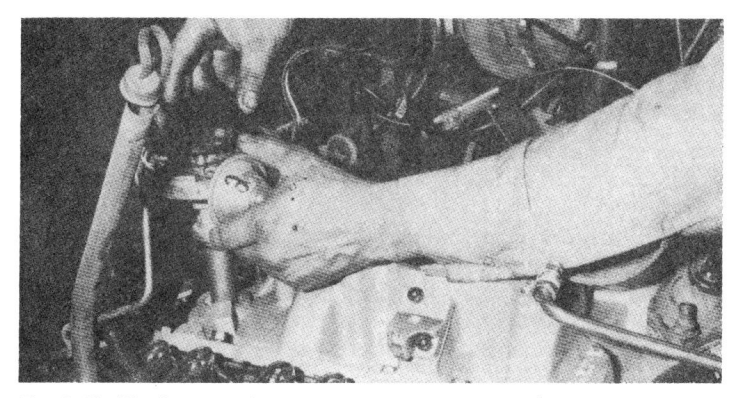

Fig. 6-42. Distributor, with rotor in correct position, is replaced through the manifold and into the engine.

Fig. 6-43. Don't forget to tighten the fuel pump back down. Then the carb goes back on, and all lines and linkage are reattached.

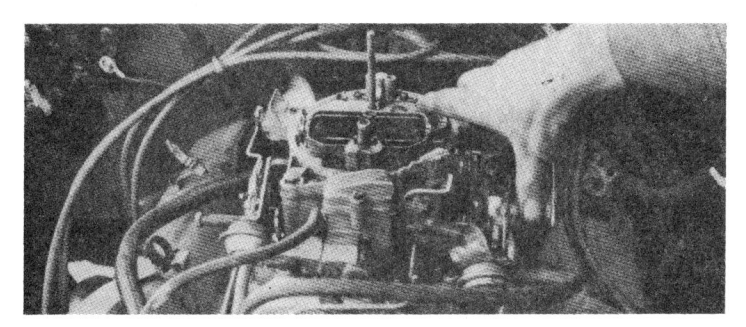

Fig. 6-44. Check to see that choke and accelerator linkages do not bind and work through full travel. Then break in the cam.

- Check the entire valve train for interference before engine is started. If there is interference, do not start engine until it is removed.
- Fill the crankcase with straight viscosity oil of 20W or 30W for break-in.
- Be sure the cooling system is filled.
- With our Sig Erson cam, the manufacturer recommended we add two cans of Sig Erson Hi-R oil additive to crankcase oil. The additive contains zinc-phosphorous additives to prevent galling.
- Engine must start immediately when cranked. Be sure timing is correct and prime the carburetor before starting.
- Do *not* idle the engine during the first 20 minutes of operation. Revs should be kept at 2500 or above to allow proper lubrication. Oil for lubrication and cooling of cam comes from the crank, and the crank will not throw enough oil for a cam below 2500 rpm.

Now that you're aware of the potential trouble spots, break out the wrenches and have a go at it.

Chapter 7

Installing Electric Windows

There's one thing about the width of a cab that's indisputable. Unless you've got arms like King Kong, there's no way you are going to raise or lower the passenger side window when you're driving alone. The answer is electric windows you can control from the driver's seat.

With this in mind, we were delighted when we ran into two old friends—Vilem Haan, one of the most noted accessory distributors and importers in the country, and Rene Pellandini—at the latest SEMA (Specialty Equipment Manufacturers Association) show. Rene was formerly the Renault distributor for Southern California. After an attempt at early retirement, he was coaxed into Vilem's organization as marketing director.

Vilem is the exclusive importer of the Unus electric window lift. He and Rene thought it might be something vanners and truck owners, would be interested in.

INSTALLATION PROCEDURE

The principle of these electric window lifts is simplicity in itself. The actual operation however, takes a good deal of engineering to build a small, powerful, reversible electric motor that can be clutch adjusted for tension. The unit replaces the manual window crank. A "tailored to fit" plastic sleeve with the correct serrations fits over the standard handle pin.

That is the first step in the installation procedure. Remove the crank handle from the pin and fit the plastic adapter. There's a whole plastic bag of these adapters along with a sheet showing which numbered one is to be used on which type of vehicle. Ours was a Number 7 (American Ford). We left the rest of them with West Coast Van Conversions who were doing the installation for us.

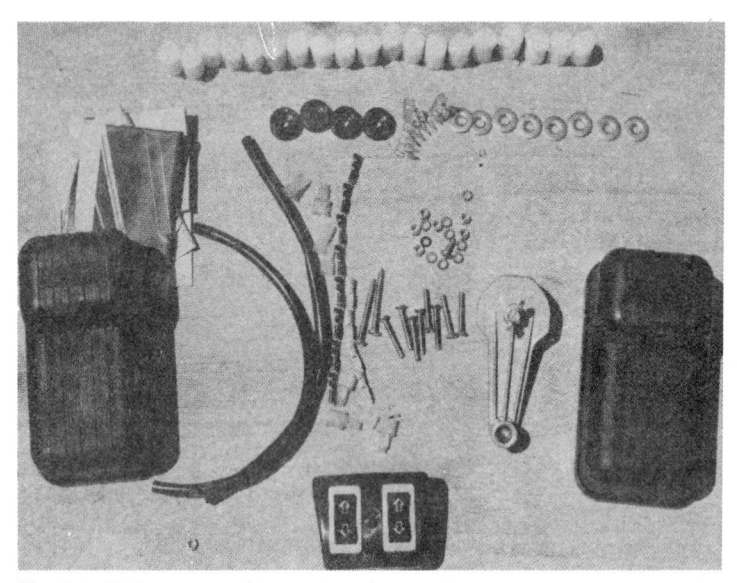

Fig. 7-1. All the parts and instructions for installation of the Unus window lifts. White items at the top are a wide variety of window pin adapters to fit virtually every make of car. Only the correct two are needed (photo by Brad Barcus).

KIT INSTRUCTIONS

The instructions that come with the kit are extremely detailed and are printed in four languages: English, French, German, and Italian. There are

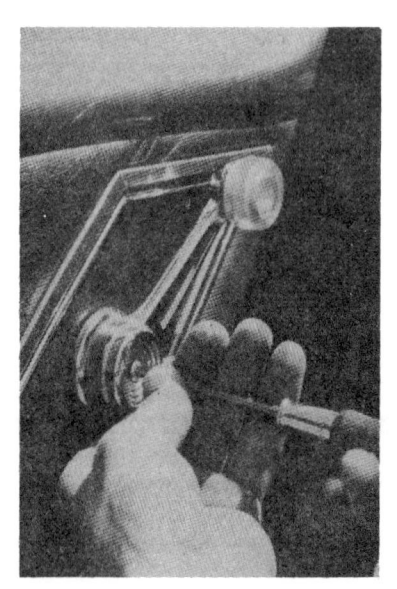

Fig. 7-2. First step is to remove stock window crank (photo by Brad Barcus).

Fig. 7-3. Plastic adapter, in our case No. 7 (American Ford), is slipped over the pin (photo by Brad Barcus).

only nine steps outlined in the instructions. One really threw us a curve but didn't seem to bother Dan of West Coast, who was doing the work. In the last sentence of instruction No. 6 it says, " . . . carry out the electrical connections in accordance with the wiring diagram supplied." Actually with the detailed schematic and the excellent instructions, it is not all that mind boggling.

Fig. 7-4. Plastic cover is removed from motor-reducing gear unit (photo by Brad Barcus).

Fig. 7-5. Unit is positioned on the door in the most aesthetic and practical position. In some cases it can be an auxiliary arm rest (photo by Brad Barcus).

The kit is supplied with an aluminum emergency crank which is also the clutch adjustment tool. This crank enables you to roll the windows up or down in case of a battery failure.

After leading wires from the cockpit up through the door (the instructions call for removal of the door panel) and making solderless connections

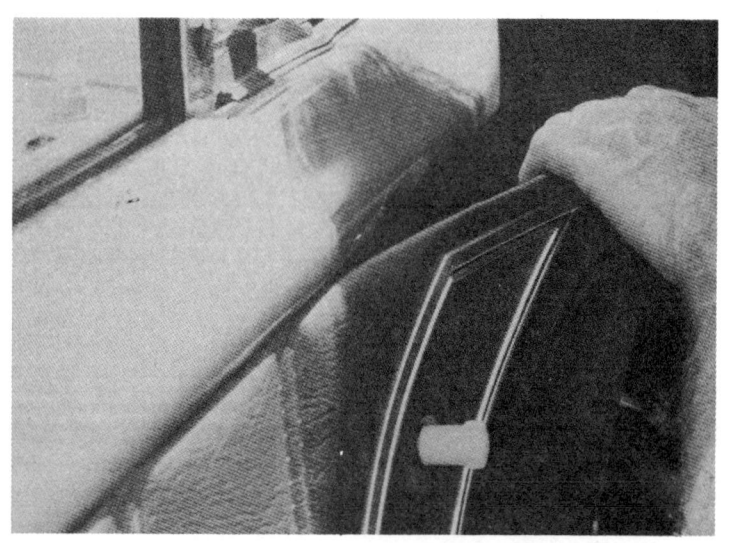

Fig. 7-6. Dan pulls the door panel loose, but not off, for routing the wire from the hot terminal to the motor-reducing gear unit (photo by Brad Barcus).

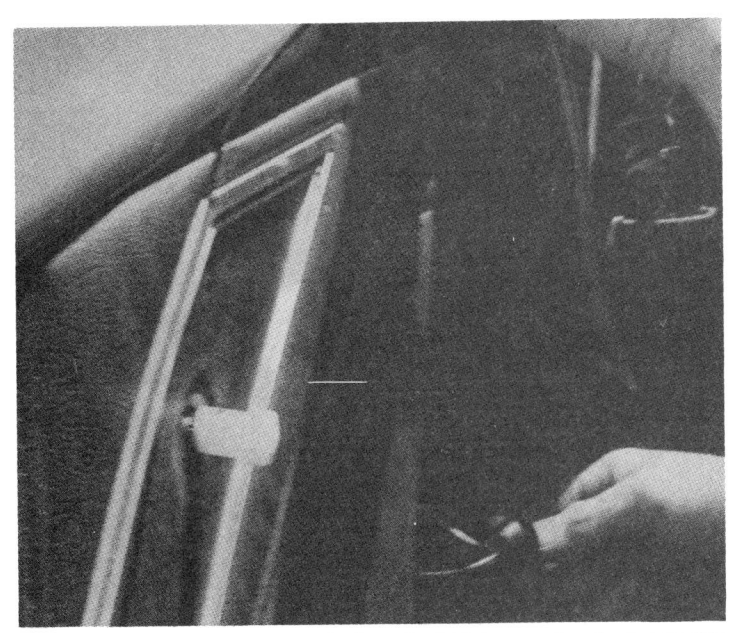

Fig. 7-7. One can usually find a hole through which to run a length of malleable wire like a coat hanger as a guide (photo by Brad Barcus).

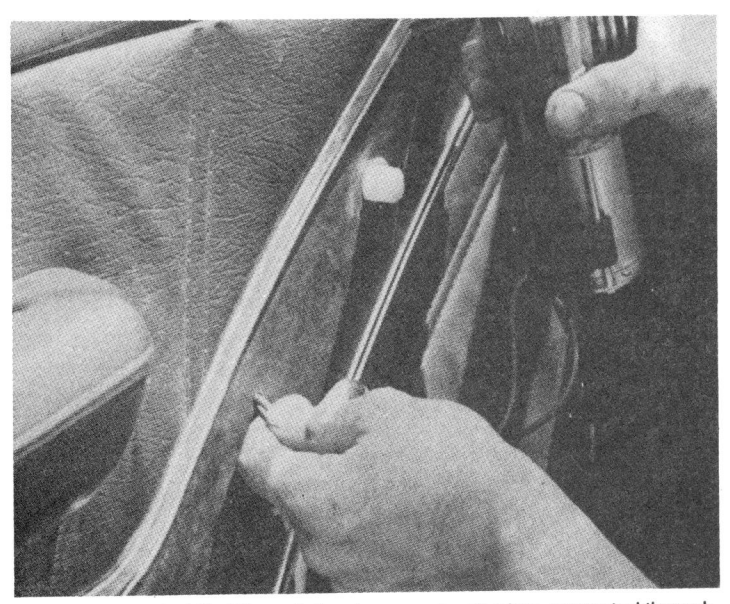

Fig. 7-8. A hole is drilled through the door panel, unit wires are routed through, then the motor-reducing gear is finally positioned (photo by Brad Barcus).

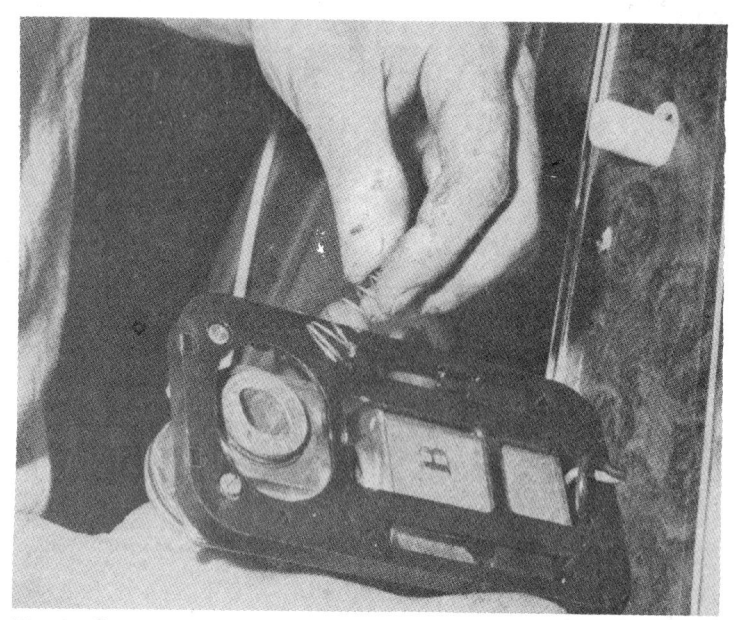

Fig. 7-9. Conical spring is inserted into the housing before attaching the unit to the door panel (photo by Brad Barcus).

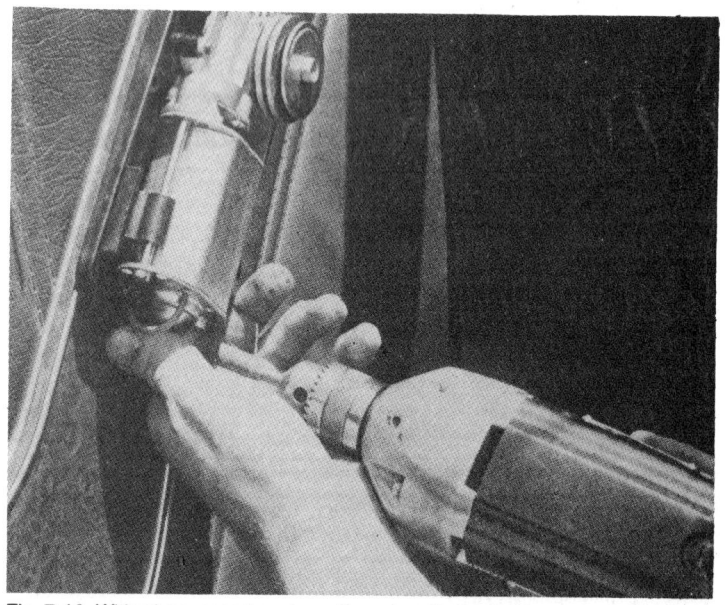

Fig. 7-10. With wires routed, motor unit can be attached to the door panel (photo by Brad Barcus).

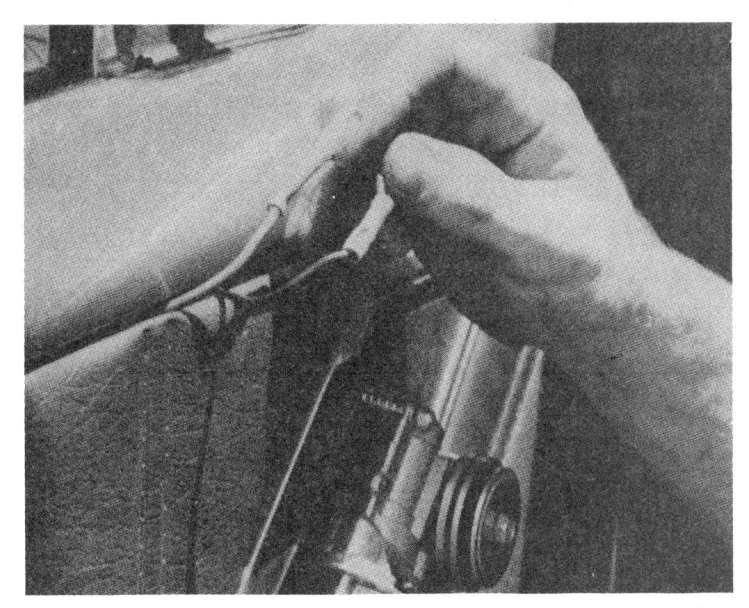

Fig. 7-11. Solderless connectors are used as a time saver to assure a firm electrical pathway (photo by Brad Barcus).

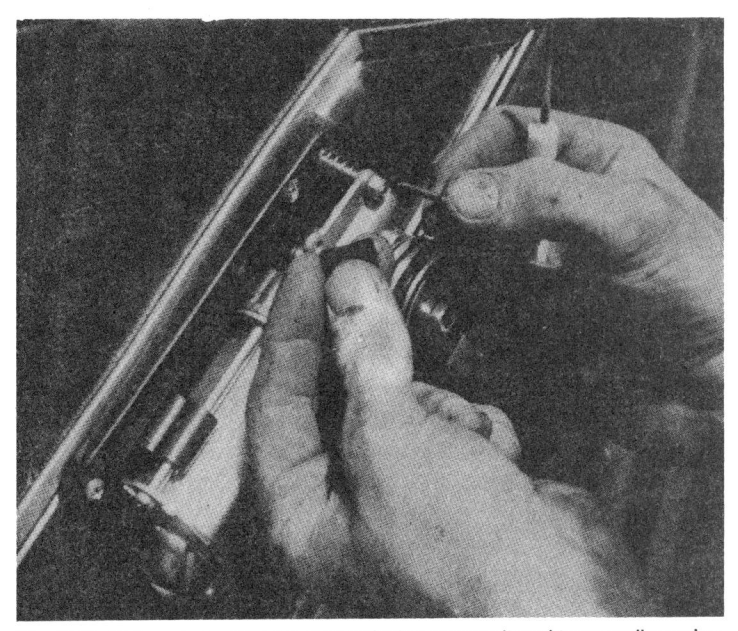

Fig. 7-12. Fixing screw of the motor-reducing gear unit and two small spacing cylinders are removed and discarded (photo by Brad Barcus).

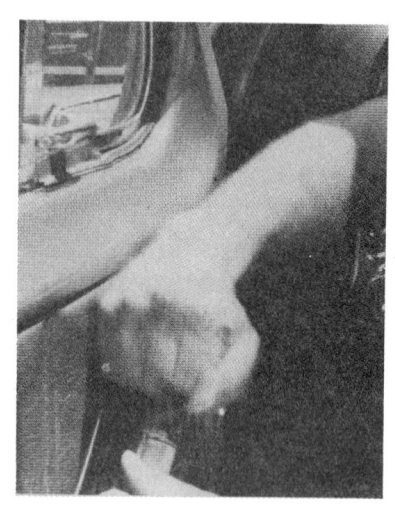

Fig. 7-13. Best method of reaffixing door panel to its clips is a sharp rap with the fist (photo by Brad Barcus).

to the wires on the unit, the motor-reducing gear unit is first positioned, then bolted to the door panel. Except for drilling out the slots for the control box installation, most of the rest of the job is electrical. One word of caution. Instruction No. 8 might be easy to misunderstand. It states, "Remove the fixing screw of the motor-reducing gear unit and withdraw the two small spacing cylinders (Fig. 7-10)." What this means is remove the screw and the spacers *and throw them away*.

After two or three days of use, it will be necessary to adjust the clutch. You don't want the mechanism so vigorous it will injure a hand; nor do you want it to slip.

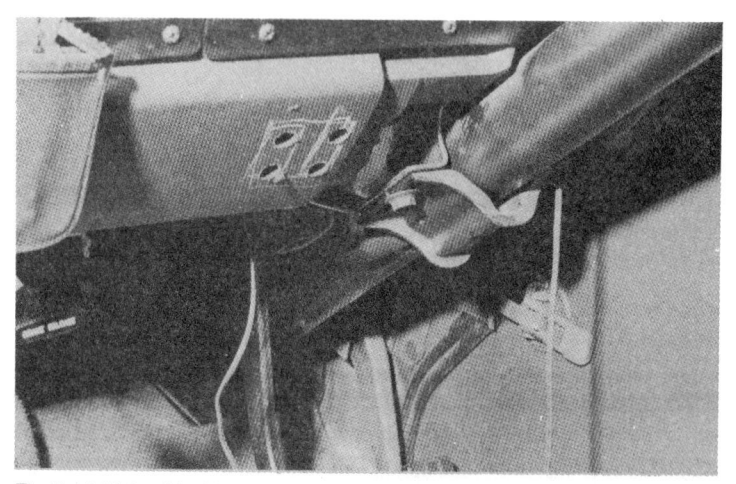

Fig. 7-14. Not an ideal location for the control box, but the driver can always open the window for the passenger. It would require quick disconnect fittings if located on the engine cover (photo by Brad Barcus).

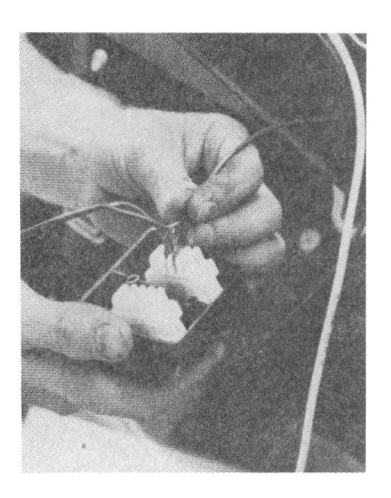

Fig. 7-15. Kit contains all necessary parts and detailed wiring diagram for connecting up /down control (photo by Brad Barcus).

Tools required for the job are: electric drill with several bits, screw drivers(s), solderless connectors, wire stripper, and a length of medium stiff wire (coat hanger).

With the excellent instructions, wiring diagram, and schematic drawing supplied with the kit, plus Figs. 7-1 through 7-19, you should be able to install the Unus window lift yourself. Dan, at West Coast Van Conversions, needed about three hours for both doors and the control.

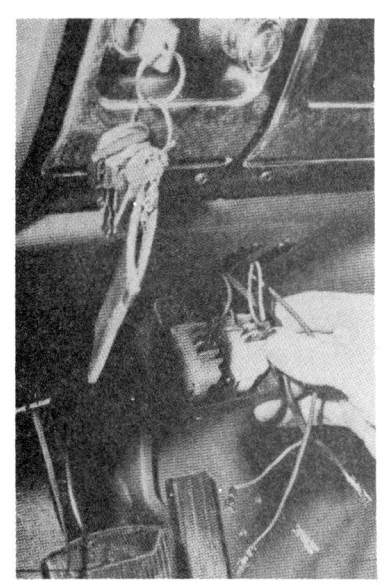

Fig. 7-16. Where holes have been previously drilled, larger slots have been made to accept plastic terminals (photo by Brad Barcus).

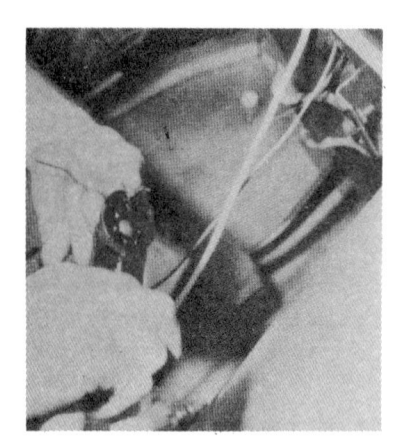

Fig. 7-17. Excessive lengths of wire are shortened for neat appearance and tidy installation (photo by Brad Barcus).

Fig. 7-18. Up/down control box neatly in position (photo by Brad Barcus).

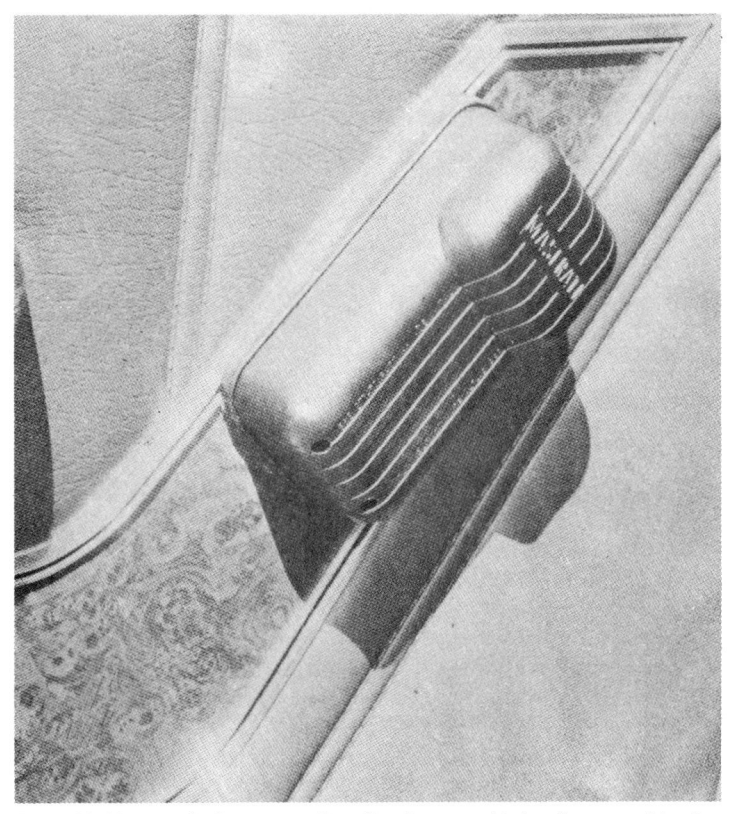

Fig. 7-19. Motor-reducing gear unit on the door panel is hardly more obtrusive than the crank (photo by Brad Barcus).

Chapter 8

Installing Headers on a 4×4

Mention the word *headers* to a drag racer or street freak, and the first thing he'll think of is speed. A good set of headers can be just as useful to the off-roader as they are to the go-fast set. Headers on 4×4s can help improve engine responsiveness, lower cylinder temperatures, and boost mileage. Getting a good set of headers, and seeing that they are installed correctly, is vitally important to their effective operation.

There are actually two parts to proper header installation. The first step is the removal of the old exhaust manifolds and the installation of the headers. The second step is the installation of a good free-flow exhaust pipe and muffler system.

The first part can be handled by anyone with some backyard mechanical experience. The second half of the job is something that can be done only by an experienced welder and should probably be left to a good muffler shop.

To see how the pros go about installing a header system, we dropped into Stan's Headers and Mufflers, 5811 Imperial Highway, South Gate, CA. 90280. Here we watched, and took notes and pictures, as a set of headers was put on a 1978 GMC four-wheel-drive pickup equipped with the 400 cubic-inch V-8 engine (Figs. 8-1 and 8-2).

Since one of the most common reasons people install headers is to improve mileage, we had the GMC's owner carefully check his mileage before the headers were installed. That way we could compare mileage afterwards to see how well the headers had done. The results were remarkable to say the least.

Doing the installation was Johnny Santana, and one of the first points he stressed was the importance of quality headers. Some headers are sold with full floating flanges. This means the header pipe is belled, and the

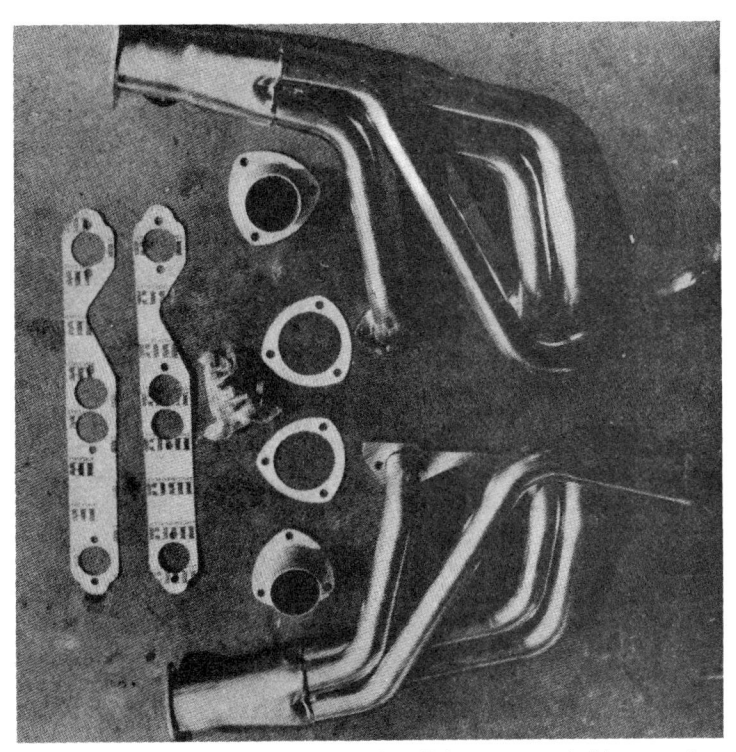

Fig. 8-1. A set of Stan's Headers includes all the parts needed for mounting, including bolts and gaskets (photo by Lin Ford).

flange that bolts to the block holds the belled portion of the pipes against the block itself. Even with the use of a gasket, leaks are still possible with this system.

Stan's Headers have the header pipes welded to the flange, and then the weld is ground down flat (Fig. 8-3). This gives a completely flat surface and insures that there will be no leaks where the headers are attached to the block.

Johnny then explained that even using top quality headers, the best results cannot be achieved if they are simply attached to a stock exhaust system. Headers work by improving the flow of gases away from the cylinders. They help to reduce back pressure and improve scavenging, so that each cylinder is completely emptied of exhaust gases and able to take a full charge on the intake cycle. Better scavenging also makes fewer combustion by-products remain in each cylinder, thus reducing cylinder temperature.

While the headers do a good job of reducing back pressure, if the exhaust is then funneled into the small diameter of a stock exhaust pipe and through stock mufflers, this will build up back pressure behind the headers,

79

Fig. 8-2. The 400-cid V-8 engine in the GMC four-wheel-drive pickup is seen here before work begins. (photo by Lin Ford).

reducing their effectiveness. A set of headers can only do their best job when routed into exhaust pipe at least 2½ inches in diameter and through low-restriction mufflers. This ensures the most effective operation of the entire exhaust system.

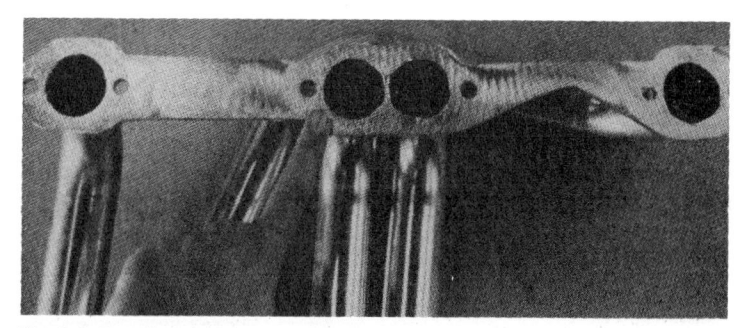

Fig. 8-3. Note how headers are ground flat to fit properly against the side of the exhaust ports (photo by Lin Ford).

REMOVING EXHAUST PIPES AND EXHAUST MANIFOLDS

Since Johnny was going to be installing headers, exhaust pipe, and mufflers all at once, the first step was the removal of all stock exhaust pipes and mufflers. Since the GMC had a GVW of over 6000 pounds, there were no catalytic converters to worry about. In vehicles fitted with such devices, it is illegal to remove the converters.

After the exhaust pipes and mufflers were out of the way, Johnny got ready to remove the exhaust manifolds (Figs. 8-4 and 8-5). On GMC's with power steering and air conditioning, it is necessary to unbolt the pumps and move them to the side to get at the manifolds. The pumps themselves do not need to be removed, merely pushed to one side.

All plug wires must be pulled from the spark plugs (Fig. 8-6). Since the brackets for the wires themselves may interfere, they can be bent up out of the way. The dipstick and dipstick tube must also be removed as well, so the headers can be slid up from underneath. The dipstick tube is simply press-fit into the block. Grasp it gently, being careful not to squeeze it too

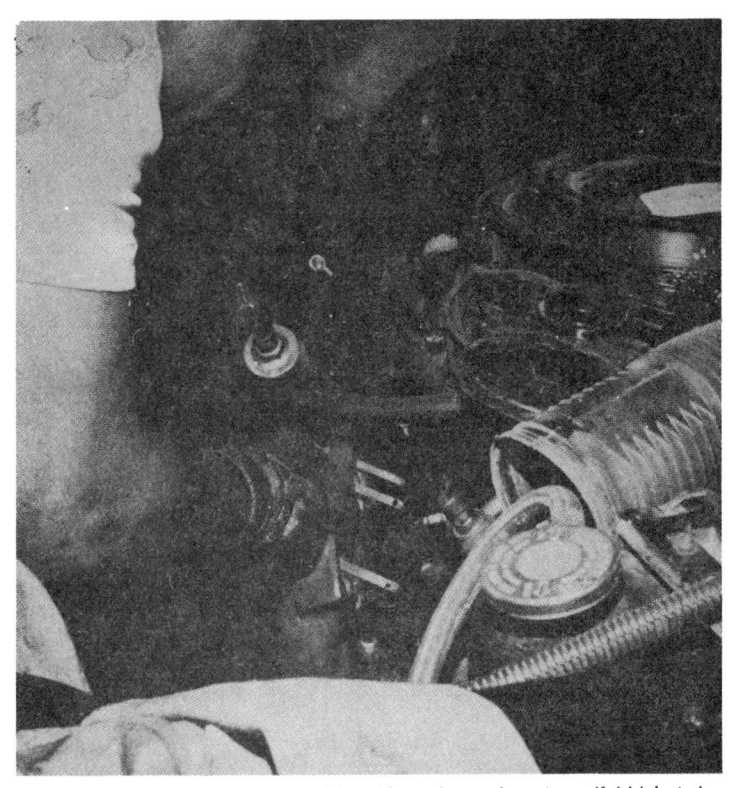

Fig. 8-4. First step is the removal of the old cast iron exhaust manifold (photo by Lin Ford).

Fig. 8-5. Headers, exhaust pipes, and mufflers are all tucked up out of the way, minimizing the danger they will be hit by rocks (photo by Lin Ford).

tightly, and twist it free. After the headers are in, it is simply pressed firmly back into place.

With a set of Stan's Headers nothing else had to be removed before the exhaust manifolds were removed and the headers put in place. Though Johnny says it is not strictly necessary, he recommends that those unfamiliar with the installation should remove the spark plug closest to the firewall on each side. Then the headers just slide up from the bottom (Fig. 8-7).

New gaskets should be used between the block and the headers, and these come with a Stan's Headers kit. The two outside bolts should be started first and then the bolts tightened from the outside inward (Fig. 8-8).

Fig. 8-6. Wires must be pulled off spark plugs so headers can be put in place. Removing the plug nearest the firewall will make installation easier (photo by Lin Ford).

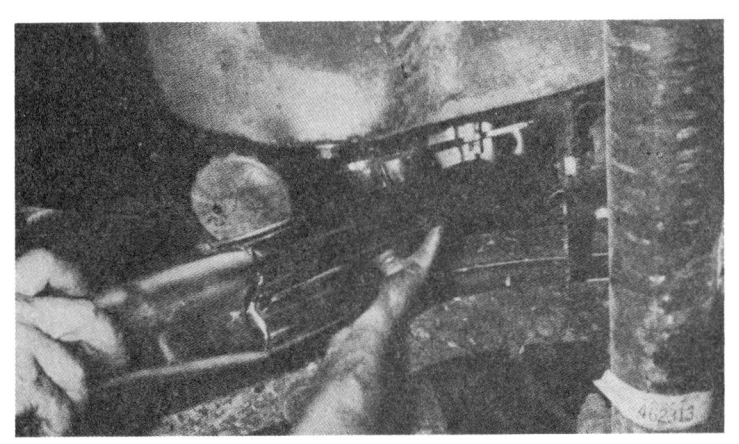

Fig. 8-7. Stan's Headers slide up easily from underneath engine, and neither oil filter (left side) nor starter motor (right side) have to be removed to get headers in place (photo by Lin Ford).

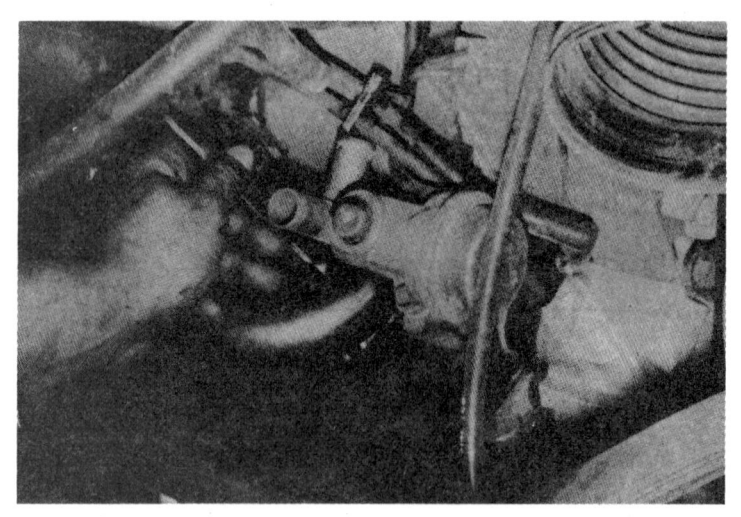

Fig. 8-8. Once headers are in, bolts should be tightened from the outside inward. Remember to retighten bolts after the engine has been warmed up (photo by Lin Ford).

After the engine has been started to check for leaks and allowed to warm up, the bolts should be retightened.

Up to this point, all the work can easily be done by a backyard mechanic. Now, however, unless the installer is a good welder and has a pipe-bending machine lying around the garage, it will be necessary to travel down to a muffler shop to have the job finished.

EXHAUST PIPE INSTALLATION

The important thing here is to insist on exhaust pipe that is at least 2½ inches in diameter and on low-restriction mufflers. Naturally, after going to the trouble of getting the headers, a dual exhaust system is the only way to go.

All the exhaust pipes and the mufflers should be kept as high as possible so that the ground clearance of the vehicle is not reduced. This also keeps the exhaust system from getting dings in it that can increase back pressure in the system. Johnny did an excellent job with the GMC, keeping all pipe along the frame rails for maximum protection (Fig. 8-9).

The exhaust pipe was exited at the rear wheel openings. While it may look like a tight fit, there was plenty of room (Figs. 8-10 and 8-11). The shorter the exhaust pipe the hotter the pipe stays, reducing the possibility of water forming in the system and causing rust.

We checked the noise level of the GMC installation after Johnny was finished, using a sound meter (Fig. 8-12). The truck registered only a slight increase in noise, well below the legal minimum. Yet the truck still had the mellow rumble a good custom system provides.

Fig. 8-9. Headers are well up along frame rails, protecting them from possible damage when the truck is used off road (photo by Lin Ford).

Fig. 8-10. At least three hangers should be used, so the system won't be shaken loose in the rough stuff (photo by Lin Ford).

Fig. 8-11. Crossover pipe between two exhaust pipes is important for equalizing exhaust pulses and reducing noise in system (photo by Lin Ford).

Once the headers have been installed, and a good listen indicates no leaks, the owner should immediately take his truck or 4×4 to a good tune-up shop with an exhaust gas analyzer. Headers may cause the engine to run leaner than it had with a stock system. In some cases the engine can run so lean (and thus so hot) it can burn a valve in less than 1000 miles.

With an exhaust gas analyzer, a shop can check to see if the mixture is correct. In some cases it may be necessary to reject the carb slightly richer to compensate for the headers.

Did the installation really make the GMC run better? Yes. The owner reported that increased power and torque were immediately noticeable. Both on the highway and in the dirt, the truck turned in better performances.

Fig. 8-12. Entire system is fully free-flowing, yet a check with sound meter shows it remains well within legal noise limits (photo by Lin Ford).

Most interestingly, gas mileage saw a healthy jump. Before the headers, the GMC had been averaging 8.2 mph in city driving and 10.8 mpg on the highway. With the headers, mileage jumped to 10.2 mpg in the city and 14.6 on the highway.

Such an installation isn't exactly cheap. The headers for the GMC cost $100, and the exhaust system installation for a pickup like the GMC runs about $175 at Stan's. For something that makes that four-wheeler run both better and cheaper, headers are definitely worth it.

Chapter 9

Engine Oil Coolers

Four-by-four owners have long been aware of the benefits to be realized when an automatic transmission-equipped vehicle is fitted out with a transmission oil cooler. When a proper size unit is installed correctly, fluid temperature drops considerably, prolonging both transmission and fluid life. What many of these same people don't realize is that a similar cooler connected into the engine's oiling system will produce similar results. Engine temperatures can be lowered sufficiently that both the engine oil and the components in that engine will perform better and live longer. This means you'll be saving money.

Engine oil will remove damaging heat from an engine when it is maintained in the 175-200 degrees Fahrenheit temperature range. It is quite hard to keep oil that cool in practice, especially if you have a late model, emissions-equipped engine and you run your machine in competitive events, pull a trailer, or just like to give your machine a good workout off-road once in a while. Conditions such as these easily raise oil temperature above 200 degrees Fahrenheit, and even if it's but for a brief period, you can be in for trouble. High engine heat tends to turn oil to tar: the oil literally burns up. We've seen oil removed from an engine pan after no more than 3,000 miles on a new emissions-controlled engine that had to be scraped out with a putty knife. It was actually tar.

Other situations that can cause oil to overheat include air conditioners, high-pressure cooling systems, and tight engine compartments, the latter often prevalent where an engine swap took place.

Due to engine-killing situations like this, a number of companies offer four-wheelers a variety of engine oil coolers. While many differ in design, if a unit of sufficient size is installed on your vehicle, it will definitely reduce engine-oil temperatures, and thereby engine temperatures.

FUNCTION OF AN OIL COOLER

In the event you are not familiar with how an engine oil cooler functions, or you need a refresher course, we'll touch briefly on what goes on when an oil cooler is rigged up on an engine. Simply put, in stock form an engine delivers oil to an externally mounted canister oil filter. After going through the filter, the oil is returned to the engine.

To utilize an oil cooler, the filter is unscrewed from the cylinder block. In its place one of two types of adapters is screwed on, using the same fitting that takes the spin-on filter (Fig. 9-1). One type adapter screws onto the filter fitting, then the filter (a new one if yours is due for replacement) is reinstalled, in effect sandwiching the adapter between filter and cylinder block.

Oil is pumped through the adapter and filter, then is delivered via a high-pressure oil hose to the engine cooler, located in front of the engine, preferably in front of the engine, preferably in front of the radiator. Passing through the cooler, the oil quickly dissipates heat, returning cooled through the adapter and back into the engine.

The second type of adapter replaces the filter on the cylinder block. Oil runs through this adapter, through a high-pressure hose to a remotely-mounted oil filter (on another adapter), then through the cooler and back to the engine-mounted adapter and the cylinder block (Figs. 9-2 through 9-4).

OIL COOLER INSTALLATION

Should you be wondering how effective a good cooler can be, here are a few words on the installation we've presented here. A Perma-Cool oil cooler was installed on a 1970 Bronco with 302-inch engine by its owner, Johnnie Rucker. The remote filter adapter was attached to the forward side of the left front fender well, where the filter would be very accessible for changing (Fig. 9-5). The cooler was installed in front of the radiator, behind

Fig. 9-1. Here's a couple of typical adapters. The one on the right attaches to the filter mount on the block, replacing the filter. The unit at left mounts the oil filter remotely. Hoses go to the cooler (photo by Bud Lang).

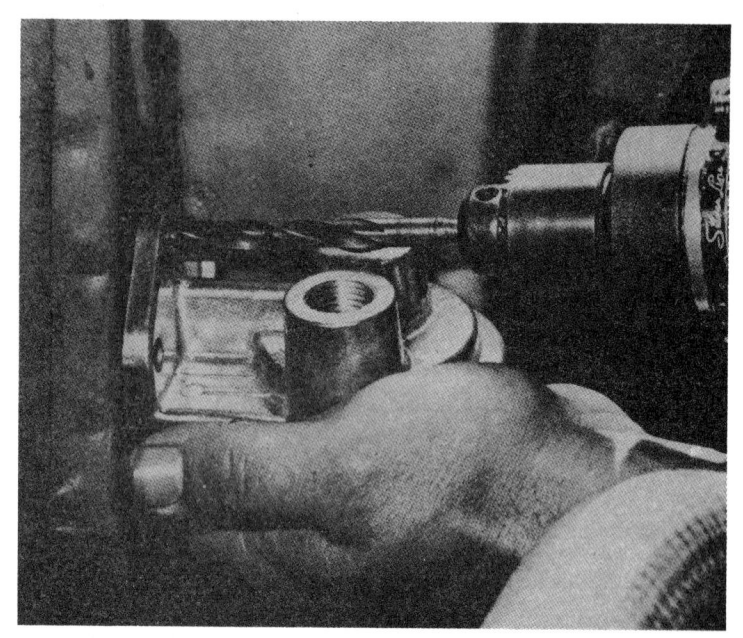

Fig. 9-2. Next step is to locate the remote oil filter mount where it will be accessible, and where lines can be easily routed (photo by Bud Lang).

the grille, a very tight fit to say the least (Figs. 9-6 and 9-7). These machines don't offer much room to play around in.

After the hoses were hooked up, the engine was started and then idled for 10-15 minutes to bring the oil temperature up somewhat and to check for leaks. One fitting hadn't been tightened enough, as oil was seeping about the treads. That was taken care of quickly. The hex-head screws on the stainless steel clamps feature a screwdriver slot, but it was discovered a box-end or socket could tighten the clamps much better than the screwdriver could (Fig. 9-8).

After this warm-up period, we could hold the hose delivering oil from the engine to the remote-mounted oil filter, and it was hot. Next, we placed

Fig. 9-3. The adapter with O-ring is next oiled and screwed onto the block where the stock filter formerly resided (photo by Bud Lang).

90

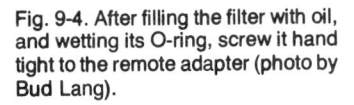

Fig. 9-4. After filling the filter with oil, and wetting its O-ring, screw it hand tight to the remote adapter (photo by Bud Lang).

a hand on the oil filter canister, which was now mounted about 18 inches from the cylinder block. It was hot enough that if we squeezed it, we couldn't continue holding on. Had this filter remained on the engine, it would have been even hotter.

Next for the big test. We clutched the hose returning oil from the cooler to the engine. It was almost as cool as it was before the engine had even been started. We both found this hard to believe. The temperature was checked with gauges, but it had to be at least 50 degrees Fahrenheit cooler, if not more. Now here was a cooler that was really removing engine heat, and this was at idle. With the engine running along a highway or back road, very likely the oil would be running a lot cooler what with air rushing through the cooler, even when you take into consideration that the engine would be working a lot harder and creating more heat than at idle.

OIL HEATING FACTS

If you're wondering just how serious oil heating can be, here are a few facts found in the Hayden Cooler catalog. If you're running an engine with

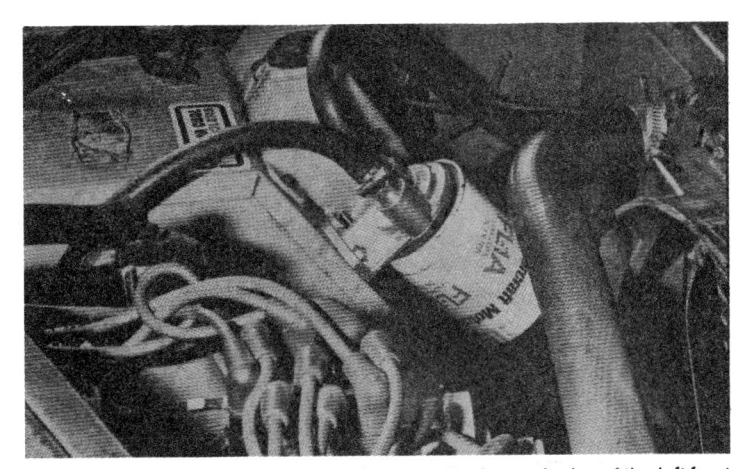

Fig. 9-5. Rucker located his remote adapter on the forward edge of the left front wheel well and routed away from the steering column (photo by Bud Lang).

Fig. 9-6. After removing the hood latch, the cooler is slipped down behind the grille to check out where it can be mounted (photo by Bud Lang).

emission controls, you can expect to get around 100,000 miles from it with normal maintenance—if the engine oil temperature *never* rises above 250 degrees Fahrenheit. Run the oil at 260 degrees Fahrenheit, and engine life will be cut 20,000 miles, or roughly a year or two. Run the engine oil at 270 degrees Fahrenheit, and engine life will be cut to around 67,000 miles. Run it up to around 295 degrees Fahrenheit, and that mill will last about 30,000 miles. Now, these figures do not mean you have to run the engine at those temperatures all the time. Just get it up there a few times during each oil

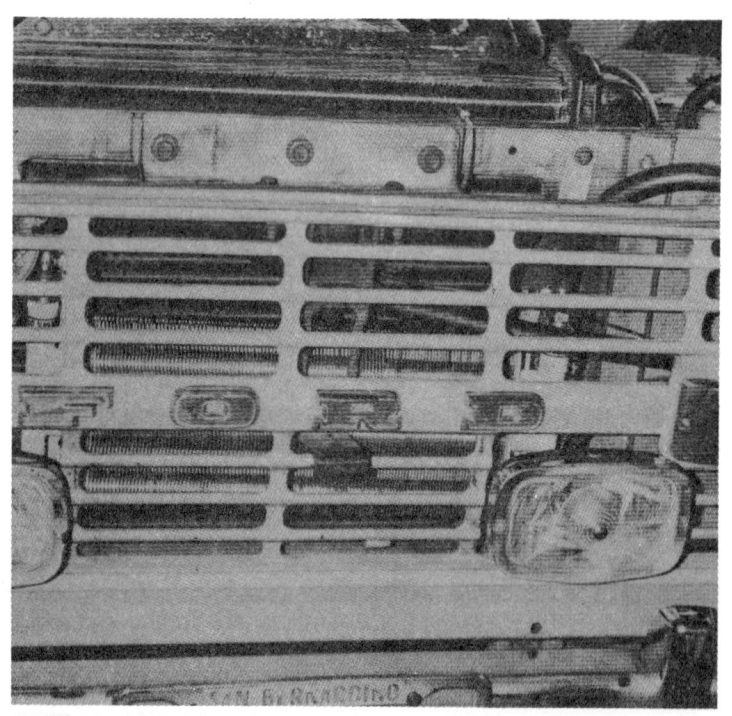

Fig. 9-7. Mounted in front of the radiator, Perma-Cool cooler is down low so it won't block too much air flow. It works super (photo by Bud Lang).

Fig. 9-8. Now the hoses can be routed to the tightened fittings, and the clamps secured. A screwdriver will work, but a socket is better (photo by Bud Lang).

change period (long enough to destroy the protective additives in the oil), and your engine will have had it.

Where you locate the cooler itself will have a direct effect on how well it cools your engine, too. If mounted directly in front of the radiator, it will be 100 percent efficient, as it's catching a full air stream. If mounted at an angle beneath the radiator and in front of the engine, it will be 85 percent efficient (Figs. 9-9 and 9-10). If mounted behind the A-C condenser or radiator it becomes less efficient because it is subjected to warmer air.

Fig. 9-9. With the cooler positioned, attaching straps from the kit are bolted on loosely, and marked where they must be bent or cut (photo by Bud Lang).

Fig. 9-10. Here are two of the straps (there are four), showing their shape and the angle they'll be mounted at after installation (photo by Bud Lang).

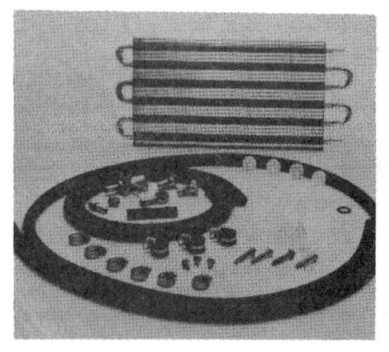

Fig. 9-11. Here is a Hayden Space-Saver cooler kit for vehicles that haven't much room in front of the radiator. The cooler is only ¾-inch thick, as opposed to 1½-inch for the heavy-duty models. Hayden provides Quik-Mount Nylon mounting rods, locking nuts, and sponge rubber pads for attaching the cooler to the radiator. This is quick and easy (photo by Bud Lang).

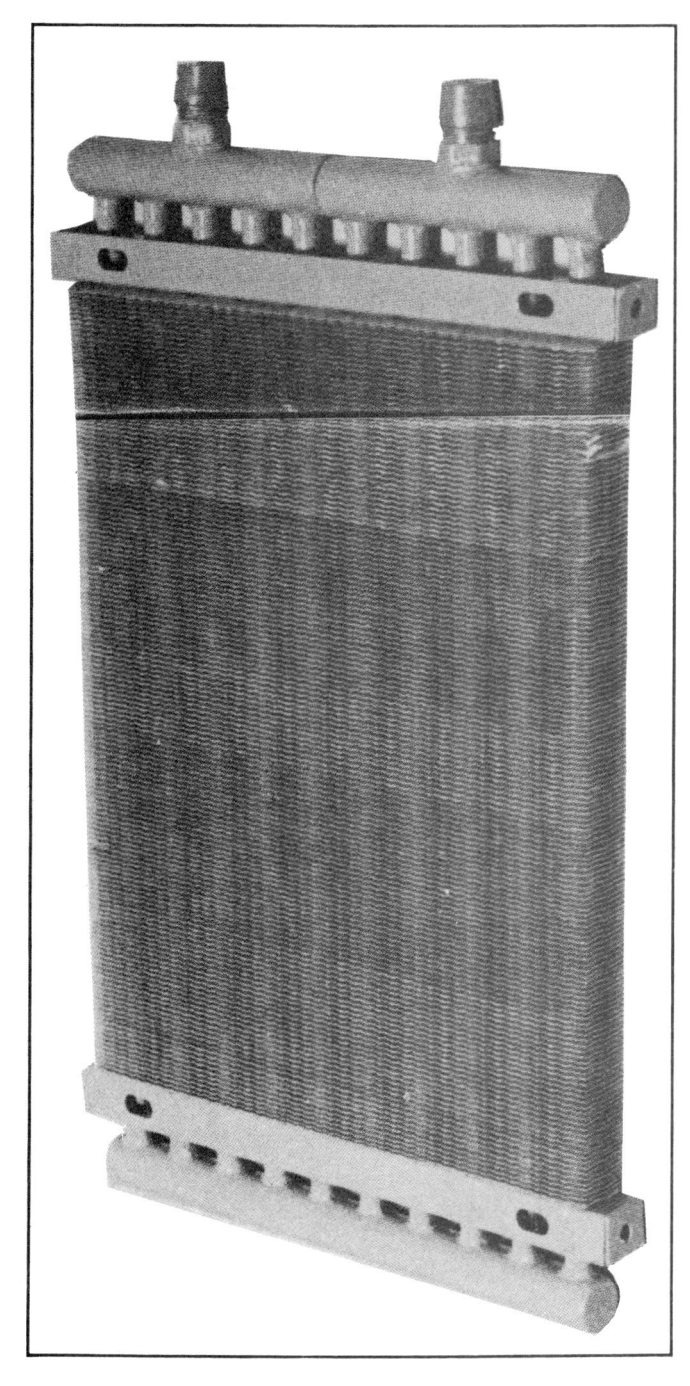

Fig. 9-12. Rapid Cool offers a number of different sizes in the Slim Line engine oil coolers. These units are designed for use where space is at a premium. Tubing used in these units is copper, recognized for its heat dissipating qualities (photo by Bud Lang).

Because of the tight fit between grille assemblies and radiators on some vehicles (like this Bronco, where the hood latch also interfered with the installation), both Hayden and Rapid Cool offer what they call their Space Saver and Slim Line coolers, respectively (Figs. 9-11 and 9-12). These units are thin enough so that they will fit just about any vehicle and still remove killing heat.

Any active four-wheeler has a definite need for an engine-oil cooler on his machine. We feel any of the coolers we've shown here are first class products (Figs. 9-13 through 9-22). If you select a model suited for your

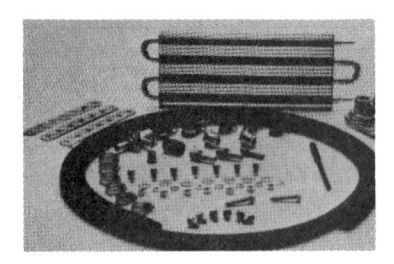

Fig. 9-13. Hayden has been producing engine oil coolers for almost 20 years now and has a line for every type of machine. Here is one of their controlled flow systems for intermittent stress driving. They also have full flow kits (photo by Bud Lang).

Fig. 9-14. Illustrated here is Hayden's #K2401 full flow engine oil cooling kit. Everything you need to hook this unit up is provided. This 8" × 21" cooler is a heavy-duty unit, recommended for four-wheelers that are going to run their engines hard (photo by Bud Lang).

Fig. 9-15. Perma-Cool's heavy-duty oil cooler is designed for high-powered vehicles. This cooler will pass up to 20 gallons of oil per minute. Large headers at each end guarantee oil is not restricted getting to and from the cooler (photo by Bud Lang).

Fig. 9-16. All Perma-Cool kits are complete. This one features aluminum adapters for a remotely-mounted oil filter. Hose supplied is more than sufficient to do the job of keeping that engine cool (photo by Bud Lang).

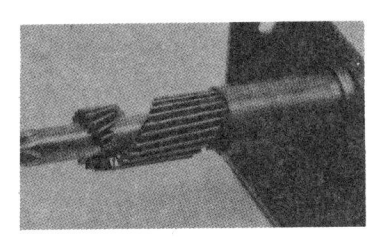

Fig. 9-17. Most coolers are designed with inner fins to tumble the oil as it passes through the cooler, making sure all of it comes in contact with the tubing walls to dissipate heat. This is the Perma-Cool method, known as a turbulator (photo by Bud Lang).

Fig. 9-18. Rapid Cool offers individual installation kits, for specific vehicles, separate from their coolers. Everything you need in these kits is furnished (photo by Bud Lang).

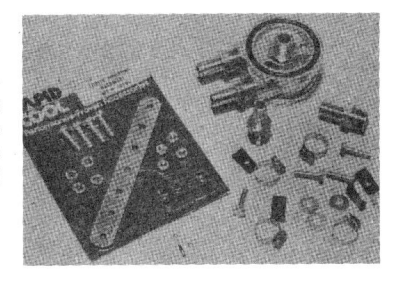

Fig. 9-19. Rapid Cool's #2300 Enginesaver oil cooler is designed for vehicles of 12,000 GVW and up, and pulling up to 500 horsepower. Twelve feet of hose is furnished with the cooler in this particular kit (photo by Bud Lang).

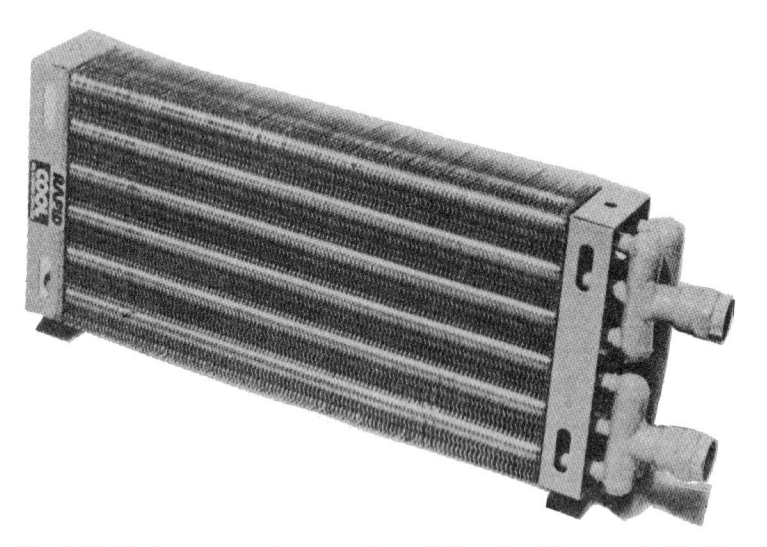

Fig. 9-20. Enginesaver coolers are also available without hose, as is this kit, #2250, designed for engines up to 350 hp, and vehicles in the 9-12,000 GVW class. Tubing in Rapid cool coolers contains a spiraled wire to provide inner turbulence of oil and better cooling (photo by Bud Lang).

particular vehicle, and mount it where it is in a full air stream, it will definitely remove excess engine-oil heat. If you mount it in a bad location, or select a cooler too small for your vehicle, it will help some. You won't be getting the benefits you're after, though, and this is to reduce engine heat and to prolong oil and engine life.

Fig. 9-21. For the lower-powered and lighter four-wheelers, Rapid Cool offers this kit, #2150. Like the others, it comes with ½-inch FPT fittings (photo by Bud Lang).

Fig. 9-22. A close-up view of a Rapid Cool cooler shows how the lines are routed through the cooling fins and into the headers (Photo by Bud Lang).

Chapter 10

Grille Guard for a Blazer

Every serious off-roader recognizes the need for some type of protection for delicate front ends. Bumper guards (or grille guards, or brush guards, or whatever else you choose to call them) are a very popular after-market item, but do not always afford the amount of protection needed. Many of them only protect the already sturdy bumper, leaving the grille exposed and vulnerable. Others are intended only as a cosmetic bolt-on and do not really afford any protection whatsoever.

We decided to build our own guard for our Blazer and get exactly what we wanted and, at the same time, save a considerable amount of money.

We used 5/16-inch steel plate for the ends and 2-inch outside diameter galvanized pipe for the bars (Fig. 10-1). This material can easily be found in a local scrap yard. You'll need a piece of sheet steel approximately 2 feet × 3 feet—depending on how large you want to make the guard—and three pieces of pipe about 3 feet in length. Total cost is in the neighborhood of $15.

The first step was to make a cardboard pattern of what we wanted. This can be trimmed or shaped easily so you can achieve exactly the shape you want—and also to ensure a proper fit.

The pattern was traced on the steel plate and the ends were cut out with an *acetylene torch*. After final shaping and finishing with a grinder, both holes were drilled to match existing holes in the frame, then bolted in place.

After both end pieces were secured tightly and positioned properly, the distance between them was measured. The pieces of pipe were cut to fit. By having both ends in place first and then measuring, a more accurate measurement is achieved and, consequently, a better fit.

The pipes were then welded in the desired positions. Although this is mostly a matter of choice, we prefer to have the bars set rather high to protect the more fragile grille, rather than the stronger bumper. A third pipe has been added for even more protection.

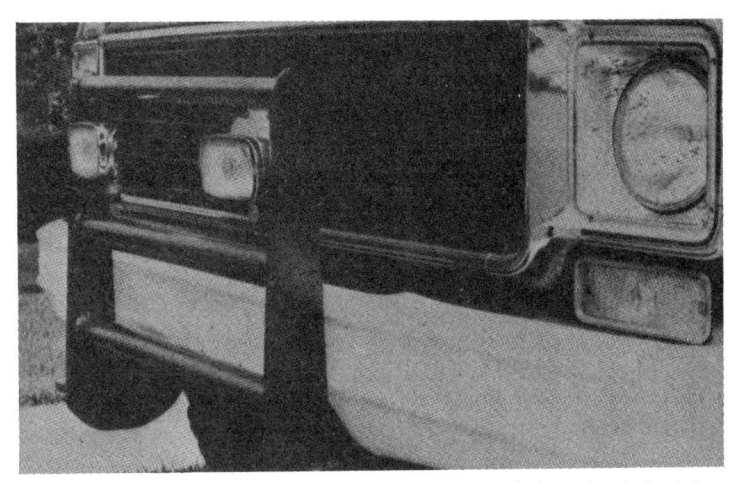

Fig. 10-1. Unit is composed of steel plate, galvanized pipe, sheet steel, tow hooks, and steel brackets (photo by Kermit Gary Henning).

We also added two steel brackets for driving lights and bolted on two tow hooks on the outside edges. It is important that the tow hooks be bolted on instead of welded in case they should bend and have to be replaced.

The last step was a paint job to match the color of our Blazer. It was all bolted in place.

Although we did all our own cutting and welding, there are many local welding shops that can do it for you rather reasonably (check the Yellow Pages). You can expect to pay about $15 for this service, bringing the total cost to under $36—about half what you would pay for a store-bought guard that only provides half the protection (Fig. 10-2).

Fig. 10-2. For under $36, the low bucks grille guard takes care of protecting the vulnerable front end (photo by Kermit Gary Henning).

Chapter 11

Keeping the Kinks Out of Your Hood

Due to an evidently faulty design, the hoods on 1973 and later GM light trucks, Blazers, and Suburbans tend to bend or kink immediately forward of the hood hinge when they're being closed (Fig. 11-1). Naturally, this is something owners really need. It's one thing to have stiff hood springs to keep the lid from coming down on you, but it's something else to have them so stiff you have difficulty closing the hood. It really isn't a case of too-stiff hood springs. It's more like the material used to make the hood is of a lighter gauge. Evidently this is being done to cut weight to improve fuel mileage so as to satisfy the latest five-year plan from Washington.

With lighter-weight hoods, and springs that have been serving truckers faithfully for years (springs that were designed for stronger hoods), it's only natural that the hoods are going to suffer. Then to compound the problem, some of these hoods feature a notch in the underside bracing, just forward of the hood hinge area, and this is where these units buckle (Fig. 11-2).

INSTALLING HOOD STIFF'NERS

The best solution to preventing or correcting, this problem that we have come up with is to install a pair of R. Milligan Engineering Hood Stiff ' Ners under that hood. These corrosion-proof steel braces are quickly and easily installed on any GM hood in a matter of minutes. Where a hood has already buckled, they will prevent further buckling once you "pop" the kink out of it. If you're smart, and your hood has not yet begun to get the bends, you'll install a set before this malady strikes.

A key reason why you should install this "preventative medicine" under that hood is because once it gets the bends, body work and painting is usually in store for you. If your hood barely shows signs of starting to bow,

Fig. 11-1. A notch in the underhood bracing of GM Blazers, pickups, and carryalls, 1973 and later, makes the hoods very susceptible to buckling when they are being lowered.

the Hood Stiff 'Ner kit will straighten it out. This repair step won't be necessary. If a kink shows up, and you take pride in your vehicle, you have to use some plastic filler and have the hoods repainted.

While most hoods buckle on the driver's side first, both sides will usually go. The way to prevent this from occurring, or to correct it if you waited too long, is to straighten the hood as best you can (Fig. 11-3). Then you remove the forward bolt on each hood hinge, one side at a time, and slip one of the Hood Stiff ' Ner braces in place. It doesn't matter which one—they're both the same. With a brace in place, you reinstall the hinge bolt (Fig. 11-4).

Now you're ready to drill through the inner hood panel, using the holes in the Stiff ' Ner as drill guides, so you can secure the braces with the metal screws furnished in the kit (Figs. 11-5 and 11-6). Use utmost caution when drilling these holes; otherwise you'll dent the outer hood skin or go right through it.

After all the screws are in place, close the hood to make sure the newly installed braces are clearing all hoses, wires, or whatever. With everything

Fig. 11-2. Only mildly buckled, this hood is ⅝-inch above the fender line. Continued use without correcting the problem will make it worse.

Fig. 11-3. A large block of wood should be placed under the forward edge of the hood so pressure can be applied to the buckled area in an effort to straighten it.

okay, remove the braces, one at a time, and apply a thin layer of nonhardening hood caulking compound between brace and hood (Fig. 11-7). This will prevent squeaks from occurring and will also lock the screws in place, preventing them from backing out should you decide to go off-roading.

Some truck hoods have different angles of bends on their inner hood panels. If one of these shapes interferes with the channel of the Hood Stiff ' Ner, you can beat this problem by simply rearranging the edge of the brace to conform to the shape of original hood paneling. This is usually required at the hinge end of the bracket (slotted end).

REALIGNING THE HOOD

As sometimes occurs when hoods have been bent, the hinge bolts have been removed, they may have to be aligned again so they'll close correctly.

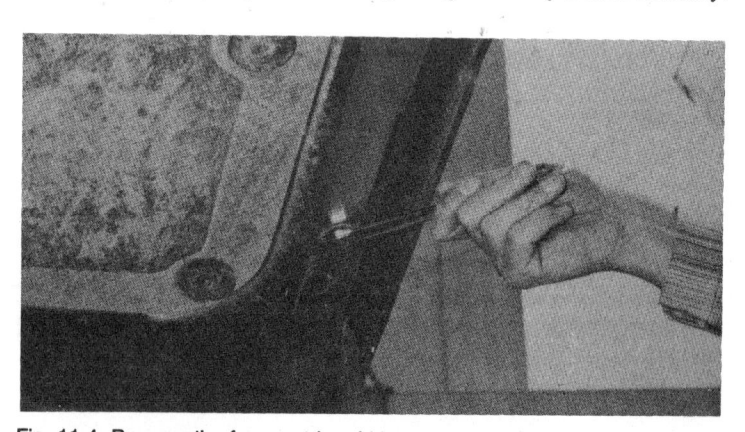

Fig. 11-4. Remove the foremost hood hinge bolt on each side. Then install a Milligan Hood Stiff'Ner on each side and reinstall the bolts.

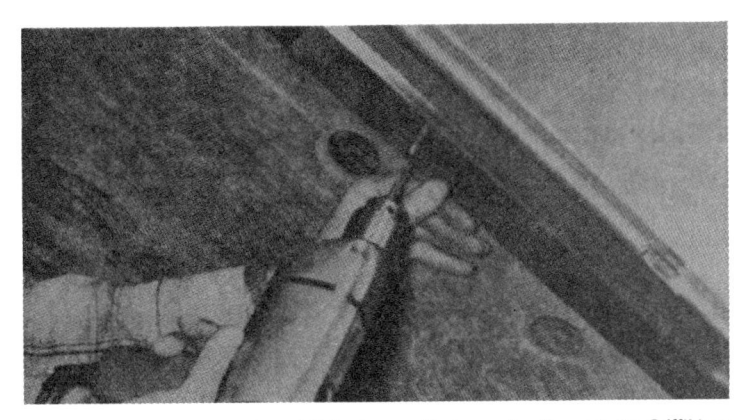

Fig. 11-5. Now you're ready to drill the forward holes, using those in the Stiff'Ners as a guide.

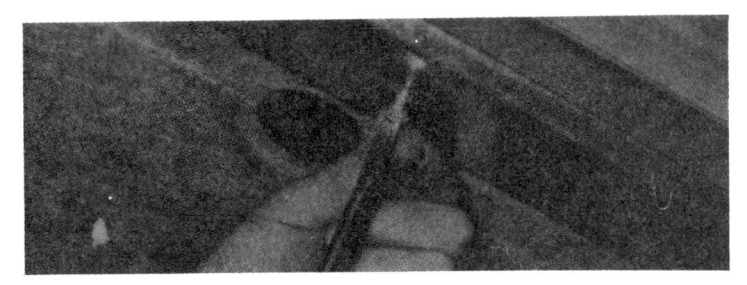

Fig. 11-6. The metal screws furnished in the kit are self-tapping, so they're easy to install.

Fig. 11-7. After all the screws are in, you should remove each brace and apply a nonhardening caulking compound between hood and Stiff'Ner to prevent squeaks and lock the screws. This will prevent their backing out.

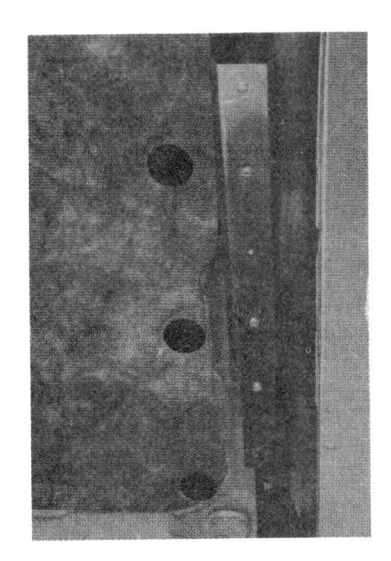

This is done simply by loosening the bolts at first one side, then the other, and manually adjusting the hood until it's aligned properly. Then you tighten the bolts again, make sure the hood is latched and closed before hitting the highway again.

If you're interested in this product, check your local RV dealer, or write direct: R. Milligan Engineering, 229 Via Socorro, San Clemente, CA 92672. Each kit retails at only $11.95 plus applicable tax and freight charges, if any.

Chapter 12

Performance Shocks for Your 4×4

Of all original equipment products installed on 4×4's as part of the overall package, one unit in particular is bound to let you down, and we mean this literally. This is a polite way of implying it is capable of holding up its end of the bargain to a point, but don't expect any more from it than that. Where other components making up your vehicle may serve you well for up to 100,000 miles or more, these pieces will literally let you down completely within 15,000-20,000 miles. Naturally, we're speaking about *shock absorbers*, quite likely the weakest component on any vehicle, two *or* four-wheel drive.

It's a well-known fact that standard-type OEM shocks are marginal at best. Unless you request and pay for heavy-duty shocks when you buy a new four-wheeler, you're going to get units that are capable of stabilizing the ride of that machine for only a brief period of time. Worse, if you load it down with a lot of safety equipment, such as roll bar, grille guard, skid plates, trusses, winch, auxiliary fuel tanks, and so forth, the shocks are going to last for even a shorter period of time, simply because they'll be working that much harder.

Unlike other components that wear out, usually in a sudden manner due to breakage, shocks are very deceptive about dying on you, and this pertains to all shocks. They don't tell you they're fading away unless something breaks. They begin wearing out from the first day they are installed on that machine. During the first year or so on a street-driven vehicle (length of time being dependent upon how many miles you drive a year), your shocks will serve you to the best of their ability for quite some time. You'll appreciate how well they do their job of controlling spring rebound and stabilizing the ride of your four-by-four. Unknown to you,

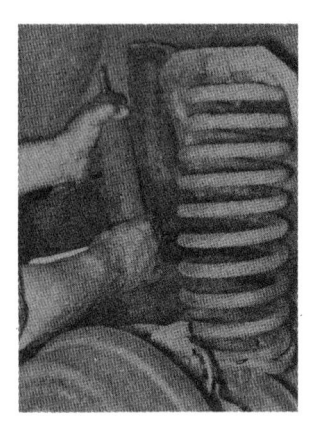

Fig. 12-1. When removing old shocks, hang on to the metal washers, just in case one is missing from the new shock box.

however, as the shocks begin to wear out, they won't be functioning as well as they did when new. You will be automatically compensating for their failings in your driving habits. The sad part is you won't even realize you're driving "differently" until the day you're tired of riding over dips and bumps as if you were on a four-wheel-drive pogo stick, and decide to install a new set of shocks.

HIGH-PERFORMANCE SHOCKS

If you've learned your lesson, you will have installed a set of heavy-duty shocks, or as we like to say, high-performance shocks, this second time around (Figs. 12-1 through 12-5). Choose a good pair of high-performance shocks, that are designed for your vehicle and the type of driving you have in mind, and you won't believe that life could be so sweet. The really scary thing about driving with shocks that are incapable of doing their part is when it comes to stabilizing a moving vehicle, or driving with shocks until they are dead, is that your vehicle is quite dangerous to be around. We've all seen some of these machines flying down a road, swaying

Fig. 12-2. Install the new M/T gas shock at the top mount first, sandwiching the bracket with the rubber biscuits.

or bouncing around with every gust of wind or after hitting every little dip or bump. They're bad news.

There are quite a few excellent high-performance shock absorbers on the market today. Some of these we're presenting here (Figs. 12-6 through 12-9). We're not going to make comparisons between brands or types because we don't feel we have the right, or the means, to fairly test and compare these products. It's our assumption the manufacturers have already spent more than we'll earn in a lifetime testing and developing their products, so we'll be content by filling you in on some of the fine points regarding these products. We must also state that just because a shock is a

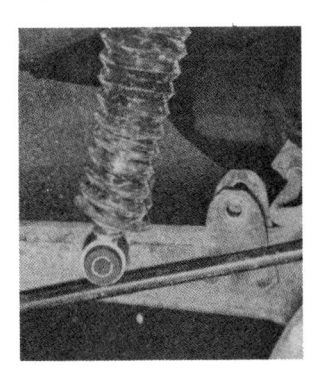

Fig. 12-3. The M/T shock was a lot stiffer than the worn out OEM, so a bar was used to lift its base onto the tie rod. Boot protects the rod.

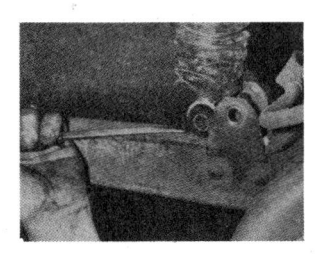

Fig. 12-4. A screwdriver was then used to slip the lower, one-piece eye into the mounting bracket. Always use new bolts, nuts, and washers when installing shocks.

Fig. 12-5. Attaching the lower end of the M/T shock takes two hands. Wheel was removed for photo purposes only. You can install shocks on a Bronco with wheels in place.

109

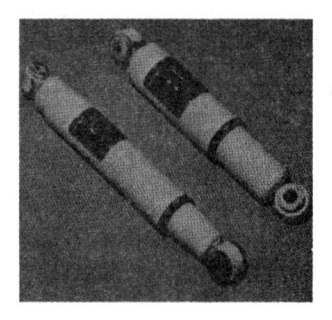

Fig. 12-6. Here's a pair of Gabriel shocks, a Strider at left, and an Adjustable "E" on the right. Both can be adjusted for regular, firm or extra firm ride. Of the two, the "E" is rated as a heavy-duty shock and is recommended for street trucking.

"high-performance" unit does not mean it is suited for all uses, i.e., racing, off-roading, etc. Just as with every other component, there are differences between products. You might do well, should you have any doubts about any specific product, to check with people who are using them. Get some personal feedback.

DEFINITION OF A SHOCK ABSORBER

A hydraulic shock absorber is simply a tube filled with fluid that connects an axle assembly to the chassis at its outer end. One end of this "tube" features a rod connected to a piston inside the tube. If a vehicle with this arrangement on it were to hit a bump or dip, your suspension system would be a total failure because the fluid in *this* shock can't be compressed. It would act like a solid link between chassis and axle.

If we were to incorporate a means of metering the flow of fluid in this shock, so that when a bump was encountered, the axle could actually drive the piston into the shock tube, forcing some of the fluid through the metering valve into another chamber, we would be in effect "dampening" the bouncing action of the axle. By precision metering, we could control how "stiff" or "soft" the shock will be, or how much damping effect it will have on the ride of the vehicle, or how much rebound control it will have.

This is the entire reasoning behind installing hydraulic shock absorbers on any vehicle, and that is to control spring rebound and keep the tires in contact with the road. Without shocks, a vehicle hitting a bump or dip will

Fig. 12-7. Bill Montague, owner of Off-Road Chassis Engineering in Buena Park, CA, installs a modified Gabriel "E" shock in the custom independent front end he built for this Datsun mini-truck.

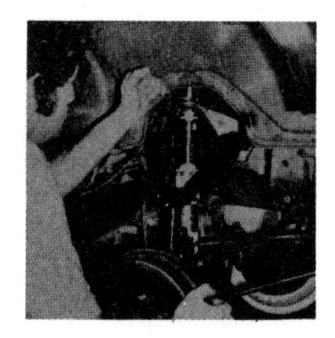

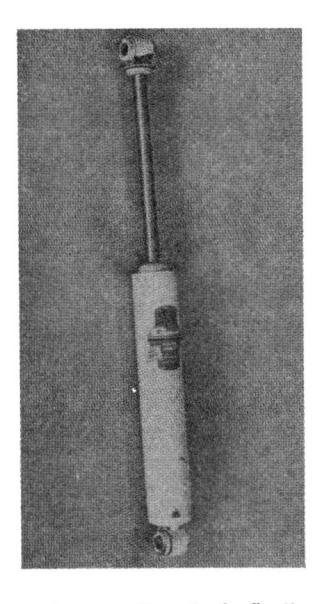

Fig. 12-8. Gabriel also manufactures a shock specifically for off-road racing. These shocks are strong, but shouldn't be used on the highway.

bounce up and down repeatedly until the springs—coil or leaf—finally "level out."

TWIN-TUBE SHOCKS

Basically, there are two types of telescopic shock absorbers on the market. One type features two tubes, the other a single tube. The two-tube shock features two chambers: the (inner) working chamber and the (outer) fluid reservoir chamber. By its very design, the outer chamber is also an air chamber. As the shock is compressed, the piston is moved by its rod into the working chamber, displacing some of the fluid through metering valves.

Fig. 12-9. Rough Country recently released this new triple-shock bolt-on kit for most 4WD vehicles. It's strictly for racing and can be used with either their standard or racing shocks.

Some of this fluid passes through valves in this piston, moving into the area behind the piston. We say some, because the rod controlling the piston displaces part of the area behind the piston. These shocks incorporate another valve at the opposite end of the working chamber that permits fluid to pass into the outer chamber.

Most twin-tube shocks feature the working chamber at the bottom end, and this can really be a problem where the shock is worked hard. This is because this lower end is attached to the axle, and every time the wheel moves up and down a fraction of an inch, this fluid chamber is moving with it. There is no way the fluid can be expected to remain free of air. Aeration is what causes shocks to fade. Air compresses under the stock piston. When this occurs, shock control of any spring action is then very marginal.

Fluid transfer from the working chamber to the reservoir and back again tends to heat up shock fluid, causing the fluid to expand. This expansion takes place in the reservoir or outer tube, thereby compressing the air space in that chamber. Excessive fluid heat will have negative effects on shock action, too, so one way manufacturers beat this problem is by designing shocks with larger reservoirs: greater fluid capacity will slow down heat buildup. This is not to imply that larger shocks are always better. Rough Country has designed shocks featuring Plyacell bags of Freon within the outer chamber. They claim this virtually eliminates aeration of fluid, but compressible air still remains in that chamber.

MONOTUBE SHOCKS

Then we have the monotube shock which is totally different from the twin-tube. These shocks, as the name implies, feature a single tube which is

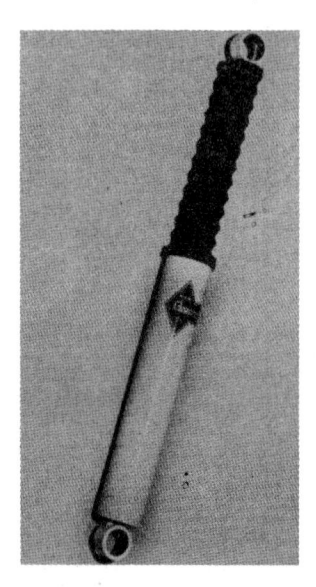

Fig. 12-10. In addition to standard and high performance gas shocks, KYB also produces special off-road racing shocks. These units feature chrome moly rods, higher nitrogen gas pressure initially, double seal piston, etc.

Fig. 12-11. Mickey Thompson "Challenger" shocks are available in a variety of lengths and diameters, as well as with various mounting ends. They are all of the gas pressure type, and aeration isn't a problem. These units really perform, on the highway and off.

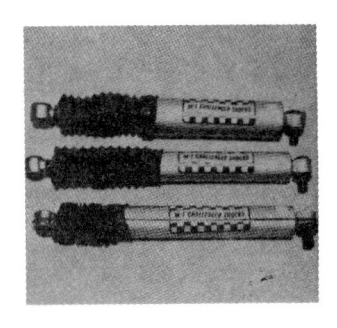

the working chamber. As the piston in this shock moves down into the chamber upon compression, it too meters fluid through the piston into the area behind the piston. While its rod displaces some of this area, fluid is not routed into a separate reservoir, as in the twin-tube shocks.

A *floating* piston separates the fluid from pressurized nitrogen gas at the opposite end of this chamber. Thus, as the piston descends into the working area, because all of the fluid cannot be metered into the area behind the piston, fluid remaining in the working chamber causes the floating piston to compress the nitrogen gas. Because there is no air in this chamber, it cannot mix with the fluid and cause aeration, the very action that produces shock fade. This floating piston moves in direct relationship to the shock and constantly adjusts the control characteristics as road conditions change. Shocks incorporating floating pistons and nitrogen gas chambers are available from Mickey Thompson, Bilstein, and KYB (Figs. 12-10 through 12-12). Yet even though these three firms offer what we call "gas"

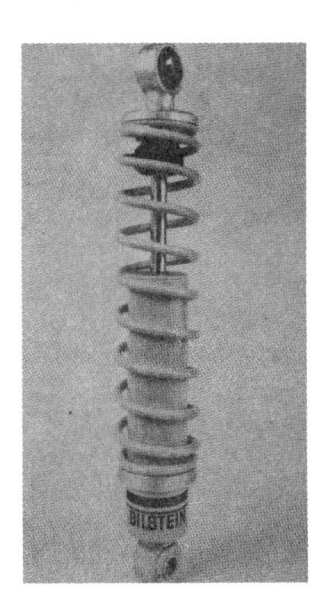

Fig. 12-12. A leader in the world of nitrogen gas shocks is Bilstein. The tube used on these shocks is extruded from bar stock to very critical tolerances. It features a patented nitrogen-gas pressure principle, and is well-known for reliability and quality.

shocks, these units are all different in the way they are designed, and in the way they function.

Manufacturers of twin-tube shocks utilize various means to improve the performance of their heavy-duty shocks over their stock counterparts. The pistons in some of these shocks feature nylon skirts, O-rings, or tetrafluoroethylene coatings to provide more efficient sealing and reduce friction (and thereby reduce heat). Hard-chromed piston rods reduce wear, heavy-gauge walls in the tubes help maintain concentricity, and Teflon impregnated multilip seals prevent fluid leakage. Naturally, all shocks do not feature all of these components, but most do. Many of these shocks also feature larger diameter piston rods, supposedly for added strength. Since these shocks perform in a near vertical manner, there is almost no side loading. It is hard to understand the reasoning. Furthermore, the larger diameter rods displace more area above the piston, and thus force even more fluid into the reservoir of the twin-tube shock upon compression, furthering chances of aeration, which is the weak point in most shock absorbers.

Two points you should consider before settling upon any particular brand or type of shock for your own four-by-four should be the type of driving you'll likely be doing and whether or not the vehicle is raised via blocks (lift kits) or aftermarket springs. If your machine is raised up, then your new shocks *must* be of sufficient length and stroke to compensate for both compression and rebound differences. If you have a race car, the shocks will naturally be valved totally different from those designed for street/off-road use. It is also recommended that the rubber bumpers on jacked-up vehicles be replaced with taller units as a means of preventing the shocks from being torn apart should the axles drop away from the chassis a greater distance than the shocks. LUV and Datsun bumpers have proven ideal replacements on jacked-up four-by-fours,.

Finally, you should not install shocks designed for the rear of a vehicle on the front end, and vice versa, just because they happen to fit. They are valved differently, and your machine won't ride safely or comfortably. Tell your dealer what you're driving, and demand shocks designed specifically for your machine. If you get the right type the first time, you'll have more control of your vehicle under all driving conditions. That's what shocks are all about. They should control your machine; it shouldn't control you.

Chapter 13

CompuSensor Ignition System

The heart of every internal combustion engine is its ignition system. This is the component that must light the fire—and deliver it at a precise time—if that engine is going to perform as designed. It's all very simple. Unless the fuel charge is ignited each and every time it's supposed to, your engine is wasting fuel (by pumping it out the exhaust). Those cylinders that don't fire are leeching power from those that do.

Until recent years, ignition distributor systems relied on breaker points to trigger the spark in each combustion chamber. When the breaker cam opens these points, the points perform as a mechanical switch—switching on and off the current supplying the coil's primary winding and routing the coil's high-voltage secondary output to the individual spark plugs.

The length of time breaker points remain closed between openings is known as "dwell" time, the time the battery is allowed to feed current into the coil's primary winding, which results in a stronger magnetic field buildup. Greater spark voltages are produced where dwell time can be increased.

BREAKER-POINT AND LED-TYPE DISTRIBUTORS

Breaker-point distributors perform pretty well under normal conditions and when the engine is in top condition, everything being relative. Rubbing block wear (which tends to reduce point gap and alter dwell) and point bounce (caused by weak springs) along with other problems encouraged OEM and aftermarket manufacturers to develop something better. Many have come up with "breakerless" ignition systems, in which an infrared light emitting diode or magnetic pulse triggering system is the spark triggering device. While many feel these systems are superior to the standard breaker-point distributor, they, too, have some drawbacks.

A weak point in some light emitting diode (LED)-type distributors is that they are susceptible to moisture and dust. A drawback of the magnetic pulse triggering system is that the output of its magnetic pickup is directly proportional to the velocity of the reluctor, and therefore at low cranking speeds, the spark can be weak.

When high performance buffs first began attempts at improving ignition systems, a common "trick" was to install a "high voltage" coil, meaning a unit that would put out anywhere from 50 to 100 percent more voltage. They were on the right track, but barely. The average engine requires between 12,000 and 15,000 volts at the spark plug to jump the electrode gap. Due to resistance in the circuit (poor wiring insulation, etc.), a coil that has the capability of delivering even 20,000 volts should be sufficient to fire most engines. You do need a coil that is capable of producing a few extra thousand "reserve" volts to take care of resistance, but that's all you need.

CAPACITIVE DISCHARGE (CD) UNITS

In recent years many manufacturers have developed *capacitive discharge* systems, or CD units, which are basically units that store electrons in an ordinary capacitor, then at the appropriate time discharge it into the secondary and then into the plug. These units came into existence as a means of breaking down resistance caused by worn or fouled plugs, a very common problem. They use a solid-state oscillator circuit to "pump up" a condenser when the primary current is flowing. When the spark is triggered, this 400 or so volts of stored-up energy literally explodes in the coil primary. This generates a high energy spark and an extremely quick rise time. Whereas these units generally work well where the air/fuel mixture is on the rich side, they don't do well where it's lean, as is the case with modern engines.

FACTS ON THE COMPUSENSOR SYSTEM

This is not to say all special or custom distributors or CD systems have been failures in their approach to producing sufficient fire to ignite every fuel charge. Far from it, but most are still lacking in one way or another. Even where an engine is in top mechanical condition, the best ignitions around are estimated to fire combustion mixes around 88-94 percent of the time. This means your engine is running on the average at about 90 percent of its efficiency, and 10 percent of that expensive fuel you're pumping through it is going to waste. So what's the answer? Take a good, close look at the Jacobs *CompuSensor computer ignition system*, marketed among others by Clifford Research & Development Co., 1670 Sunflower Avenue, Costa Mesa, CA 92626 (Fig. 13-1). This unit appears to be the ignition system to end all ignition systems.

Available for four, six and eight-cylinder engines with point or breakerless and OEM electronic distributors, six or 12-volt negative or positive

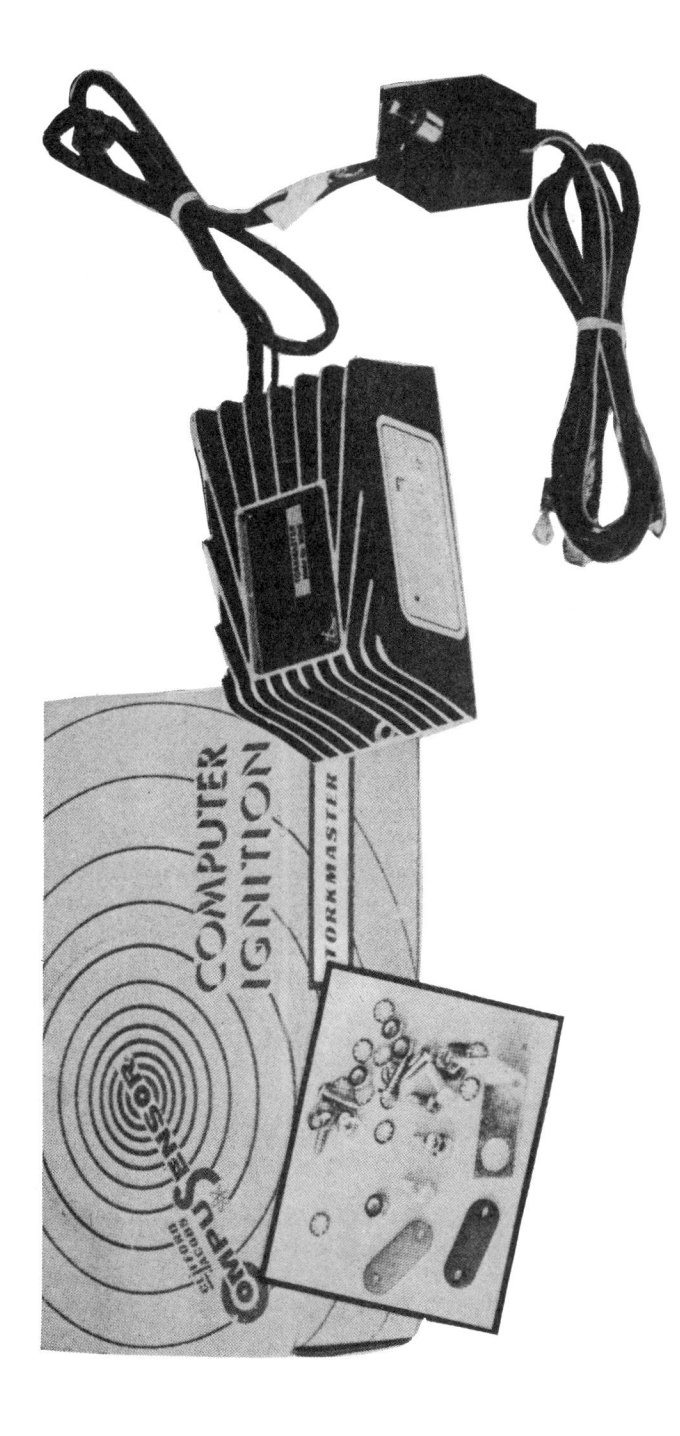

Fig. 13-1. The Clifford CompuSensor Kit, Torkmaster computerized box, wired-in selection switch, instructions, and all the necessary hardware (photo by Bud Lang).

ground systems, the Jacobs ignition will work with gasoline or propane-powered cars and trucks. It is a thoroughly tested system that is most unusual when compared to other capacitive discharge systems (Fig. 13-2).

First of all, its traditional "black box" is home for 103 major electrical components and subcomponents which include 14 major, solid-state devices which are equal to over 10,000 transistorized circuits. Compare this to the average solid state electronic ignition system which has but three transistors and four diode circuits and the average CD ignition with its two transistors, six diodes, and one silicon rectifier. So what we have inside the black box of the Jacobs ignition system is a miniature computer, a device capable of sensing engine spark requirements and completely adapting spark voltage, duration energy, etc., in response to the engine needs.

This ignition is fully adaptive to the needs of your engine at any given moment. When a hotter spark is necessary, it is fully capable of matching or exceeding any ignition system currently on the market. The CompuSensor responds to battery voltage, engine temperature, load and rpm's just as easily. It adjusts its output to compensate for all of these conditions. A cold engine, for example, requires a hotter spark to get things moving than does a warm engine. The CompuSensor will adapt to this condition, making the otherwise hard-starting engine an easy-starting one. It does this by reading spark plug resistance at every stroke of the engine and even has the ability to read differences in resistance between plugs. With this inherent ability, misfires are just about a thing of the past, providing every other component in your engine is set up right. Cracked or burned spark plugs, frayed plug cables, worn distributor caps, etc., will shoot down even the best distributor system. Jacobs estimates their CompuSensor has the ability to deliver efficient firing 99.999991 percent of the time, and do it up to 7500 rpm.

Because this ignition system can "read" spark plugs and deliver the exact amount of voltage required to fire a fuel charge, the engine is bound to produce more power, fuel economy has to improve, your engine will run much smoother, and the coins will stay in your pocket a lot longer. This system costs more than many others, but it does things the others only dream about. At most it takes but an hour or so to install a CompuSensor, and if you decide to sell your vehicle, you can remove it in a matter of minutes and install it on any other vehicle. Where everything else on the engine is functioning as it should, it is estimated a minimum increase in gasoline mileage of 10-20 percent in cars and 7-15 percent in vans and pickups can be realized.

There are many other key features that should be stressed, too. For one, it is recommended that a standard ignition coil, such as a Delco #D511, be used with the CompuSensor, regardless of type of engine. A high-performance coil is not required, simply because this ignition system regulates secondary voltage and is capable of delivering up to 60,000 volts. The breaker points, LED, etc., act merely as a switch, signaling the CompuSensor when to fire. When this distributor system is operating in the

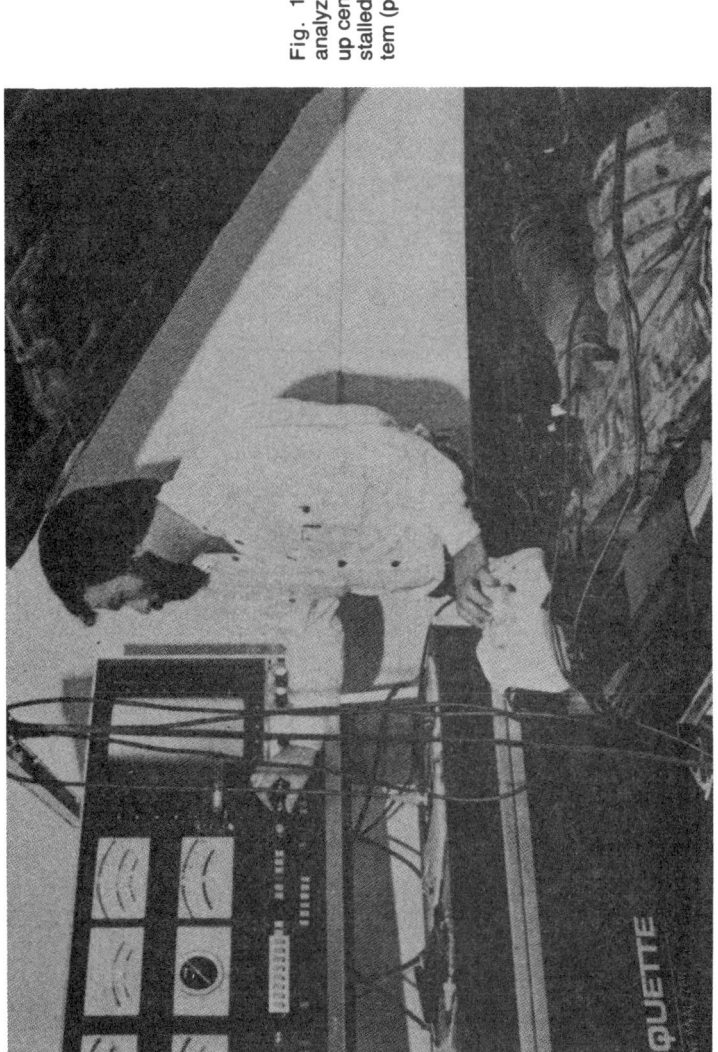

Fig. 13-2. A Marquette engine analyzer is used at a Compu-tune-up center to check out the newly installed CompuSensor ignition system (photo by Bud Lang).

starting mode, it uses only 13 percent of the current required by the conventional ignition system. The smaller drain on the electrical system by the ignition allows more juice to be available to the starter, thus reducing the strain on the starter and battery. Because it also has the ability to sense proper gasoline burning, it can "turn off" the voltage at the proper time, thus enabling spark plugs to last as long as 40,000 miles before needing replacement. This is because the hotter spark capability of this unit does not wear the electrodes down as rapidly.

Relative to spark plugs, it is recommended you use the same heat range of plugs as you would with a stock ignition. Resistance type plugs shouldn't be used unless you experience excessive radio noise. Autolite plugs, particularly the "T" series, feature very hard electrodes and are suitable for highly extended periods between ignition services. Champion plugs have very hot burning electrodes and are ideal where spark plug fouling is a problem. The ac plugs are somewhere in between both.

To achieve the greatest benefits in running the CompuSensor ignition, plug gaps should be opened to the folowing specs: .050-inch with breaker point ignitions, .060-inch with breakerless ignitions, and .075-inch with GM HEI ignitions.

Each CompuSensor finned heat sink (the black box) features four wires that lead to a three-way toggle switch (Figs. 13-3 and 13-4). The computer box should be attached to a fender panel away from heat while the switch can be installed inside the engine compartment, on the fender well with the toggle facing down through a hole in the sheet metal so it is hidden, or even inside the car, under the dash or on the inner firewall (Figs. 13-5 and 13-6). With the switch in the "computer" position, you are utilizing the Jacobs CompuSensor ignition system. Flip it over to the conventional" position after turning the engine off, and you can run on the conventional ignition system. Nothing made by man is infallible. If the CompuSensor ever fails, you can immediately switch back to conventional. This brings to mind the

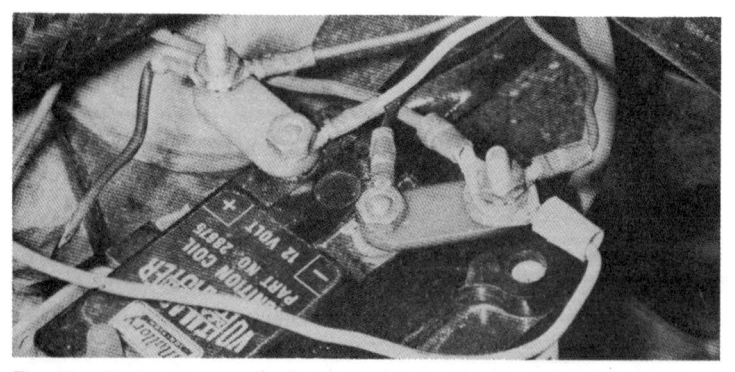

Fig. 13-3. Red and green plastic tabs and fasteners, furnished with the kit, are used to connect the four wires coming from the computer box (photo by Bud Lang).

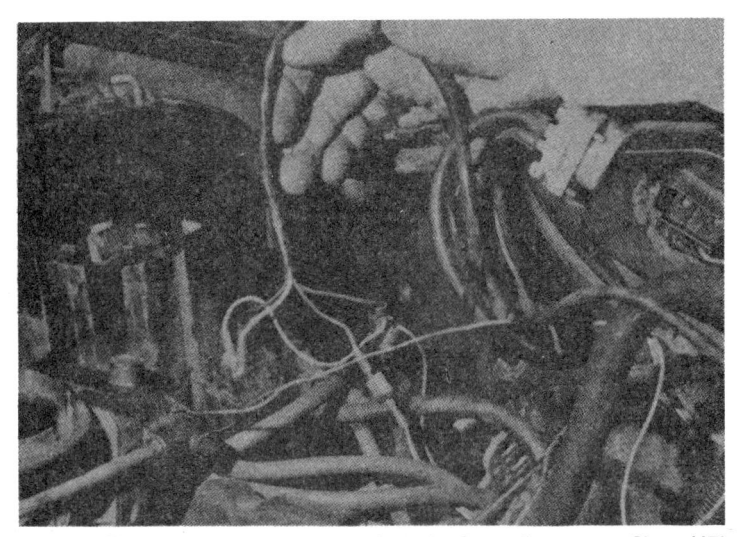

Fig. 13-4. This view of the wires that run from the CompuSensor to a Chevy HEI distributor cap shows that the wiring is very simply set up (photo by Bud Lang).

guarantee behind this unit. If it fails to live up to any of the claims made for it, you can get your bread back if it's returned to the dealer with the original receipt within 120 days. If it fails within two years, it will be repaired or replaced, or if it fails to allow two years or 40,000 miles between tune-ups (whichever come first), it will be replaced. Now this is hard to beat

Fig. 13-5. The Clifford/Jacobs computer box as installed on the inner fender panel, away from exhaust heat (photo by Bud Lang).

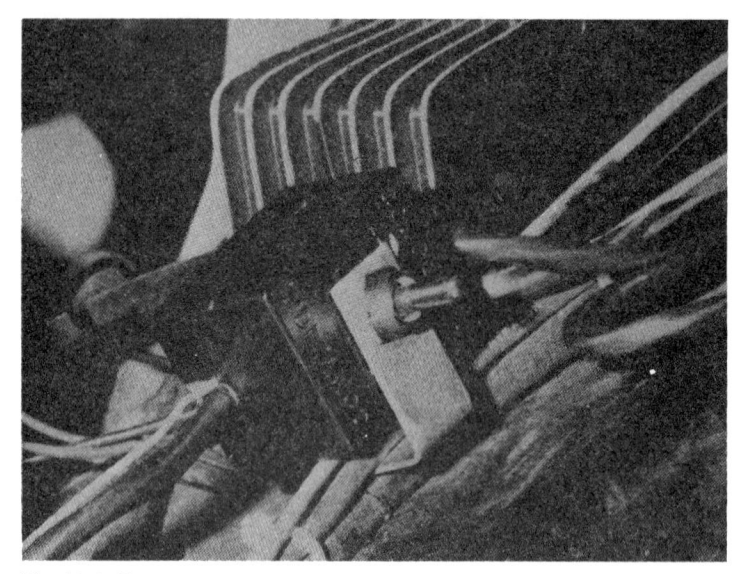

Fig. 13-6. The three-way switch is mounted close to the fender-well-mounted computer itself, where it's easy to reach (photo by Bud Lang).

anywhere. Back to the three-way switch. When moved to the neutral position, it works as an antitheft device by cutting current flow to the ignition, so you may wish to hide the switch under the dash, etc.

The CompuSensor was developed and is manufactured by Jacobs Electrical Products, Dept. T4, 3578 Eagle Rock Blvd., Los Angeles, CA 90065.

To make any further claims about how an investment in the CompuSensor can cut your fuel and maintenance bills while improving performance would be redundant. We're sure you agree that this unit is not just another CD ignition system. It is *the* system and one you would be wise to consider if you aren't satisfied with the performance and mileage you're getting from your current ignition setup. This is the ignition that starts where the others stop.

Chapter 14

Security Systems

Sophisticated security devices for your truck or van help to deter thieves. This chapter will include how-to information on some effective security systems. Chris Jacobs, president of Jacobs Electrical Products, Los Angeles, California, did much of the research.

VEHICLE THEFT

The current trend in vehicle theft is no longer just to steal a CB or other accessories. Now the vehicle theft industry, netting an estimated 1.9 billion annually, takes the whole vehicle, then gives it back 48 hours later with a "clean" look, unencumbered by an engine, transmission, custom wheels and, frequently all the interior as well.

Now that we've given you the bad news let's start you thinking like a crook. You've got a master key or copy you've made. A friend is waiting in his car with stolen license plates, just in case.

You look for a truck parked where its appearance is normal—you don't want to attract attention. Try to get between the target truck and another vehicle.

For three reasons you'll want to open the passenger side door. First, many people forget to lock that side. Second, for some reason people always think that a crook would enter from the driver's side. Third, as soon as you enter the vehicle you're going to reclose the door, lock it, and lie down on the floor so no one can see you while you are working the key, jumping wires, or pulling the key locking assembly out of position. A pin about the diameter of the lead in a pencil is all that holds most ignition locks in place.

Now you're going to start the engine while you are on the floor and work the throttle with your hand. If the truck's engine doesn't start right away, don't keep on cranking. While an alarm won't attract much attention, an engine which is cranking but not starting attracts everybody's attention. If it's cranking but not starting, chances are there's a kill switch. The switch will be located where the driver can reach it.

If you are following the first procedure, you're on the floor anyway in a good position to find the switch. Turn it off. The truck will start right up because you've already precranked it. Come off the floor and drive away like you owned the rig.

An alarm by itself isn't much protection, nor is a kill switch by itself. Both together can be an effective deterrent if you'll always remember to throw the switches on both. Seventy-eight percent of the vehicles that have security devices are stolen anyway because that one time the rig's owner had forgotten or become too lazy to turn on his system(s). Every thief has a raincoat. If you're in a big hurry when it's raining, that's a good time for a thief to pounce.

Now we're certainly not trying to discourage you from installing one or more security devices on your precious truck. Just the opposite. What we're trying to do is acquaint you with some of the very best antitheft devices available. As we have mentioned, a combination of systems is the best approach.

JACOBS STOP ACTION

There were nearly 143,000 vehicles stolen in California during 1977, according to a report from the California Highway Patrol. A fair share of these were pickup trucks, vans, 4×4s, and other recreational vehicles. In the 4×4 pickup category there were 865 thefts, and only 386 of them were ever recovered intact. Another 183 were recovered with most of the parts missing, and at the end of the year there were still 296 missing. The intact recoveries of 4×4 and utility vehicles runs less than half, and even if we include the vehicles that were recovered "stripped," the figure only climbs to 66.6 percent. That compares with a recovery rate of nearly 94 percent for automobiles.

There is a way to avoid becoming one of the statistics. The market has been flooded in recent years with antitheft devices that do everything from play the national anthem if someone sneezes nearby to just making the vehicle lie there like it's dead. There are pros and cons to every system, and a sharp salesman can convince you that each has exclusive dominion over all the others. We've recently come into contact with a system that makes a lot of sense to us, and it presents so little hassle to the owner that it can essentially be forgotten and still function. It's called Stop Action, and it's made by Jacobs Electrical Products Corporation at 3578 Eagle Rock Blvd. in Los Angeles (Fig. 14-1).

The Stop Action system does allow the thief to start the car and drive it for about 20 seconds, whereupon it dies and goes to heaven. Presumably, in the first 20 seconds, the thief has gotten the vehicle out into traffic, and its

Fig. 14-1. The stop action system is an effective deterrent against auto theft.

death causes an embarrassing situation that prompts the crook to search elsewhere (immediately) for his transportation. An automatic sensing device will allow the vehicle to be restarted after a wait of about 30 seconds, if the key is immediately removed when the engine initially dies. If an attempt is made to restart the engine without the 30 second wait, and without locating the tiny reset switch, the system dives deeper and deeper into its coma. The harder the criminal tries, the worse the situation gets, and the objective is to frustrate the auto thief to the point that he abandons the rig and you make an intact recovery.

Our strong desire to retain what is ours helped up make the decision to have one of these devices installed for testing and for protection. Installation was simplicity itself, requiring all of about 15 minutes time and a few standard tools (Figs. 14-2 through 14-5). We can report that after several months of use in the hazardous southern California crime jungles, the Land Cruiser still hasn't strayed.

GORA FUEL LOCK

One of the most interesting theft deterrents is the *Gora Fuel Lock* (Fig. 14-6). This is a system that has no hidden swiches or locks. The switch and the key lock, two separate entities, are in plain sight where the driver can readily operate them. A special key switch, the tubular type, is required to open the fuel lock and permit fuel to flow to the carburetor.

Fig. 14-2. With all the parts and pieces laid out on the fender for inspection, it is easy to see that this isn't going to be a very complex installation. Total time investment is about 15 minutes.

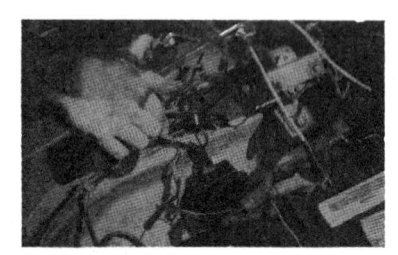

Fig. 14-3. We decided to place the Stop Action box under the hood, next to the coil. That kept all the wiring short instead of having it strung all over the vehicle.

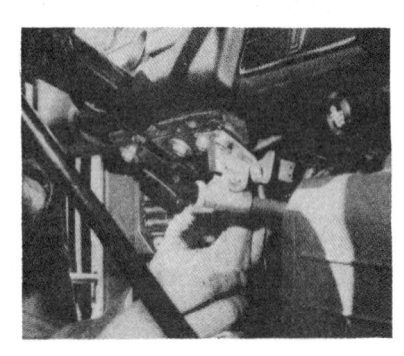

Fig. 14-4. After running the switch wire through the firewall, we located a handy spot under the dashboard for its installation. A more unconventional location will help deter thieves who are familiar with this type of device. After installing the switch, all that's left is to hook into the vehicle's fuse box with the handy fuse connector. Then, test the system, and rest peacefully at night knowing you've done your best to stay off the statistic list.

The fuel lock itself is just a part of the whole system; everything depends on everything else. To make it all the more confusing for the would-be thief, there are 60 different combinations in its wiring system to deter anyone attempting to overcome it electronically.

For maximum protection, here's what you do. After the Gora Fuel Lock is installed and tested, flip the special circular key lock (spring-loaded) to the right. It returns to position instantly. Now you are ready to drive. When you park for any length of time, push the adjacent bottom when you are a couple of blocks from your destination. As you are parking, rev the engine a few times and you'll "run out of gas." Now the would-be thief can crank your engine until the battery runs down, but he won't be able to start

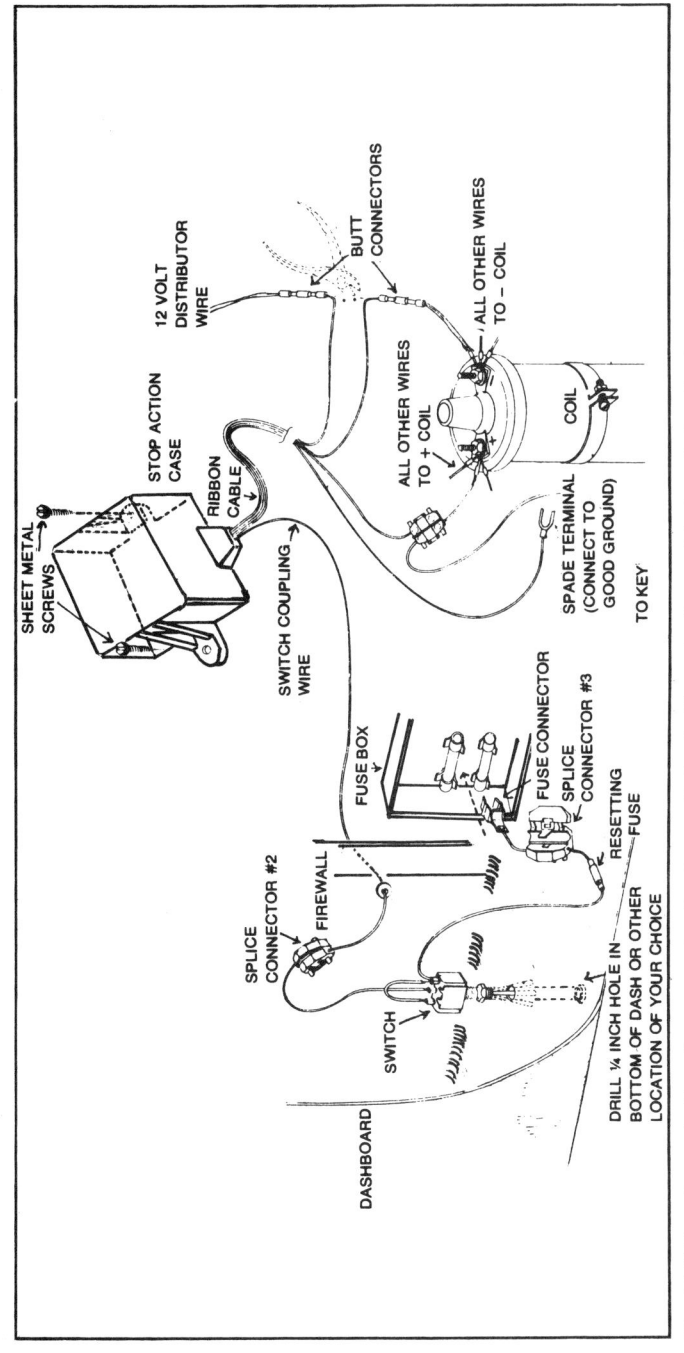

Fig. 14-5. Easy-to-read wiring diagram makes hookup pretty basic. The only phase of the installation that is even challenging is trying to decide where to hide the tiny operation switch.

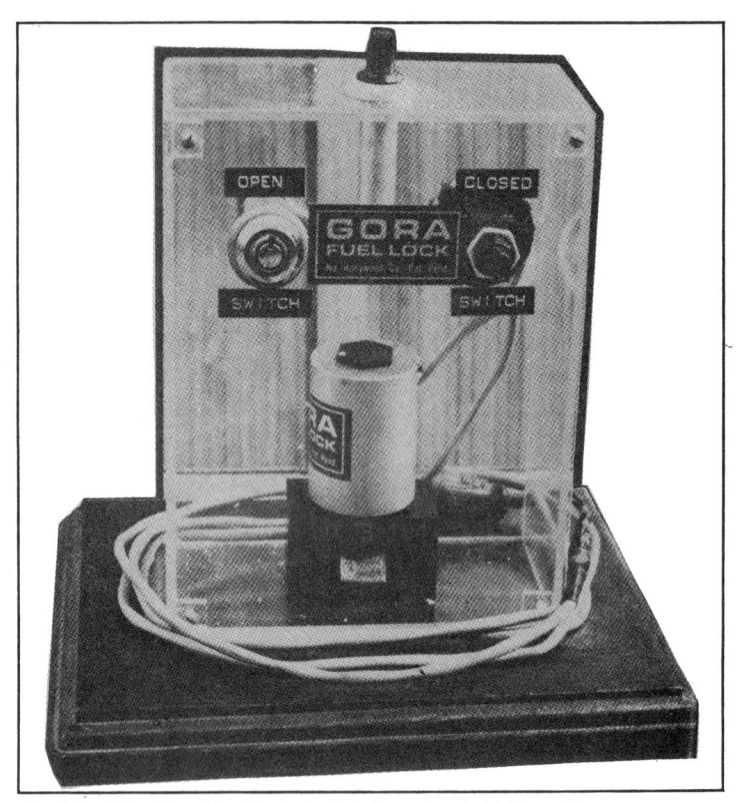

Fig. 14-6. The Gora Fuel Lock is an interesting theft deterrent.

your rig. If he should try to hot wire the fuel lock, it will remain in the closed position. The unit operates on a secret amount of reduced current so direct application of 12 volts, either at the fuel lock or the key switch, is fruitless. Another security precaution is that parts from one Gora Fuel Lock will not interchange with parts from another set. All sets are matched. The Gora is marketed nationally by Gora Fuel Lock, Dept. T4, 5905 Sepulveda Blvd., Van Nuys, CA 91411. They're interested in hearing from dealers around the country.

Mike's Automotive of Van Nuys did the installation on our rig while we photographed the procedure (Figs. 14-7 through 14-20). The Gora Fuel Lock should be installed as close to the carburetor as practical, but it can be anywhere between the fuel tank and the carb. Units are guaranteed for life on workmanship but not for incorrect installation.

CLIFFORD COMPUTERIZED PREPROGRAMMED LOCKS

Clifford is the name of the system manufactured by C.P.P.L., Computerized Preprogrammed Locks, Dept T4, 74ll Laurel Canyon Blvd.,

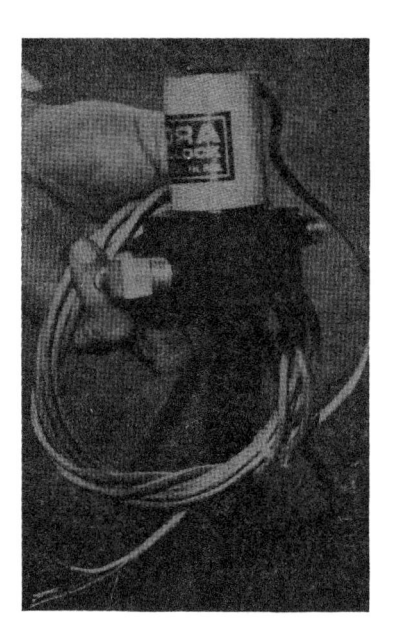

Fig. 14-7. The lock assembly with fittings. Depending on the location, an elbow may or may not be required.

North Hollywood, CA 91605. The Clifford system is, perhaps, the most sophisticated we encountered. Operating on the principle that there's no way one can keep a determined thief out of your rig, the next best thing to do is to frustrate him from moving it and make him obvious at the same time. There he is sitting in a truck he can't start, engine cranking, with a pair of air

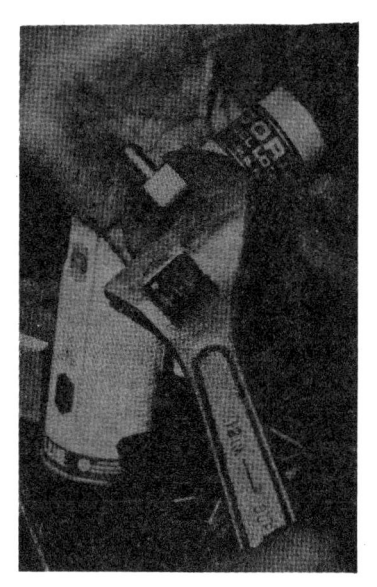

Fig. 14-8. A length of Teflon tape on the threads before tightening will assure leakproof fittings.

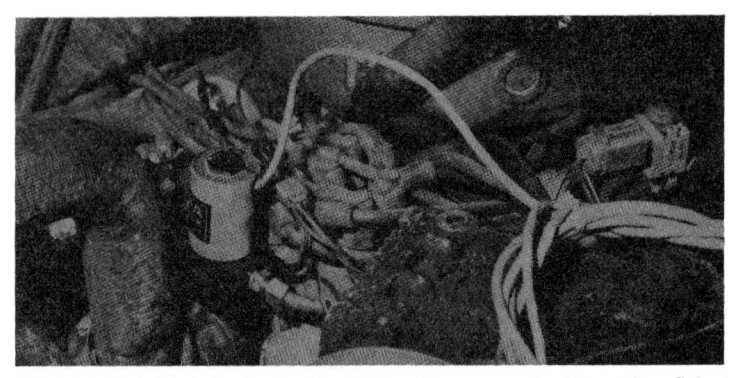

Fig. 14-9. Inlet side to the fuel lock is visible with compression fitting. Hose fitting goes to the elbow fitting on the lock.

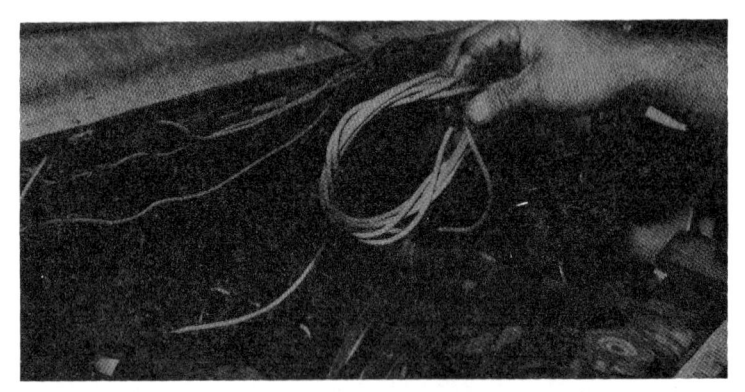

Fig. 14-10. This cable contains 11 coded strands of wire. Enough is provided to reach from the fuel lock to any reasonable location in the cockpit. Cable will be fed through any convenient hole in the firewall near the driver's position.

Fig. 14-11. Parts to be wired and installed in the cab include the set button and the lock switch. A matched pair of keys is provided.

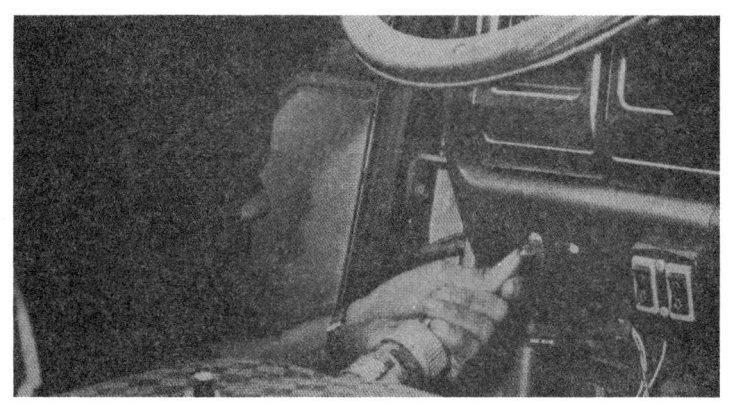

Fig. 14-12. Mike's installer, Smitty, drills the first hole for the key switch.

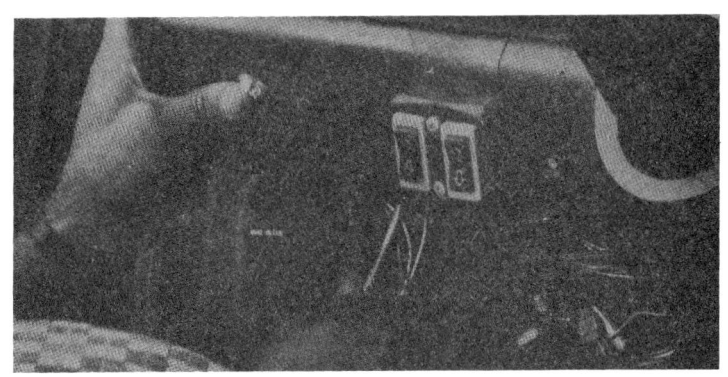

Fig. 14-13. Key switch in position. Wire is drawn down for connection to the interior valve control.

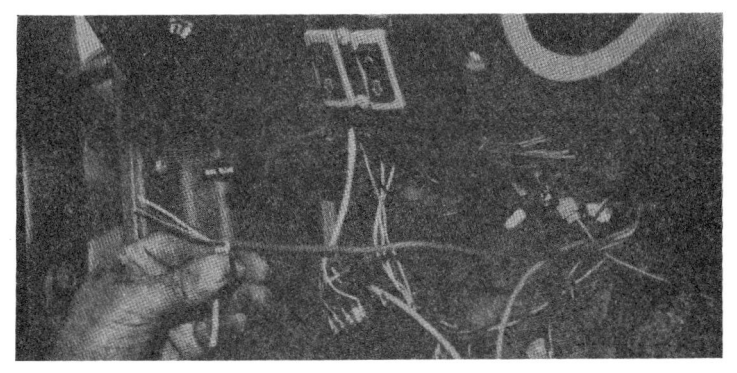

Fig. 14-14. Insulation is stripped from the cable revealing the color-coded wires for key switch and button switch. The key switch is already wired to valve-switch body.

horns blasting and no amount of electronic know-how is going to get him anywhere. Unlike many devices which use a concealed switch or even an obvious key switch and/or alarm to discourage the malefactor, the *Clifford Electronic Lock System* utilizes a totally integrated system designed to prevent *even* the most skilled and experienced thief from stealing your rig.

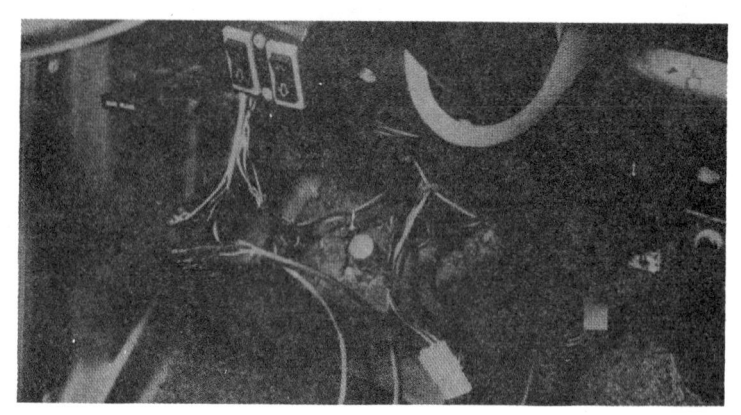

Fig. 14-15. Wires are now connected to both the valve side and the key lock side. Each kit is wired differently giving 60 different combinations to deter efforts to overcome system electronically.

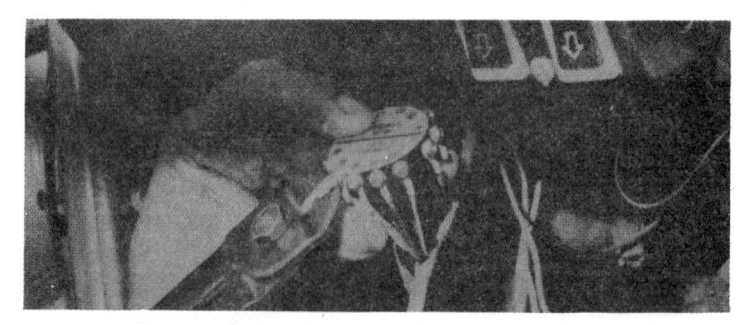

Fig. 14-16. For maximum integrity of connections, each is crimped.

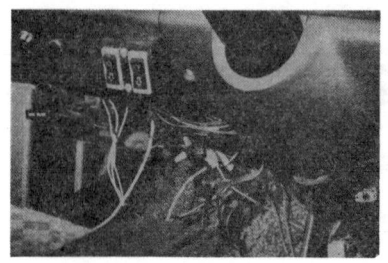

Fig. 14-17. Interior installation nearly complete. Excess wire will be tied and concealed.

Fig. 14-8. To assure a solid ground, an eyelet is crimped to the coded ground wire.

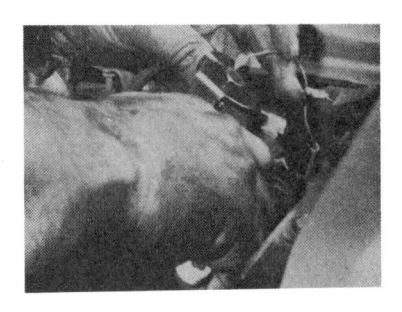

It has a minicomputer, a logic circuit with a combination preprogrammed into its memory bank. The minicomputer has various control circuits leading to the key components of your van's electrical system, the doors and others. This electronic system and its subsystems cannot be "jumped," overridden, or short circuited. The only way to activate the system is by punching out the proper sequence on a keypad resembling that on a pushbutton telephone. Also included in the system is a piercingly loud pair of air horns, a motion detector, and a keypad-controlled hood lock so strong that the only way a thief can open your hood is with a chain saw.

While we were at Clifford shooting the installation, the cars coming in for protection were to say the least impressive—Turbo Porches, BMWs, Rolls, and the like. There is one Southern California dealer who will not sell a Turbo Porsche without the Clifford system.

A narrative description of the Clifford System can't really tell the story. With Figs. 14-21 through 14-37, however, you will see in detail the various components and how they operate.

The Clifford system is by no means inexpensive, but what's your rig worth? Its installation requires a fair amount of know-how in automotive electrics. The instructions are very complete and detailed and include a wiring diagram. Once you have one and have memorized your keypad combination, you'll be impressed with how well it works.

UNGO BOX

Among the very sophisticated devices now available is the *Ungo Box*, which has three operating-condition memories and switch-selected vari-

Fig. 14-19. System is grounded to a convenient body bolt.

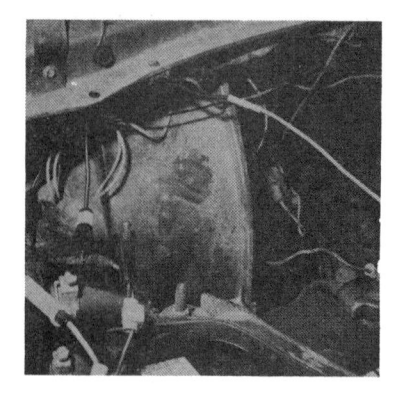

Fig. 14-20. Final installation step is hooking up the hot wire. Here a ScotchLok connector clamps Gora lead to an existing hot wire. In-line fuse is a must.

able sensitivity for varied parking conditions (Fig. 14-38). The Ungo Box is engineered to be a complete, virtually foolproof alarm system with no hidden switches.

The unit is delivered with a factory set combination (an individualized combination can be ordered) and is equipped with exit and entry delays. The alarm is triggered if the truck is moved or jostled whether on level ground or on a hillside. When the alarm is triggered, the Ungo Box sounds the horn and disables the ignition which effectively immobilizes the vehicle. The alarm sounds for a minute, then shuts off and automatically rearms for continued protection. If one should punch up a wrong number combination, the Ungo Box will go through a full alarm cycle ignoring all command inputs. In this way, in case of an emergency, the unit can be triggered to attract attention. Needless to say, there is override provision so that the vehicle can be serviced, or if it is left momentarily and the owner doesn't wish the arming capability to operate automatically.

The Ungo Box comes with complete hardware and detailed instructions for what is said to be "quick and easy installation." As with other devices with computer memories and multiple transistors and diodes, the

Fig. 14-21. Although the entire system functions as a unit, the computer and the keypad might be considered the brains and the heart of the Clifford system.

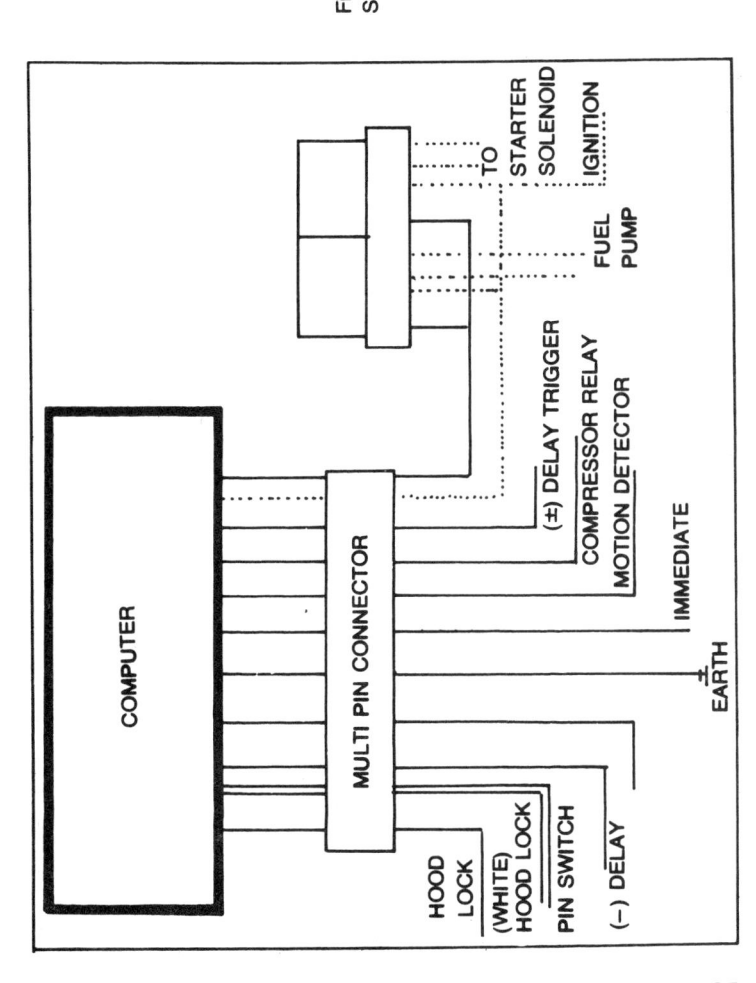

Fig. 14-22. Wiring diagram for the Clifford System.

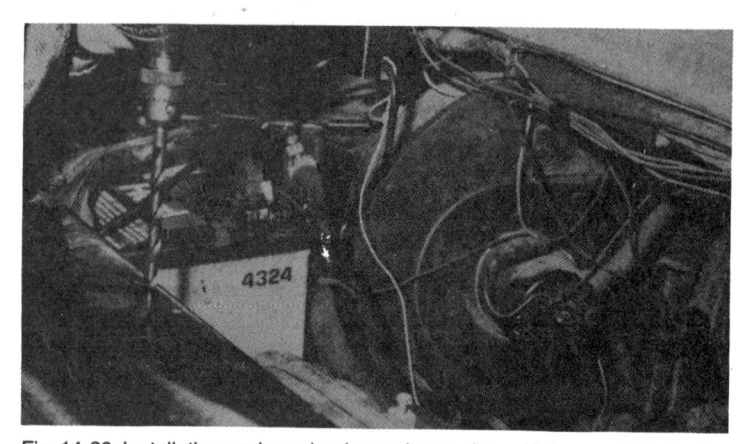

Fig. 14-23. Installation work can begin nearly anywhere. Holes are drilled for the hood lock.

Ungo Box is not inexpensive. The manufacturer is Techne Electronics Ltd., Dept. T4, P.O. Box 5760, San Jose, CA 95150.

UNISTOP STOP HIT

One of the theft deterrents you might consider in your efforts to keep your truck out of the hands of the enterprising thief is the *Unistop* (Fig. 14-39). This device, which locks both the steering wheel and either the clutch or brake pedal, is handled by Vilen B. Haan Incorporated. Dept. T4, 7531 Coldwater Canyon, North Hollywood, CA 91605. It has the advantage

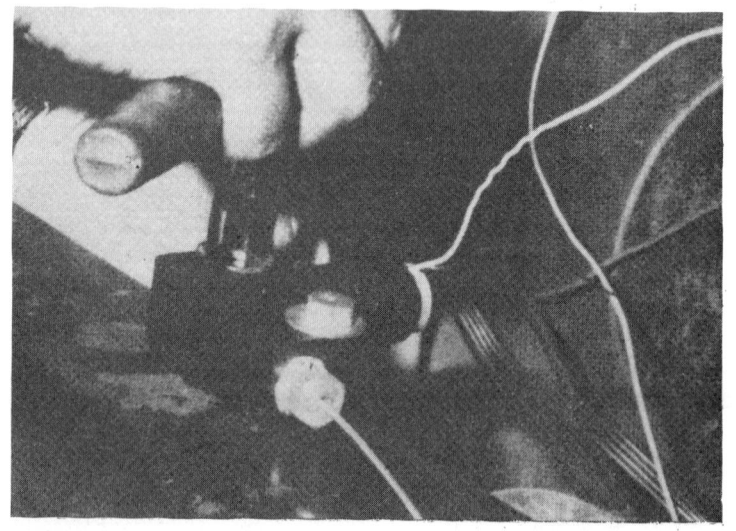

Fig. 14-24. The hood lock is secured with aircraft-quality steel bolts.

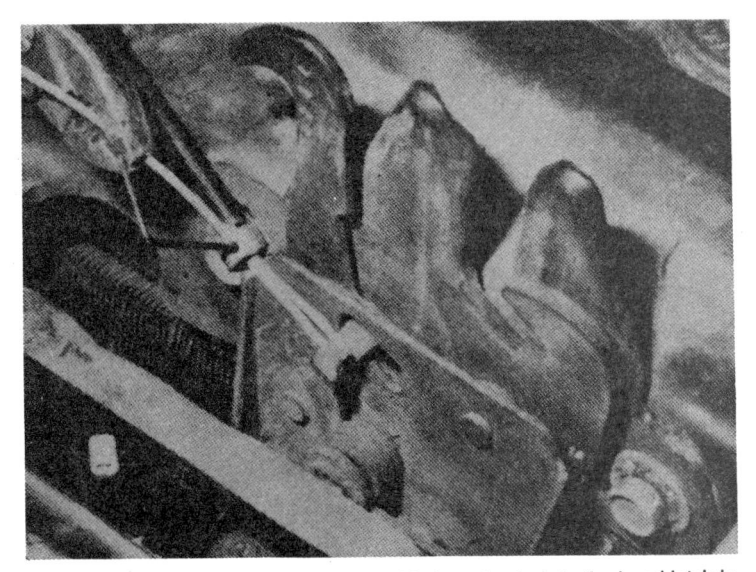

Fig. 14-25. Also of aircraft quality, the cable from the lock to the hood latch is adjusted for tension, then securely clamped.

of being quick and easy to use while being, at the same time, inexpensive. Curved at both ends with a kink at the bottom, it is adaptable to vehicles with pedals through the floor. There are over 1000 key variations so that your security is assured.

Fig. 14-26. Loom from the computer is fed through a slit in the firewall boot.

137

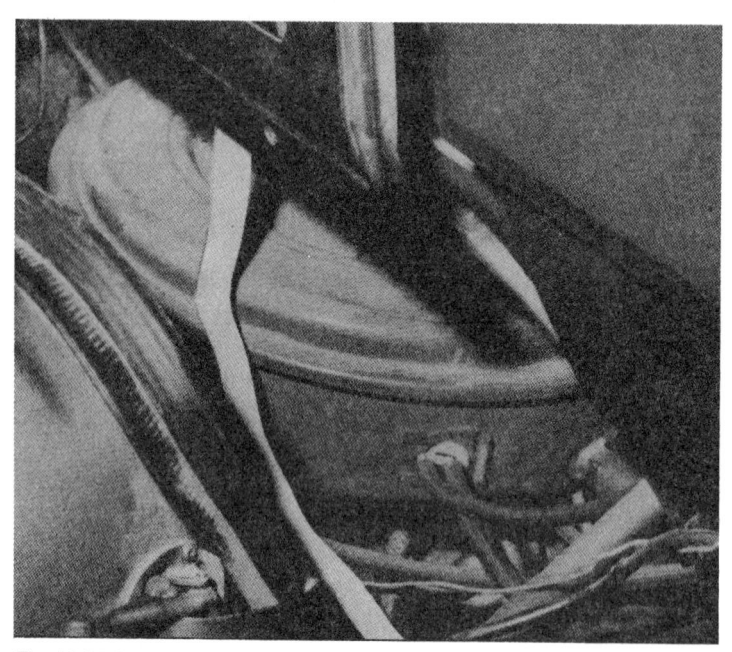

Fig. 14-27. Inside the truck the loom is brought to the area where the keypad will be located.

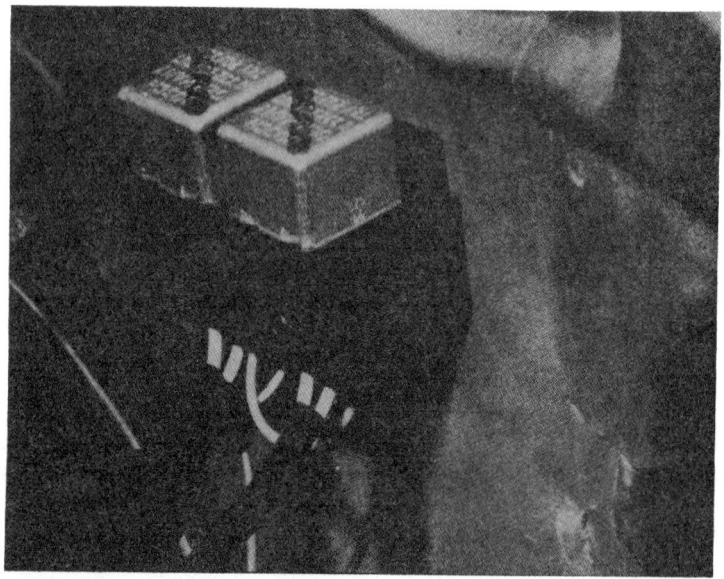

Fig. 14-28. Under the hood, adjacent to the fender well, is the relay pack which controls the starter and the fuel supply.

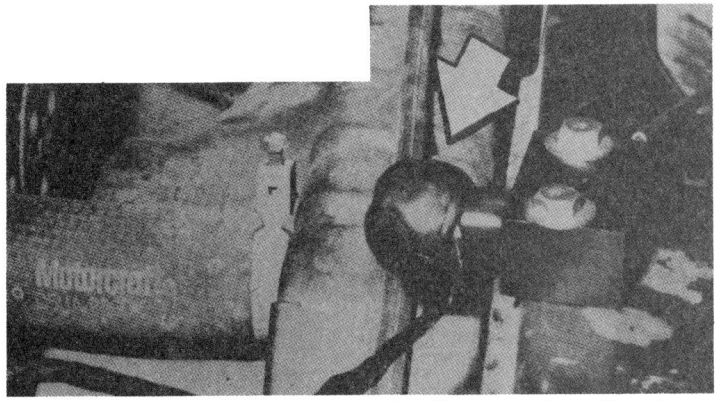

Fig. 14-29. After wiring, connections to the hood lock are protected from dampness by a ball of caulking compound.

Fig. 14-30. Multipole male and female quick release connectors can only be joined one way. These join the main loom and the computer.

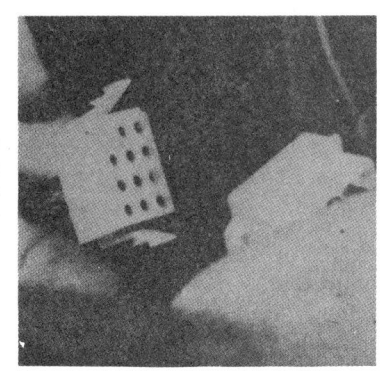

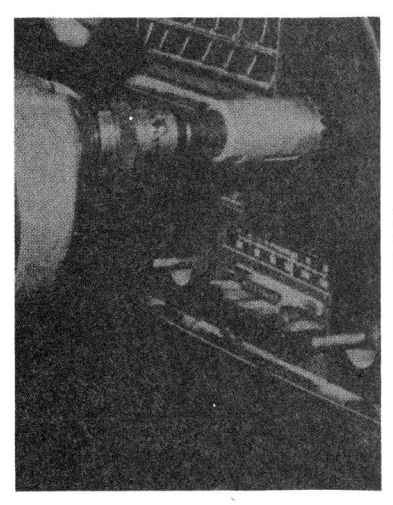

Fig. 14-31. A hole saw makes quick work of cutting through plastic. A large hole is not required.

Fig. 14-32. Keypad is a press fit in the panel. No mounting screws are required.

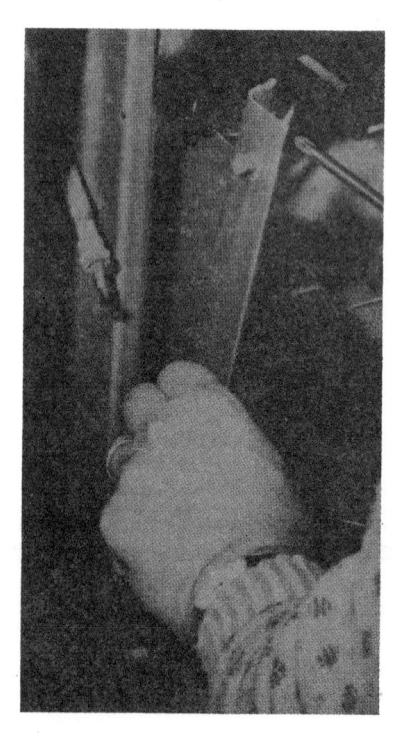

Fig. 14-33. Courtesy light switch button on the driver's side door is hooked into the system. Just wiring this one switch brings all other doors into the circuit.

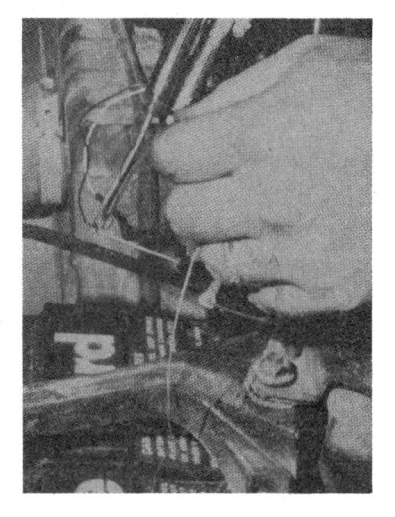

Fig. 14-34. For connection integrity, the hot wire to the battery's positive side is soldered.

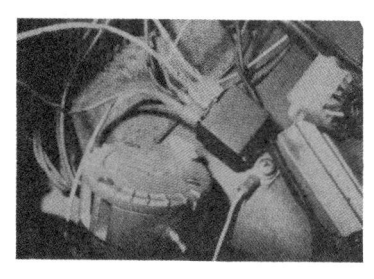

Fig. 14-35. In the foreground is the compressor for the air horns. Above it are the compressor motor relay and ground.

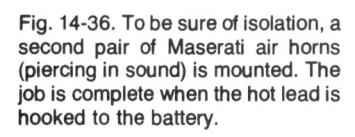

Fig. 14-36. To be sure of isolation, a second pair of Maserati air horns (piercing in sound) is mounted. The job is complete when the hot lead is hooked to the battery.

Fig. 14-37. In the cockpit the Clifford keypad adds a touch of class. To the knowledgeable thief it means one thing—forget this truck.

Fig. 14-38. The Ungo Box is a sophisticated device.

Fig. 14-39. The Unistop locks the steering wheel and either the clutch or brake pedal.

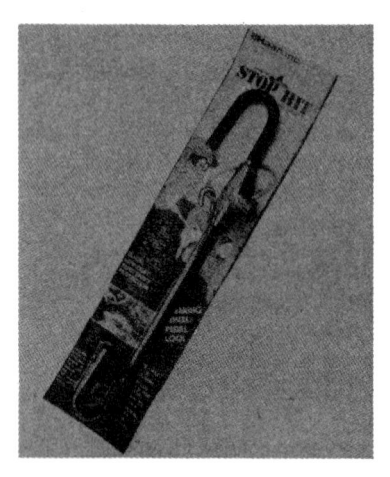

Chapter 15

Trans-Go Kit

A Trans-Go reprogramming kit makes each shift faster and more efficient. As a result, durability of the transmission is immediately doubled.

GIL YOUNGER'S WORK

Now it has to be the cumulative efforts of a bunch of geniuses to come up with the fairly efficient stock automatics we have. A lengthy section could be (and has been) written about the man who founded Transco, the parent firm from which Trans-Go evolved, Gil Younger was first a mechanic, working for a number of Southern California new car dealerships in the 1940s. He saw the arrival of the automatics and set out to learn all he could about these marvels.

Being a mechanic, Gil was performance oriented. As a young man, he got heavily into drag racing.

When the sanctioning bodies introduced drag classes for automatic shift cars, Gil considered this a challenge. With his self-taught engineering knowledge, he decided something had to be done to make the automatics more efficient and far more durable. So successful were his innovations that drag racers sought his help in building transmissions for their competition efforts.

By this time Gil was a major partner in a shop which specialized in transmission rebuilding and was also the owner of Mercury Tool and Engineering Company. His practical knowledge, coupled with business savvy, led to the creation of Transco, transmission rebuilding kits, and to Trans-Go, which is a kit that offers greater efficiency and durability to the modern automatic transmission. All of which leads us to why we felt a

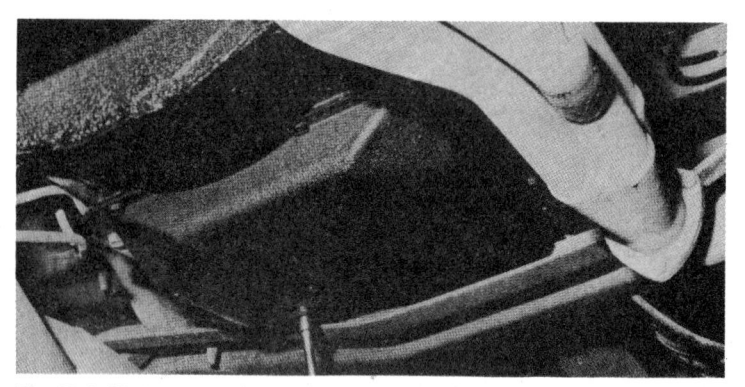

Fig. 15-1. Obviously, the first step is to remove the 17 bolts holding the transmission pan. Use a ½-inch socket.

Trans-Go kit was the only way to go on our Ford truck. Shifts were sloppy, first to second gear came in much too early, and half throttle downshifts were a sometimes thing.

If your truck has an automatic transmission, we're sure there are times when you've been vaguely dissatisfied with its performance. You have reason to be. We'd like to pass along a quote from the Trans-Go catalogue—Trans-Go being probably the first name in automatic transmission reprogramming kits.

"The automatics coming off the assembly lines in Detroit are truly masterpieces of engineering. But engineers have been asked to program the shifting for smoothness and comfort. Also, consumer attitude surveys show that drivers believe a smooth shift is easier on the transmission. *Actually, just the reverse is true.*

"To add comfort, Detroit engineers have had to subtract a considerable amount of efficiency and durability. They've achieved comfort by

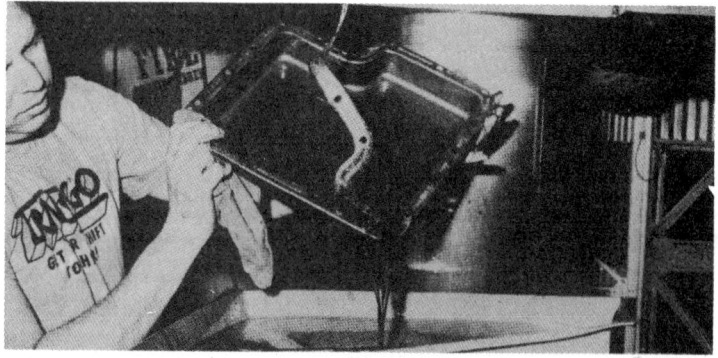

Fig. 15-2. If transmission oil is good and can be reused, it should be drained into a clean container. Ours was due for replacement.

Fig. 15-3. The valve body is removed, using a ⅜-inch socket.

Fig. 15-4. First step in disassembly of the valve body is removal of two bolts on the top.

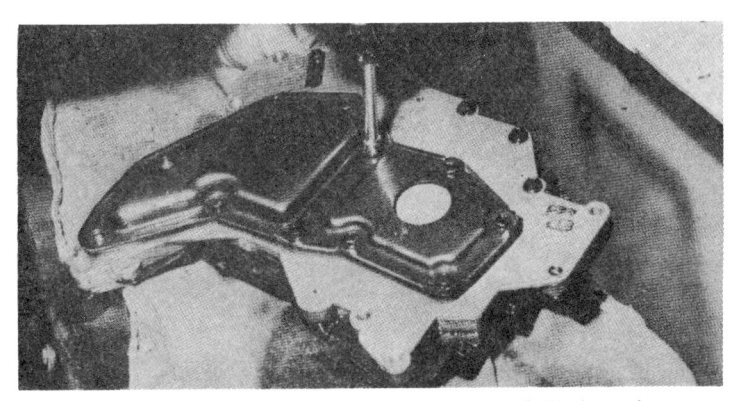

Fig. 15-5. Valve body is turned over, and the oil screen and all bolts on the screen side are removed.

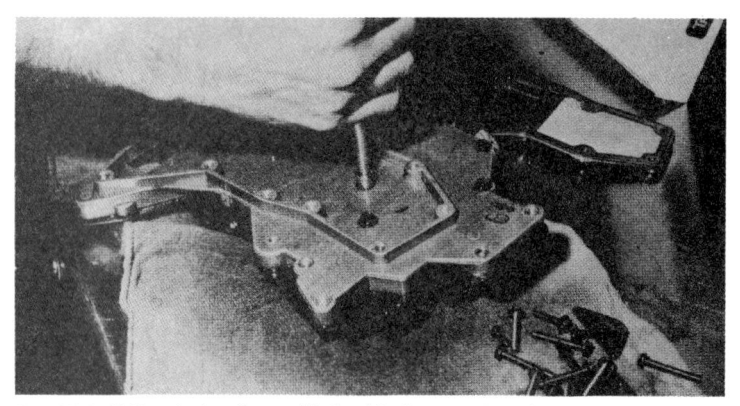

Fig. 15-6. Follow instructions with the kits for complete disassembly.

extending the time duration of every shift. Not only does power slip away during this extended shift, but all friction surfaces receive excessive wear because they're asked to work overtime.

"So, inversely, if you are willing to accept a faster shift, which will subtract some comfort, you can restore full performance and durability."

RESEARCH COMPANY

Before we get down to the actual Trans-Go kit installation, there's an interesting sidelight to Gil Younger's operation that bears mentioning. Generated by demand, a separate company called *Research* has been set up which costs Younger thousands each year but yields, in direct profits, not one penny. Research is a service company for the automatic transmission mechanic wherever in the world he may be. Since he started as a mechanic, Gil is highly sympathetic to the needs of the transmission serviceman. Therefore, if you are a mechanic and are having trouble rebuilding an

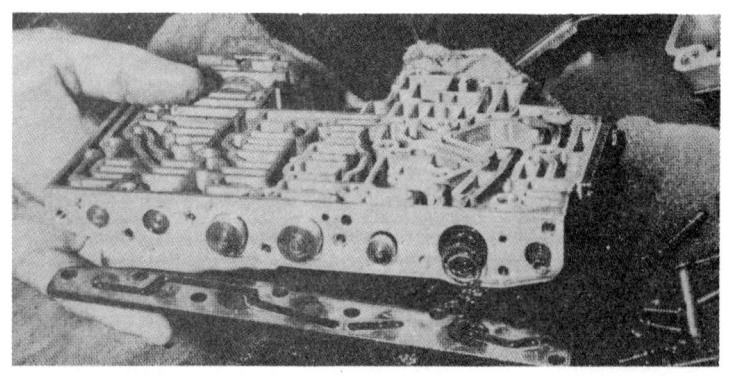

Fig. 15-7. Care is taken to lift the channel casting straight up to prevent dislocation of check balls.

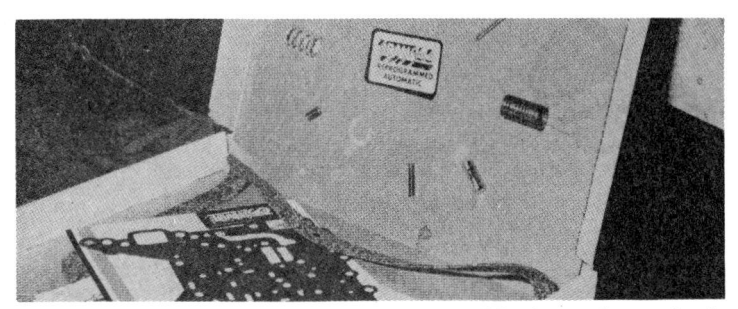

Fig. 15-8. Everything required to transform a sloppy shifter into a crisp gearbox is supplied.

automatic transmission you may call Research collect from anywhere and get precise knowledgeable information from the experts at Trans-Go. They often take as many as 50 calls a day, some lasting 15 minutes or more.

Research also does development work and builds prototypes for continuing performance improvement in automatic transmissions as well as improved economy of operation.

Cleanliness counts. A good clean work area is very important. A sheet of cardboard on the bench makes a good working surface once the valve body has been drained of oil.

The excellent instructions that are provided with the Trans-Go reprograming kit are so easy to follow that even a "shade tree" mechanic should be able to make it a do-it-yourself project. We do, however, strongly recommend your using a hoist. On your back, on a creeper, can get you a face full of hot transmission oil.

Here in photos, are the basics of our Trans-Go kit installation at the Research Center, 2621 Merced Ave., South El Monte, CA 91733 (Figs. 15-1 through 15-20). For your installation of the Trans-Go kit here are the tools you'll need: ¼ inch drill, 5/16 socket, ⅜ socket, ½ socket, speed handle or ratchet, 5/16 spin tight screwdriver, 5/16 wrench, 13/16 wrench, and an inch/pounds torque wrench (optional).

Fig. 15-9. Replacement springs are color-coded with explicit directions.

Fig. 15-10. It is not necessary to completely remove this plate. Remove one bolt and loosen the other.

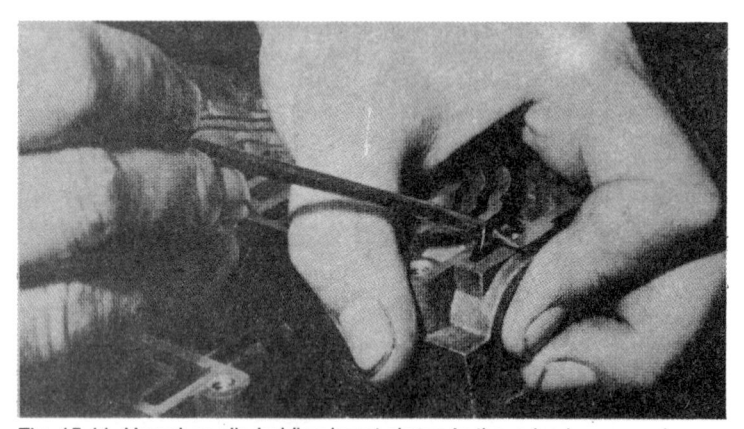

Fig. 15-11. Horsehoe clip holding boost sleeve in the valve is removed.

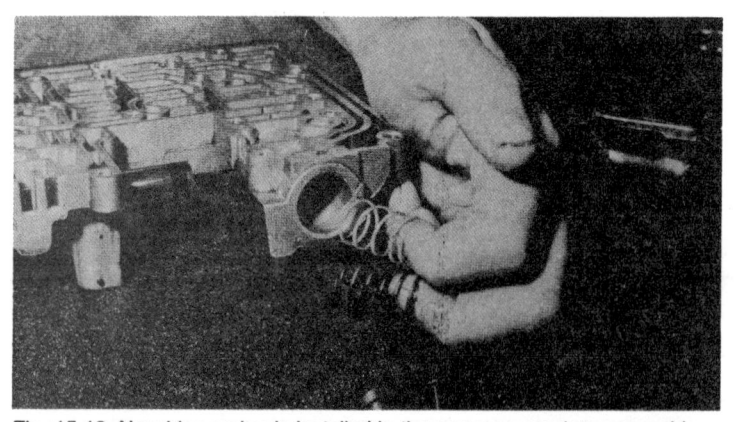

Fig. 15-12. New blue spring is installed in the pressure regulator assembly.

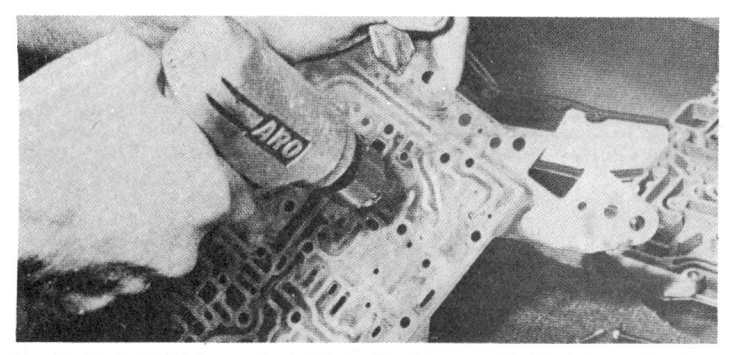

Fig. 15-13. A drill bit is supplied with the kit. If the specified hole is smaller than the drill, the hole is enlarged.

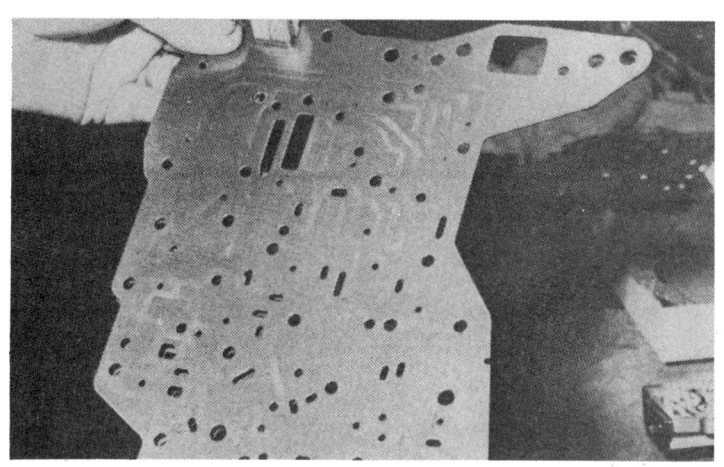

Fig. 15-14. Two gaskets are furnished. Use only the one whose holes line up with the separator plate.

Fig. 15-15. Plate hold-down screws are installed but not tightened.

Fig. 15-16. Care must be taken not to overtighten bolts on the assembly. Valve body is easily warped. If torqued, use 18-20 inch pounds.

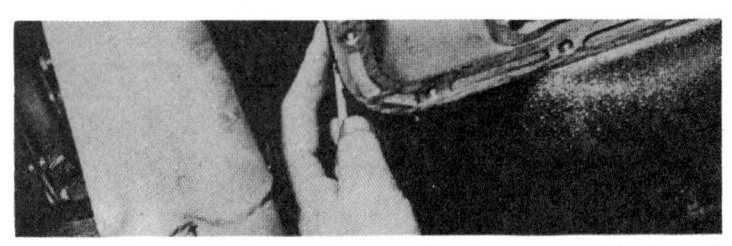

Fig. 15-17. Front band adjustment is snug, with a short wrench. Then back off one-and-a-half turns.

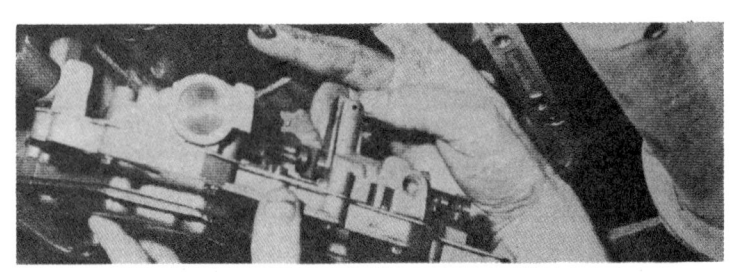

Fig. 15-18. While installing the valve body to the transmission, actuate the downshift lever to engage the valve slot.

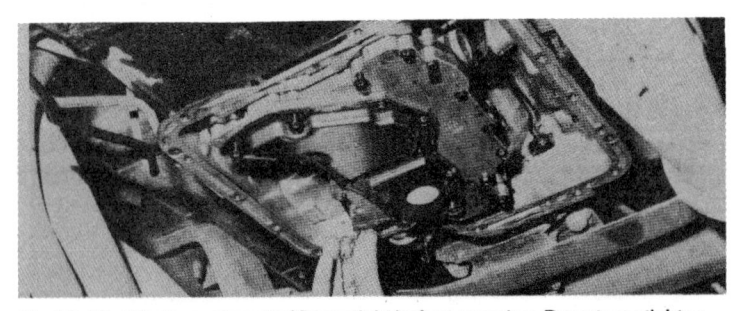

Fig. 15-19. All bolts are inserted finger tight before securing. Do not overtighten.

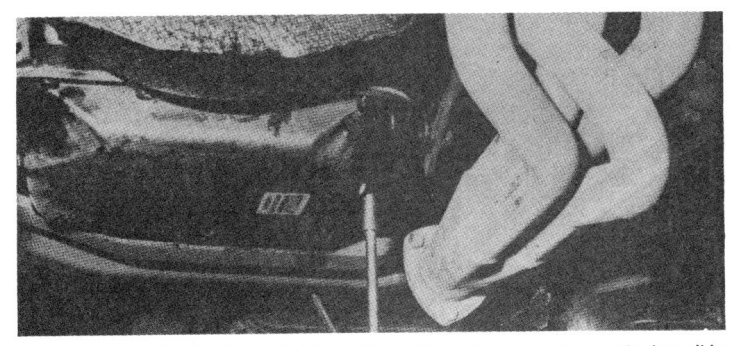

Fig. 15-20. The job is almost finished. Pan will be tightened, transmission oil is replaced, and then the truck will be road tested.

Chapter 16

Facelifting the Chevy Blazer

Today's van and pickup market demands more just than the factory look, and nobody knows that better than the people at PVT Plastics, manufacturers of van and pickup accessories that reflect today's modern age. When a new product comes along, it's usually received with mixed emotion. PVT has come up with a grille for Chevy Blazers and pickups that makes most other grilles look pale in comparison.

RUFF RIDER GRILLE

Big, bad, and bold, the *Ruff Rider Grille* is eye catching. The flashy chrome shell and rectangular headlight with chrome bezels creates a look that's more than just exciting. The metamorphosis takes only an hour and a half (Fig. 16-1). Simply remove your old grille and bolt in the Ruff Rider. We've all seen literally hundreds of stock Chevys. The Ruff Rider Grille has got to be one of the best things that's happened to the Chevy in years. Naturally, the grille kit comes complete with all necessary hardware and brackets. A couple of tools, an hour and a half of time, and you're on your way. When the opportunity presented itself, we jumped at the chance to see a Ruff Rider Grill installed.

Mike Trippedi of Ray's Custom Shop in Brooklyn, New York performed the transformation on a '74 Blazer. Mike first removed the existing grille. Then he assembled the Ruff Rider Grille (Figs. 16-2 through 16-4).

Next on the agenda was the mounting of three aluminum brackets on the bottom of the grille. Once the brackets were fastened, Mike drilled four ¼-inch mounting holes into the sheet metal on the Blazer (Fig. 16-5).

In order to allow for clearance of black plastic spacers between grille and truck, Mike cut out a 1-inch notch in the sheet metal lip under the drilled

Fig. 16-1. A "before" look at a classic "before and after" series (photo by Jerry Schembari).

Fig. 16-2. Step one invovles removing the stock grille (photo by Jerry Schembari).

holes (Fig. 16-6). After placing black plastic spacers onto screws from the bottom, and mounting the grill by putting his hands through grill opening, Mike then fastened the screws to the grille (Fig. 16-7). Finally three small holes were drilled through bottom brackets into sheet metal screws. Much to our surprise, after a glance at our watch, only 45 minutes had gone by. Now, it was on to the headlights.

HEADLIGHTS

Mike first removed the original headlight bezel to get out the round headlights (Fig. 16-8). Once the headlight was removed, he remounted the

Fig. 16-3. The Ruff Rider Grille must be assembled before installation (photo by Jerry Schemabari).

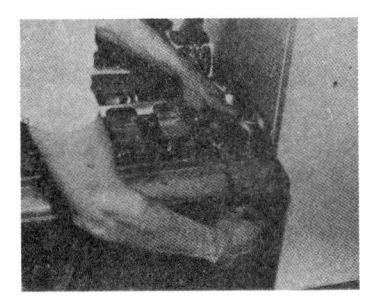

Fig. 16-4. A final assembly step is mounting the bracket at the base of the grille (photo by Jerry Schembari).

Fig. 16-5. Four mounting holes are drilled, following the excellent instructions (photo by Jerry Schembari).

Fig. 16-6. A one-inch notch is cut to allow for black plastic spacers under the previously drilled holes (photo by Jerry Schembari).

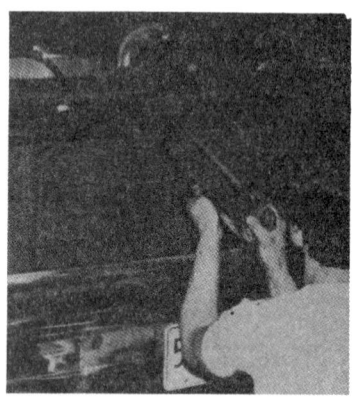

original headlight bezel. After both headlights were removed, Mike fastened the focus screws and springs to the supplied headlight bucket (Fig. 16-9).

Using a small drill bit and sheet metal screws, the headlight bucket was mounted to the original headlight bezel on the Blazer (Figs. 16-10 and 16-11). Next the headlight was mounted into the bucket, and the existing

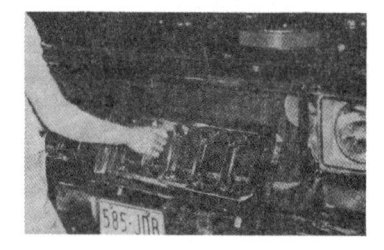

Fig. 16-7. The grille can now be placed in mounting position (photo by Jerry Schembari).

Fig. 16-8. Mike removes the original headlight bezel to remove a stock round headlight. After headlight removal, the bezel is reinstalled (photo by Jerry Schembari).

Fig. 16-9. Focus screws must be mounted to the new headlight buckets (photo by Jerry Schembari).

wiring was plugged in (Fig. 16-12). We took a quick check and turned the lights on for a second. All systems were go. Next we mounted the chrome bezel by drilling four small holes into the bucket (Fig. 16-13). The transformation was complete, and another quick check at our watches told us an

Fig. 16-10. The new headlight bucket is checked for position (photo by Jerry Schembari).

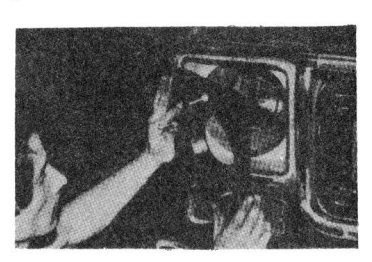

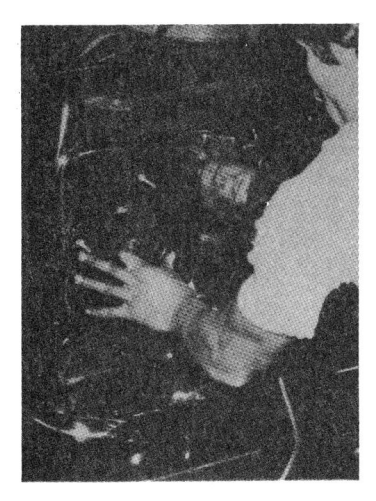

Fig. 16-11. Mounting holes for the new headlight bucket must be drilled (photo by Jerry Schembari).

Fig. 16-12. Headlight is positioned and mounted in the new bucket (photo by Jerry Schembari).

Fig. 16-13. Headlight outer bezel is next installed to the bucket (photo by Jerry Schembari).

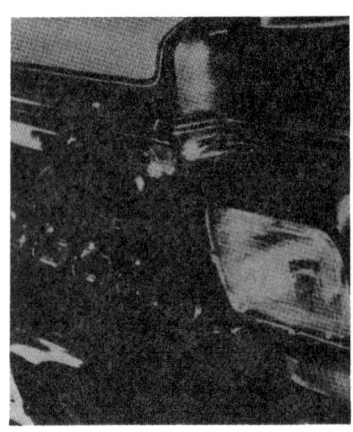

Fig. 16-14. The job complete. Ruff Rider Grille with chrome headlight bezels and new square lights (photo by Jerry Schembari).

additional 45 minutes had gone by—a total of only 1½ hours. You've finally got it all, Chevy owners. It is a grille that not only looks impressive but installs in no time at all (Fig. 16-14).

The Ruff Rider Grille is also manufactured for Chevy vans, Ford pickups, and Broncos. Further information can be obtained by contacting: PVT Plastics Corp. Dept. T4, 300 Richardson Street, Brooklyn, NY 11222.

Chapter 17

Installing Superior Running Boards

We have noted the increasing popularity of running boards as add-ons for pickups over the last year or so. Now more than ever the movement has gotten past being as groundswell and is really taking hold. One of the reasons is the increasing number of manufacturers who are creating easy-to-install kits of striking beauty.

One is the handsome EZ-Sider running board from Superior Industries. We thought you might be interested in a running board installation on a late model Chevy pickup.

We asked West Coast Vans, 607 So. Victory Blvd. in Burbank, California, to let us know when they were about to begin such an installation. They did, and we arrived armed with camera and loads of film.

Everything you need for the job, along with a completely detailed set of instructions, comes in the box with the running boards—everything, that is, except the tools. These include a ¼-inch drill, drill bits, ¼ and 3/16-inch wrenches, 7/16 to 15/16-inch, box or open end; C-clamp or vise grips, Phillips head screwdriver, regular screwdriver, and a spirit level.

In big bold letters the instructions say, "Read carefully." And, "This unit must be assembled prior to use."

There are also some front page general notes that will help with the installation on different vehicles, for the running boards are designed so that they will fit a variety of machines. Figures 17-1 through 17-14 outline the procedure in such detail that a running narrative would be pointless.

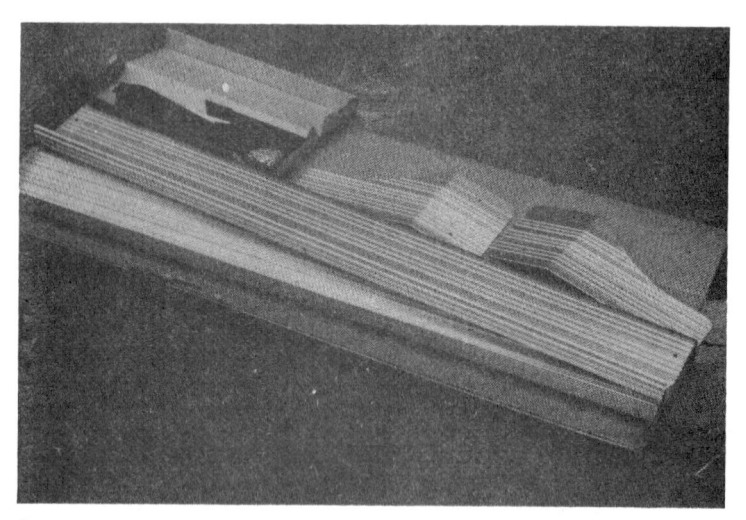

Fig. 17-1. All the parts needed for the running board installation are included in the box.

Fig. 17-2. First step in the assembly process is fitting the angle bracket to the running board.

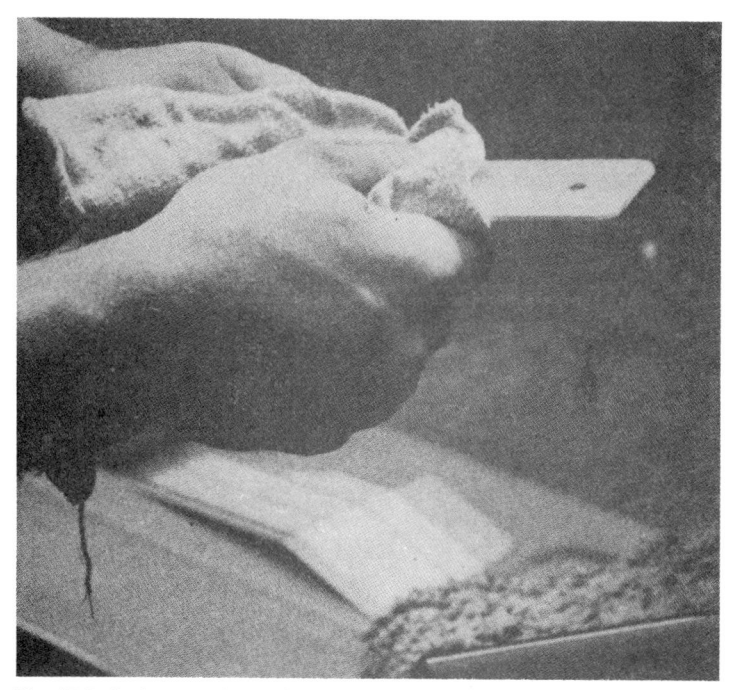

Fig. 17-3. A clean rag is used to clean off oil from the nameplate.

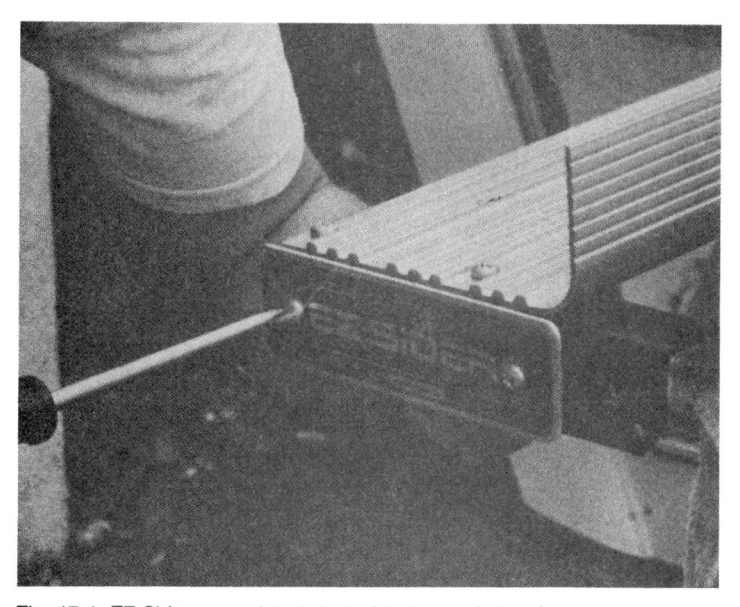

Fig. 17-4. EZ-Sider nameplate is bolted to the angle bracket.

Fig. 17-5. Mud guards are next bolted to the front angle bracket.

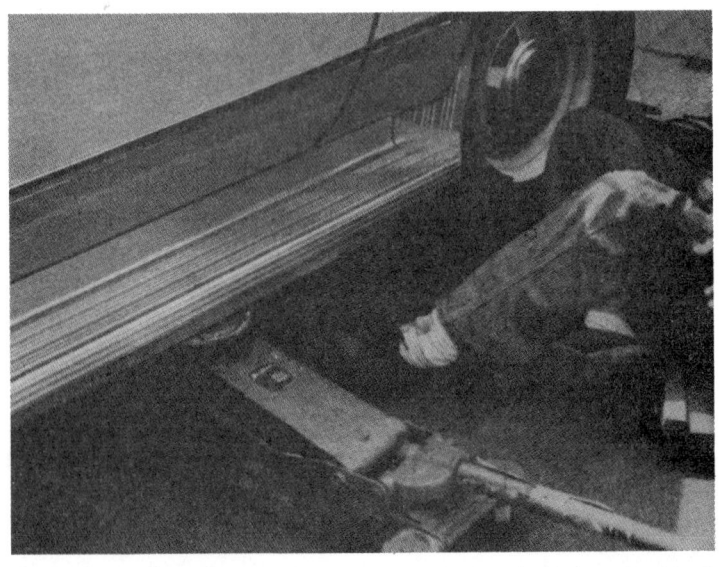

Fig. 17-6. Here a floor jack is used to line up running board with the rocker panel. Vise grips or C-clamp can be used in the absence of a floor jack.

Fig. 17-7. First of four holes is drilled through the mounting flange and rocker panel.

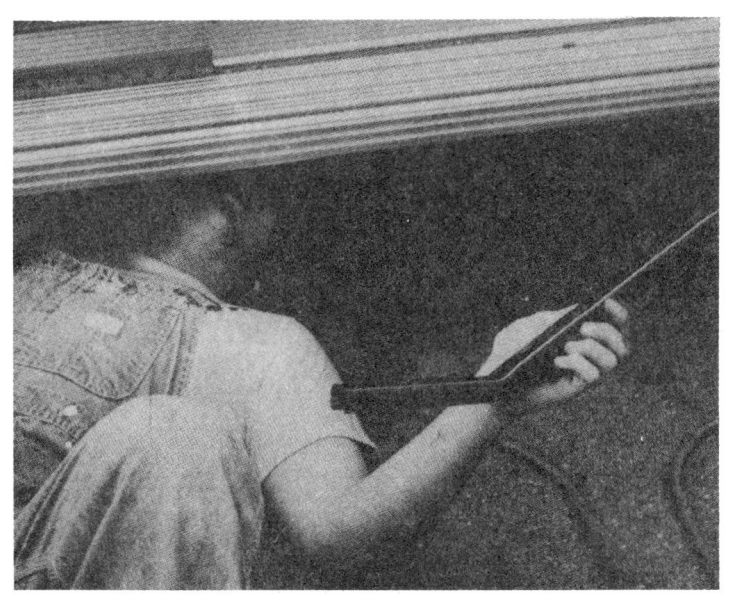

Fig. 17-8. With a running board bolted to the rocker panel, an existing hole is found on the frame for mounting the support bracket.

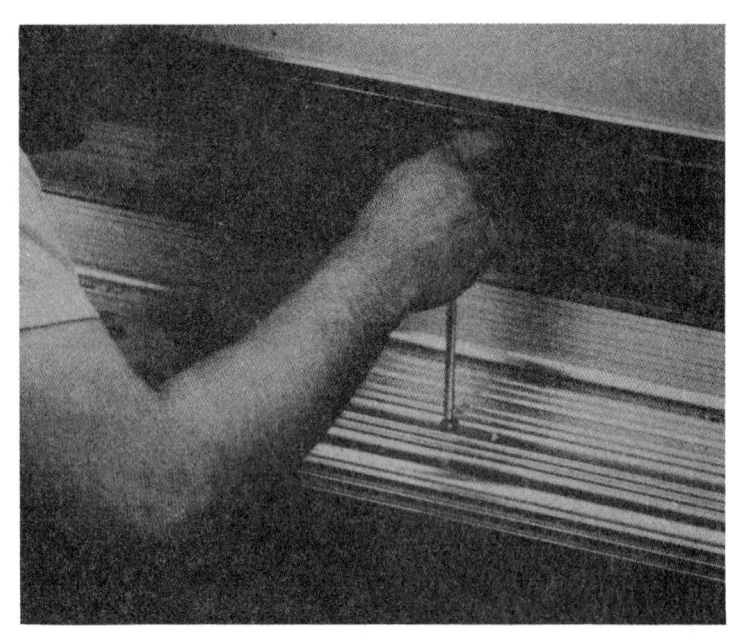

Fig. 17-9. After drilling a hole from beneath, the running board is bolted to the support bracket.

Fig. 17-10. A second bolt will be installed to secure the support bracket.

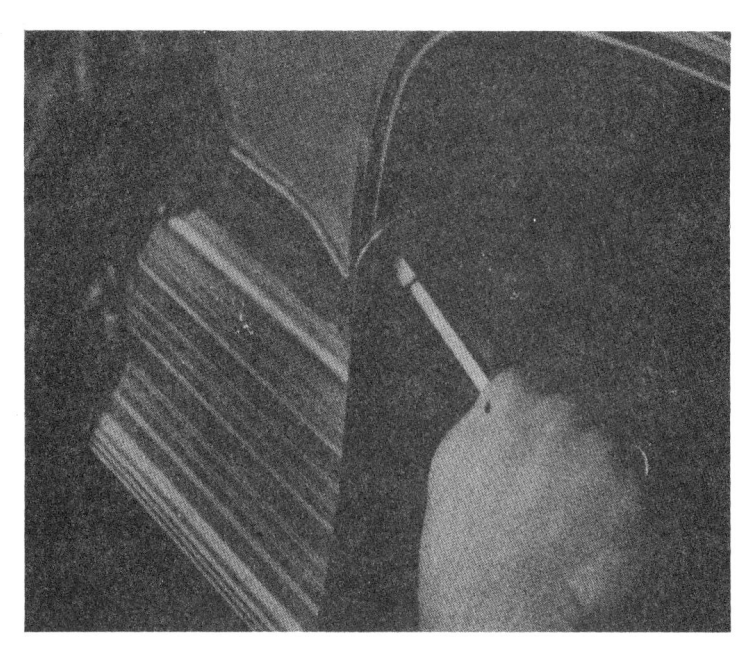

Fig. 17-11. A mud guard is secured to the fender lip with metal screws. Several are required.

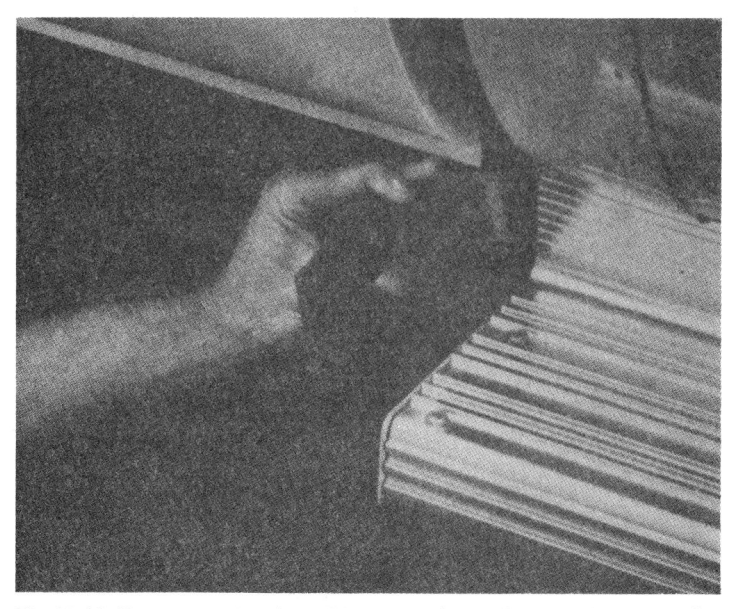

Fig. 17-12. Rear support bracket will be secured to the frame and to the running board.

Fig. 17-13. Ric of West Coast Vans demonstrates the strength of the Superior EZ-Sider.

Fig. 17-14. The running boards are a neat dress-up touch and practical, too.

Chapter 18

Building a Swinging Step

Getting into and out of your high-clearance vehicle can be a real crotch splitter. You can remedy this with a few scraps of metal and an hour of work by putting some handy cab steps on your machine to ease those exits and entrances.

Manufacturers of accessory equipment provide a variety of fixed and folding steps; however, none seem to work really well on four-wheel-drive vehicles. Fixed steps become crushed and mangled in travels over rocky terrain. Folding steps, although they take more off-the-road punishment, have to be folded down each time before they are used. Even more elaborate are the sliding steps which automatically position themselves when the door is opened. They are of rigid construction and can be easily damaged by rocks and by high-centering on mounds.

Another common complaint about fixed and folding steps is that they tend to collect grass, mud, and assorted debris along the backcountry trails. You'll have to pay a lot for some of these manufactured steps.

What's the solution? It is a swinging step made from some of your old metal scraps. Always ready and waiting for your foot, the swinging step cannot be damaged on any terrain, nor will it pick up debris. We installed two steps on our Jeep in 1974, after 110,000 miles of travel throughout the North and South American continents. They function just as well now as they did before.

CONSTRUCTION TIPS

To make the swinging step, you will need two long bolts, some chain, and some scraps of channel bar. We used 3½-inch long 5/16 bolts, 5/16 linked chain, and 2-inch channel bar because this is what we had lying around at the time. We see no reason why other combinations would not work equally well.

First, determine exactly where you wish to have a step. By piling up boxes, bricks, books, or whatever, alongside your vehicle's door, you can simulate a step into the cabin. Once correct positioning and height have been determined, record the figures and start to work.

Cut a 6-inch piece of channel bar (or longer if desired). The holes in the rocker panel where the top ends of the chain will be fastened must be 2 to 4 inches farther apart than the length of the channel bar. The greater the spread of the holes, the more stable the step will be. Cut two pieces of chain to fit between these holes and the ends of the channel bar.

Next, weld the two lengths of chain to the ends of the bar. Ideally, the bolts should be the same width as the inside diameter of the chain's links; also, they should be about 1½ inches longer than the width of the rocker

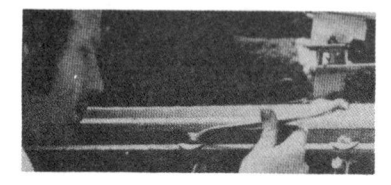

Fig. 18-1. The last step is securing the bolt to the rocker panel. The part of the bolt extending above the nut should be cut off to avoid interference with the door.

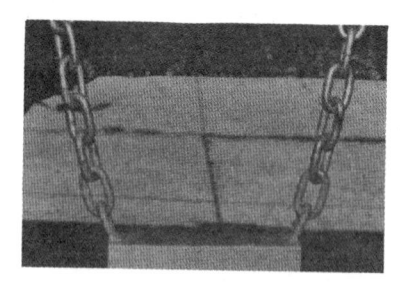

Fig. 18-2. Shape of the finished product is a "V." The more pronounced the "V," the more stable will be the step.

Fig. 18-3. A swinging step greatly facilitates entering and exiting this Jeep Wagoneer.

panel. Heat the bolts an inch from the heads and bend them to a little more than a right angle (about 100 degrees). Now slip the free ends of the chain through the bolts. In less than 30 minutes you should have your first swinging step ready for installation.

MOUNTING THE STEP

To mount it, drill the two holes through the rocker panel in which the bolts are to be inserted. Push the bolts through and cap them with a flat washer and nut (Fig. 18-1). Make sure that the chain is not twisted and the channel bar is level. Tighten down the nuts and check to see if the bolts interfere with the closing of the door. If so, the protruding end of the bolt and possibly the nut will have to be trimmed down.

After a couple of hours of work, you can wipe the sweat from your brow and step easily into your vehicle's cab (Fig. 18-2). No matter how rough or muddy a trail becomes, your swinging step will always be ready and waiting (Fig. 18-3).

Chapter 19

GMC Sierra Truck

Tim Sweeney is an avid four-wheel-drive enthusiast. A member of Connecticut Central Four Wheelers, he was married in Norfold, Connecticut in an open park surrounded by 15 off-road trucks. He had planned to take his vows in front of his GMC Sierra pickup, but the minister objected. The honeymoon was a two week trip to Colorado by 4×4. Tim and Melissa headed out west, drove up Colorado's 14,000 foot high Pike's Peak, and returned.

"Most people have family portraits. Not us," says Melissa. The Sweeneys have albums of 4×4s and four-wheel drive races. On the walls are pictures of his GMC. A glass case is filled with plastic models of trucks. Tim reflects, "When I'm not building trucks, I'm building models." Out in back is a two-wheel drive '55 Chevy step-side that needs body work but "runs like a charm." Tim eventually plans to enter the show circuit with it. Behind the garage is a Commando Jeep that's going to be fixed up and raced.

Tim's '77 Sierra GMC half-ton gets a steady diet of dirt as well as the normal highway mileage of a family vehicle. After such use, the truck is surprisingly competitive on the show circuit. Tim attributes this to "good engineering with an eye to the practical." He wanted a truck that was going to perform superbly off the road, yet look great back in civilization.

SUSPENSION

His first concern was the suspension. The front end was scrapped. Rough Country shocks were thrown in place coupled with Rough Country five leaf springs (Fig. 19-1). In back, Tim stuck with GMC's heavy duty springs and matched them to another set of Rough Country shocks. The back end was picked up with a pair of 4-inch raiser blocks.

Fig. 19-1. Tim swapped the factory suspension for Rough Country shocks and springs (photo by Anthony Esposito).

Lots of GMC's break off U-bolts, and Tim was determined not to be left stranded somewhere. He replaced his U-bolts and nuts with aircraft-quality substitutes. A skid plate under his gas tank was installed to keep the rocks out of the fuel system.

CAB PROTECTION

The cab is protected by a 3-inch House of Steel Mushroom Bar supporting two KC lights with internal wiring for additional night vision (Fig. 19-2). Matching the roll bar, Tim opted for a House of Steel grille guard as well (Fig. 19-3). Both the bar and grille were sandblasted and repainted in GM's blue white.

Tacoma Stars are highly functional rims offering greater strength while reducing mud buildup and assisting in the brakes' cooling. Tim popped these into four 11½ × 15 Goodyear Wranglers.

Up front, KC fogs coupled with Marchal quartz iodides proved to be ideal for illuminating the way home at night. The Marchals are wisely protected from scrub and branches by screening.

Inside the cab is a seat and dash combo ripped out of a Blazer. The headliner is heavily padded to keep bruised scalps and crushed vertabrae to a minimum. A GE 40-channel CB takes care of communication problems while Sun gauges monitor engine conditions. One interesting instrument was a tilt gauge which measures, as Melissa puts it, "the chances of us using the roll bar." See Fig. 19-4.

Fig. 19-2. The House of Steel Mushroom Bar supports a pair of KC lights (photo by Anthony Esposito).

Fig. 19-3. A stury brush guard adorns the front end of Tim's GMC Sierra (photo by Anthony Esposito).

Fig. 19-4. Factory indicators have been replaced with Sun instruments and a Lev-O-Gage which tells Tim when he's about to use the roll bar (photo by Anthony Esposito).

Though few believe it, the Sierra does have its original paint. Lots of hand-rubbed wax has kept the tons of brush, mud, and rocks from marring the truck's appearance. Pinstriping on the body, roll bar, and grille was executed by Gary, "the local brush." An attractive custom cover reduces the amount of topsoil Tim brings back with him after each outing while protecting whatever he carries around with him.

Tim's tasteful work and care has proven that a four-wheeler can be used off the road and still catch eyes on the road.

Chapter 20

Removing and Replacing Locking Hubs

A lot of us have the savvy to change the linings or pads on our front brakes or lube the bearings. We have put out unnecessary bucks to a dealer though, because we felt incompetent to correctly remove and replace our locking hubs. It's a lot simpler than you think.

Take the Warn hub, the most common (after all they started it all) hubs on our 4×4s. The whole idea of getting into the innards of something as seemingly complex as locking hubs can needlessly put you off from what is really a simple job if you have basic tools.

What makes it simple is a kit, (cheap, too) that has all the necessary parts to put things back together right. This isn't a repair kit. That should never be necessary with Warn or anybody else's locking hubs, but they do have to come off and go back on again every now and then.

Perhaps you want to replace the pads on your front brakes (another simple job). How do you go about getting the hubs off without messing up? Thats's just what we're going to show you.

First, though, next time you're at your friendly off-road parts and supply house, pick up a hub service kit for your brand of hubs. If they're worn, you'll get gaskets, O-rings, and tab-lock washers. With these correct parts you'll never have to worry about a leak or sheared mounting bolts, which can happen if you use substitute washers rather than the tab locks.

Now that you've got all the pieces you need, how do you go about it? Just follow Figs. 20-1 through 20-6 and you, too, will be an expert.

Fig. 20-1. Two different types of locking hubs.

Fig. 20-2. Different front lockers call for a different kit for each. Packaged in plastic, you can see what you're getting.

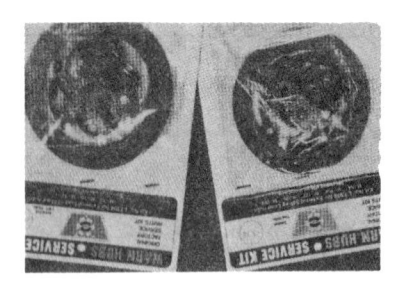

Fig. 20-3. Remove the socket head screws from the outer edges of the clutch assembly and pull it off. Replacement parts are on the clean shop rag below the wheel.

Fig. 20-4. Remove the snap ring from the end of the axle as well as the heavy retaining ring that is seated in a groove in the wheel hub. The hub body will now slide out of the housing. Complete hub has now been removed.

Fig. 20-5. Installation is the reverse of removal. Be sure to replace "O" ring seal with a new unit from the kit. Snap ring and retaining ring should also be replaced since they are easily deformed during removal.

Fig. 20-6. Turn control dial to "lock" position, install clutch assembly, and put socket head screws in loosely. When all are in place, tighten to 18-21 inch-pounds torque. Turn the control dial to "free" position.

173

Chapter 21

Liquid Petroleum Gas Conversion

Ever since our companion magazine, *Travelin' Vans*, had one of their project vans converted to run on LPG, (liquid petroleum gas), we've been on the lookout for an installation on a 4×4 so we could acquaint you all with the advantages, and the economy of this "better idea" in alternate fuels. We had left our number with Gary Moody Automotive, 9531 East Valley Blvd., El Monte, CA 91731, along with a request that Gary call us when he had an LP conversion scheduled on a four-wheel-drive vehicle.

SONNY BONO'S JEEP WAGONEER

Gary called the other day saying he had a truck coming in that we'd be especially interested in—a Jeep Wagoneer belonging to singing and comedy star Sonny Bono. Needless to say, we jumped at the chance. We would get a good installation story and a Celebrity Jeep along with it.

Gary Moody is a long time professional in LPG conversions. He's tried every product on the market, and now has settled on using only Manchester tanks and Impco carburetion. He says, " . . . Like in racing, why monkey with a going machine? Manchester and Impco never let us down. They may be back ordered at times, but the products are always tops."

The installation on Sonny Bono's Jeep called for all the expertise of the talented crew at Gary Moody's. Normal installation in a Jeep type vehicle is for the tank to sit in the bed directly behind the cab. The Wagoneer, being a station wagon type 4×4, presented a different ball of wax. Bono didn't want the tank inside, so this called for under floor mounting. See Figs. 21-1 through 21-29.

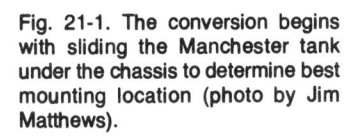

Fig. 21-1. The conversion begins with sliding the Manchester tank under the chassis to determine best mounting location (photo by Jim Matthews).

Fig. 21-2. After marking and drilling for the mounting bolts, tank is moved into permanent position (photo by Jim Matthews).

PROPANE

We've known about propane as a motor fuel for quite some time. As far back as 1967, we tested two identical cars on a drag strip. One was gasoline powered—the other propane. Times were identical except for the more experienced driver.

Fig. 21-3. Only highest quality steel bolts are used for securing the tank (photo by Jim Matthews).

175

Fig. 21-4. Sliding ring in Impco carburetor determines which fuel, gasoline or LPG will be fed to the engine (photo by Jim Matthews).

Off-roaders have known about propane as a motor fuel for a long time, too. In 1969 Spike Cooper was busy winning the Mint 400 with his AMC Jeepster outfitted to run on LPG. In 1972, Spike was at it again for the Baja 1000, but this time he was joined by Impco, the foremost manufacturer of

Fig. 21-5. Aluminum plenum (right) will carry fuel/air mixture to existing carburetor (photo by Jim Matthews).

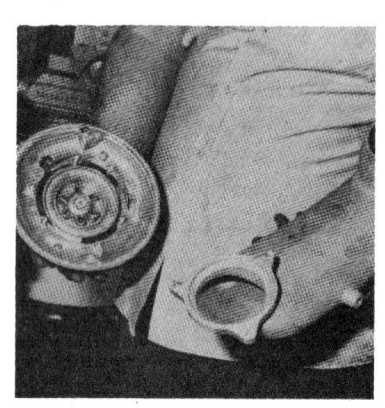

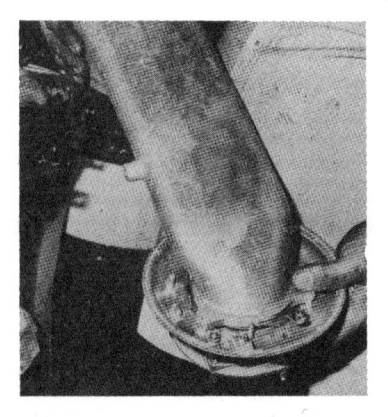

Fig. 21-6. Plenum mounts to carburetor in this fashion. Bolt pattern permits a variety of positions. (photo by Jim Matthews).

Fig. 21-7. Mandatory air cleaner completely surrounds carburetor and air intake (photo by Jim Matthews).

Fig. 21-8. Air cleaner cover with fittings attached bolts to assembly (photo by Jim Matthews).

carburetors for LPG use. The engine in Cooper's Jeepster was "built" by Impco's Don Bass to NORRA specifications for a stock engine. It had to have a broad horsepower range for supplying the necessary power at both high and low rpm for the various high speed and terrific torque applications

Fig. 21-9. The Impco converter warms the entering LPG. Some fitting holes are protected with plastic caps which must be removed (photo by Jim Matthews).

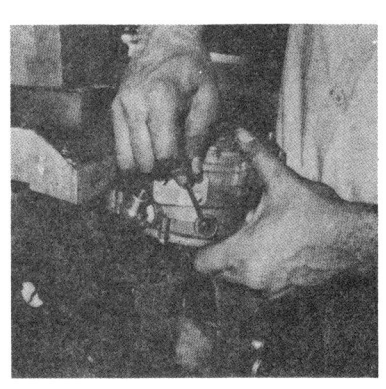

177

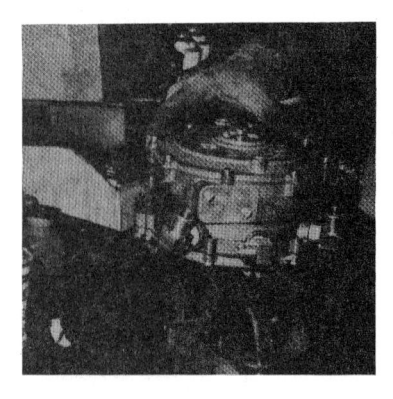

Fig. 21-10. All brass fittings are coated with sealant on the threads before installation (photo by Jim Matthews).

that are required in the varied and grueling 1000 miles of Baja. Spike Cooper didn't win the race due to an out-of-balance wheel and sheared center bolts on the front end springs. Even so, he did finish the race and the engine in the LPG powered Jeepster worked perfectly.

Propane is a colorless, flammable gas obtainable from petroleum and used as a fuel. Most of the time we think of it as being used in

Fig. 21-11. Holes are drilled into top of fender well for anchoring of the converter (photo by Jim Matthews).

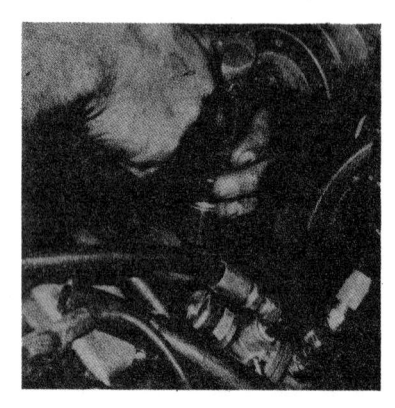

Fig. 21-12. Once secured, heater hose lines are cut and routed to converter. Warm engine coolant ensures gasification of the extremely cold LPG (photo by Jim Matthews).

178

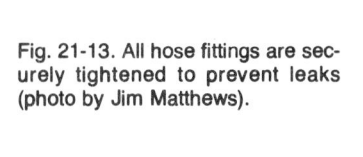

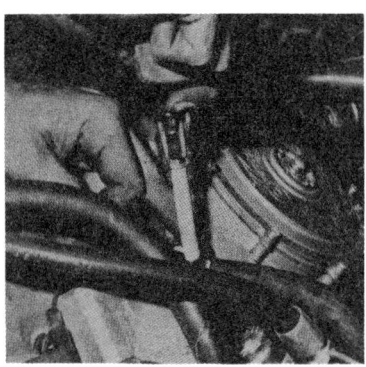

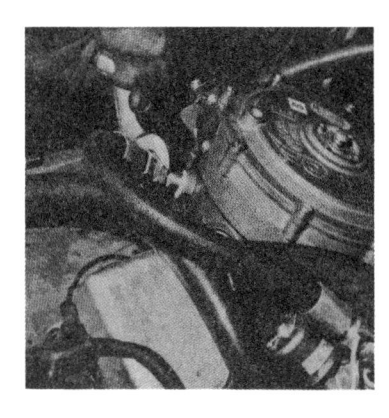

Fig. 21-13. All hose fittings are securely tightened to prevent leaks (photo by Jim Matthews).

Fig. 21-14. LPG fuel line to the converter is also securely tightened (photo by Jim Matthews).

recreational vehicles for cooking and heating. With gasoline now in the triple digit figures, and diesel rapidly approaching the same stratosphere, it bears some heavy thinking as a fuel for your off-road vehicle.

CONVERSION ADVANTAGES

Now here's a big plus. With LPG there is no float to bounce around to slosh gasoline out when you need it most. So far as carburetion is con-

Fig. 21-15. Assembled carburetor, air cleaner, and plenum are carefully positioned for maximum air flow to the cleaner (photo by Jim Matthews).

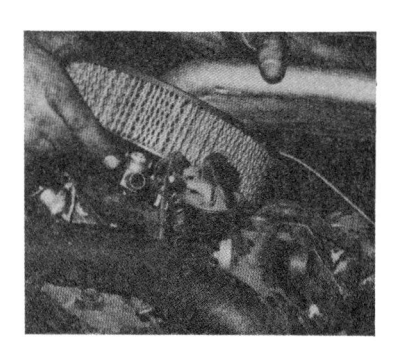

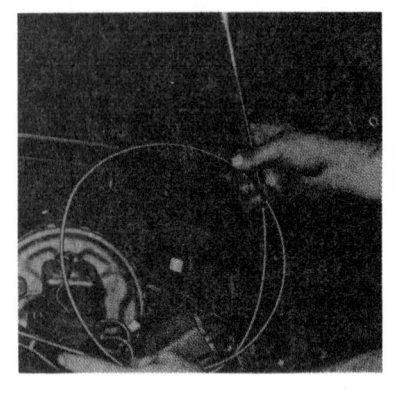

Fig. 21-16. Flexible push/pull cable reaches from cockpit to carburetor—in for LPG, out for gasoline (photo by Jim Matthews).

cerned, your LPG powered 4×4 doesn't care if it is running upside down, although your bearings might complain of oil starvation.

Before carburetion can occur, however, the liquid propane, which is extremely cold and under pressure, must first pass through a converter, vaporizing the fuel and reducing the pressure. The propane entering the

Fig. 21-17. Cable is routed through firewall to carburetor with as few bends as possible (photo by Jim Matthews).

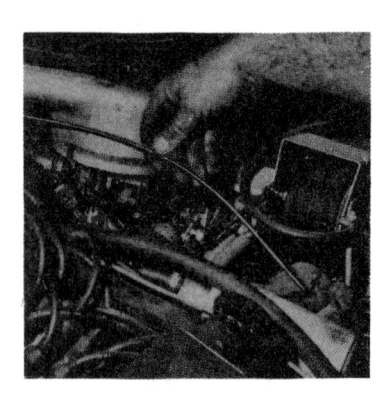

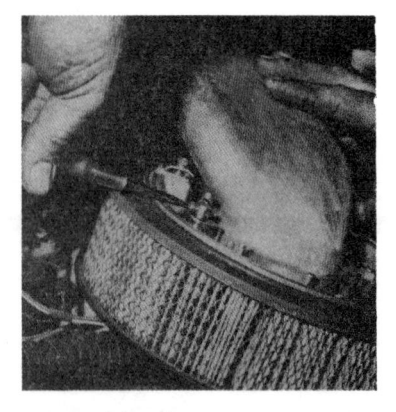

Fig. 21-18. After being cut to length, the cable is secured to the carburetor selector plate (photo by Jim Matthews).

Fig. 21-19. Both the LPG and gasoline supplies must be fitted with fuel locks to ensure that only the fuel desired gets to the carburetor (photo by Jim Matthews).

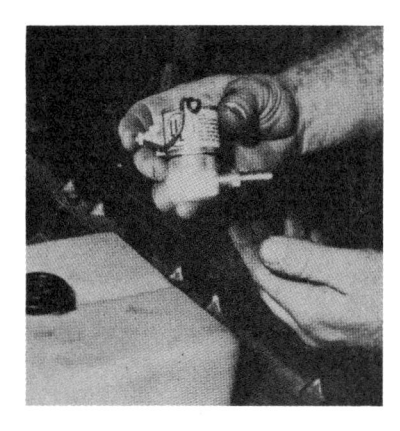

Fig. 21-20. Close-up of gasoline fuel lock in position (photo by Jim Matthews).

converter is still quite cold. In order to keep it from freezing, water from the engine radiator is circulated through the converter supplying a heat source from which the propane can draw as it transforms into a vapor. Once a vapor, it readily mixes with the air in the carburetor regardless of the vehicle's position.

Fig. 21-21. Main LP fuel line from rear tank to converter is positioned out of harm's way at the top of the firewall (photo by Jim Matthews).

Fig. 21-22. Underhood installation virtually complete. Wing nut atop the plenum is to be added (photo by Jim Matthews).

As a bonus, the manifold pressure remains relatively constant, extending the life of bearings, pistons, cylinders, and other vital engine parts. Also on the plus side is the lack of carbon deposit buildup. Spark plugs last longer. The interval between oil changes is extended, and your engine just plain lasts longer.

Fig. 21-23. Since tank filler is virtually inaccessible, remote fill is required. All fittings here are also coated with sealant (photo by Jim Matthews).

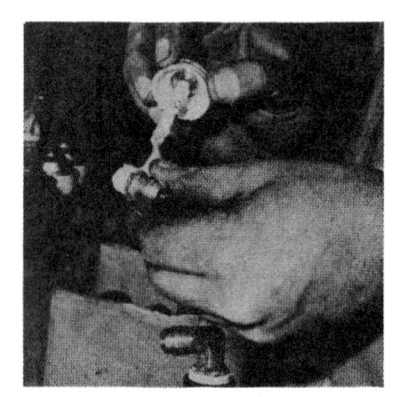

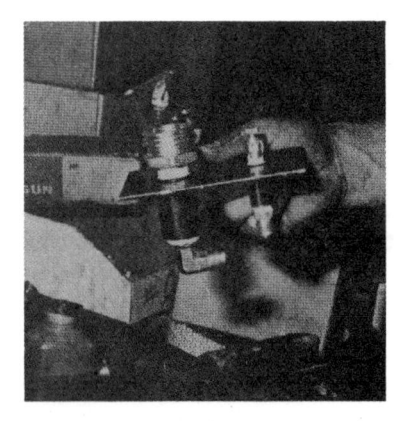

Fig. 21-24. Complete remote fill assembly ready for installation (photo by Jim Matthews).

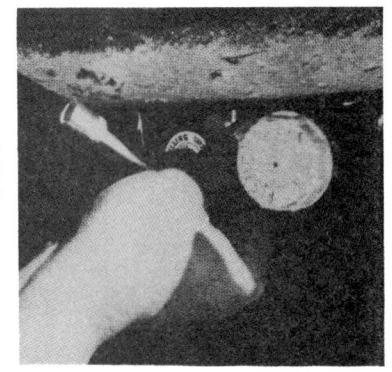

Fig. 21-25. On Sonny Bono's Jeep Wagoneer, the remote fill is located on the left rear fender skirt (photo by Jim Matthews).

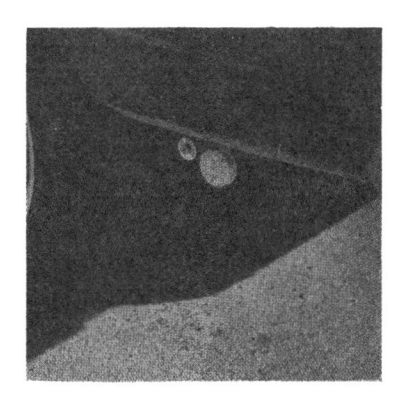

Fig. 21-26. Remote fill is unobtrusive. Few observers will understand its significance (photo by Jim Matthews).

Special attention must be paid to your ignition system when switching to LPG, since the ionization voltage required for the spark is 20 percent higher than with gasoline. Although normal silicone wiring will handle the voltage requirements, chances are your stock coil will not, resulting in misfiring problems. It's a simple matter to install a heavy-duty coil or computerized ignition such as the CompuSensor.

Fig. 21-27. Final touch is fitting the fuel gauge alongside fuel selection controls. Separate gauge gives a more accurate reading than tying in to the existing gas gauge (photo by Jim Matthews).

Fig. 21-28. The interior installation, as neat and unobstrusive as remote fill (photo by Jim Matthews).

Fig. 21-29. Departure angle is somewhat reduced by underchassis location of the Manchester tank. The conversion is complete on Sonny Bono's Jeep Wagoneer (photo by Jim Matthews).

CONVERSION DISADVANTAGES

So far just about everything we've discussed has been on the plus side. What about the minuses?

Just about the only major deterrent comes from the cost of the conversion. On an open 4×4 where the tank can be mounted behind the cab, the installation cost including tank, carburetor, converter, lines, fitting, and labor will run from $700 to $800. On a more complex operation, such as mounting under the frame, as with Sonny Bono's Wagoneer, the cost, because of the extra labor and longer lines, will come in closer to $1000. Against that you have to balance the savings in fuel costs.

If you're thinking about doing a propane conversion as a do-it-yourself project, stop. It would be virtually impossible unless you are already an expert in the field. Providing you live in or near a major city, you should have no problem finding a qualified conversion shop. Your only problem will be getting your name on the waiting list. Once there, you can look forward to cleaning up your act.

Chapter 22

Installing Rigid Racks

Right after World War II brothers Alva and Herb Stephan began business in Grayling, Michigan, as manufacturers of wooden clothespins. Thousands of laundry days later, Stephan Wood Products has evolved into a large and diversified woodworking complex which provides a number of items for both the military and commercial markets.

Recently the company completed production on 27,000 combination side rack-troop/seats for the U.S. Army. These units enable the adaptation of the standard Dodge pickup to utility-troop transport configuration. As a natural extension of this program, Stephan Wood Products is now offering similar but more attractive side racks for the consumer pickup market. These *rigid rack* units feature a 6-inch wide steel support channel which runs the length of the pickup bed. Models are available for 6- or 8-foot Chevy-GMC, Ford, Dodge, or Jeep trucks.

Figures 22-1 through 22-6 show the installation of the Sportsman Bench model on a Chevy pickup. Upright it is a strong functional side rack, and when folded down it serves as a practical bed, seat, or storage shelf. These units come completely assembled with all the hardware needed for installation and a complete set of instructions. Only a few simple hand tools are required: hand drill, hammer, scissors, and a ½-inch socket or box end wrench.

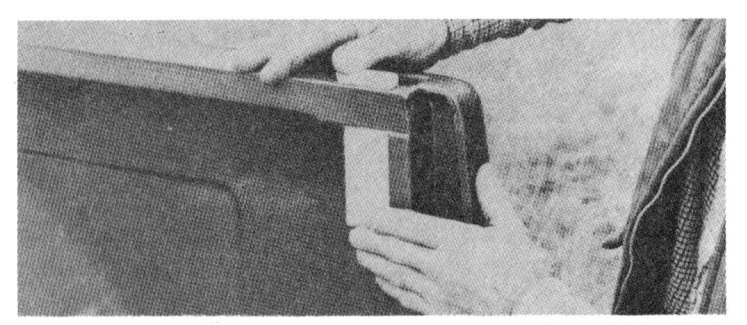

Fig. 22-1. Cut two, 2½-inch long foam pads from the 1½-inch material furnished, and place them on the face of the two rear pockets. Next cut six 2½-inch long pads from the ⅜ × ½-inch material and place these on the top rail at the edge of each stake pocket as shown. Cut six additional 2½-inch long pads from the 1½-inch wide material and have these ready to use (photo by Don Geiss).

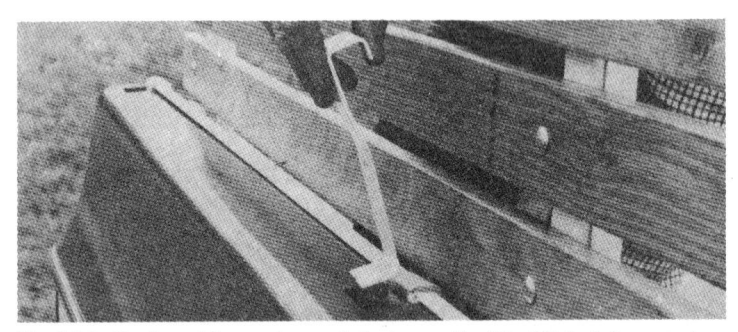

Fig. 22-2. Starting at the center pocket, place a ¼ × 1½ × 2½-inch foam pad on the top edge of the panel at the stake pocket, then install J-hook. The bolt on bottom of the J-hook must go through the hole in the bottom of the stake pocket and the hole in the bottom of the 6-inch steel support channel. Pressure against the panel may be necessary to force the J-hook to lap over the top edge of the panel. Repeat procedure for the front pocket (photo by Don Geiss).

Fig. 22-3. Drill a ⅜-inch hole in the face of the two rear stake pockets. Use the hole in the 6-inch steel support channel as a guide (photo by Don Geiss).

Fig. 22-4. Place the J-hook with rubber spacer and weld-nut in the rear stake pocket and hook over the top edge of the 6-inch support channel. Thread one of the 5/16×1-¾-inch hex bolts through the rear pocket into the weld-nut on the J-hook (photo by Don Geiss).

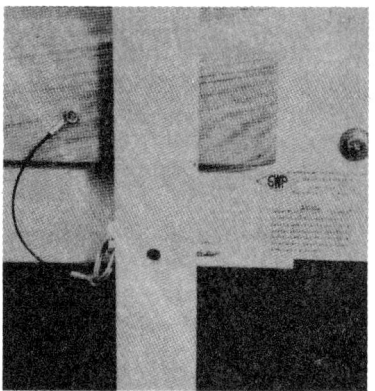

Fig. 22-5. Tighten the hex bolt at the two rear pockets. Now place one of the rubber boots on each of the seat legs, and the installation is completed (photo by Don Geiss).

Fig. 22-6. The Sportsman's Bench installation completed (photo by Don Geiss).

Chapter 23

Improving Basic Suspension on Vans

Suspension systems on American cars and trucks have not seen much innovation since the 1940s and 1950s (Figs. 23-1 and 23-2). The idea of the leaf suspension now utilized on the vans of today was born in the horse-and-buggy days.

REAR SUSPENSION

The longitudinal leaf spring used on the rear suspension of today is basically made up of a main leaf with one or more shorter leaves held together by a center bolt and aligning clips. The number of leaves and the broadness and thickness of the leaves determines the load rating of your van. This is why your van rides better when there is some weight in the tail end. The front of the main leaf is securely attached to the chassis, while the rear is attached by shackles that allow for longitudinal movement of the spring but no sideways end movement.

This system, although archaic, is still effective. It allows for maximum vertical movement of the rear end and rarely comes out of alignment.

FRONT SUSPENSION

There are basically three types of front suspension systems used on the newer vans. The first type is control arms with coil springs in between. The control arms are "A" shaped and pivot vertically while allowing for no horizontal movement. They are attached to the spindle by ball joints. This type of system could use some innovation as the joints receive a lot of wear and tear, so alignment is occasionally needed.

A second type of front suspension is the independent "I" beam supported by coil springs (Fig. 23-3). Each "I" beam is pivoted on the chassis

Fig. 23-1. A hard hat isn't what you need most when driving the average stock van—it's plenty of padding elsewhere.

side opposite the side on which the spindle and wheel are. This allows for maximum vertical movement in a wide arc. Pivoting braces extend perpendicularly back from the "I" beam to the chassis.

A third type is the leaf spring mentioned earlier, which is utilized in the newer four-wheel-drive conversions (Fig. 23-4).

SHOCK ABSORBERS

The tubular telescoping, vertical shock absorbers of today don't actually absorb the shock of hitting bumps (Fig. 23-5). Instead they dampen the oscillating motion of the spring suspension once the bump has collasped the spring. Internally, telescoping in either direction is dampened by fluid being forced past a damping piston from one chamber to another.

The front shocks are usually attached to the lower control arms and extend up through the coil springs to where they are attached to the chassis

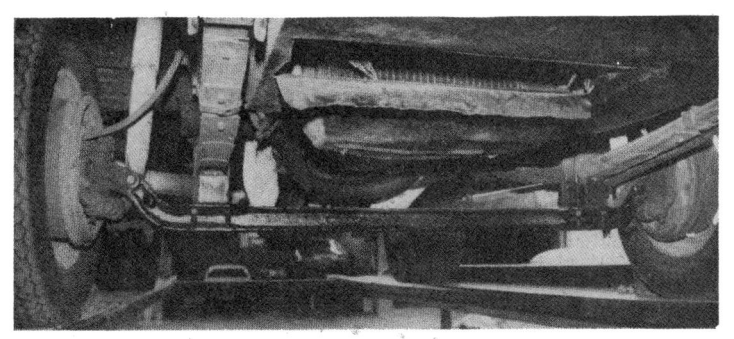

Fig. 23-2. Here's a mechanic's-eye view of a typical suspension system. It looks businesslike, but not much more.

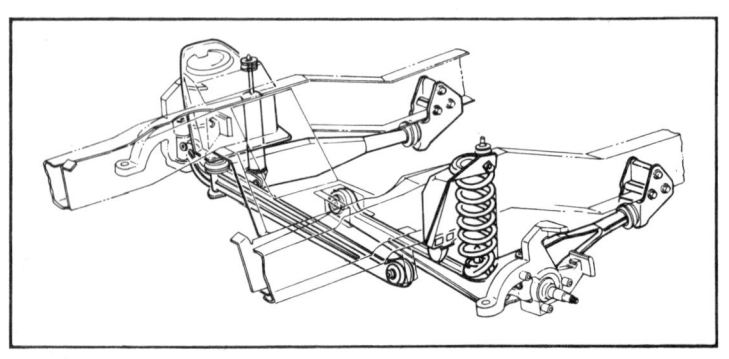

Fig. 23-3. Here's a setup using twin I-beams with coil springs. The shock absorbers here are inside the coils.

above. In the rear, the shocks extend from the mounting pads on the axle housing vertically or near vertically to the chassis or cross member above.

There are several adjustable-type shocks on the market. The first and foremost is the *Dutch Koni*, produced with high quality and workmanship. All the internal parts are perfectly engineered and matched. They contain no plastic, rubber, or leather parts. They can be adjusted for a harder or softer ride by collapsing the shock and turning the bottom until it clicks. Two other noteworthy types of adjustable shocks are the *Gabriel* and *Armstrong* adjustables. These, however, do not allow for infinite adjustment as the Konis do.

Air shocks are very popular these days. They are not to be confused with adjustable shocks, as the damping ability of the shock isn't changed. Instead, the length of the shock can be altered by filling an air bag or

Fig. 23-4. The leaf spring goes way back in history. The number and length of the leaves make a big difference in the ride.

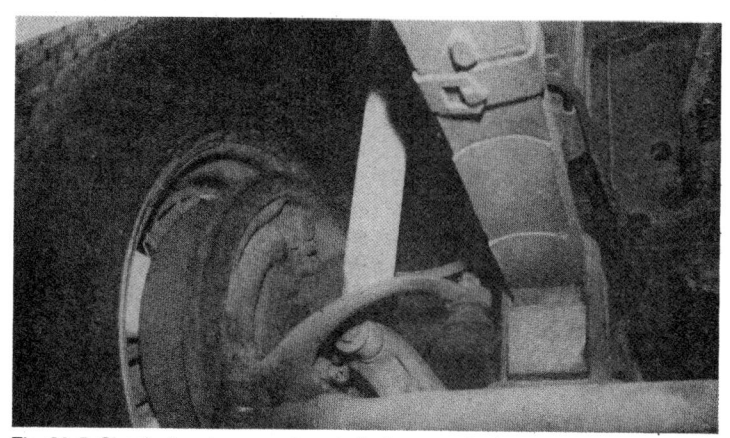

Fig. 23-5. Shock absorbers, contrary to their name, don't actually absorb shocks. "Dampers" would be a better name.

chamber. These shocks are used more to adjust a load or just give your van a lift.

STABILIZER BARS

Obviously, the Detroit manufacturers could provide improved suspension systems right from the factory, but they probably won't do so as long as they can sell all the vans they make so easily in any case. Aside from the adjustable shocks and such things as wider wheels and tires, one of the most important devices you can add yourself is a *stabilizer bar* (Fig. 23-6).

Due to a van's higher center of gravity, stabilizer bars are needed more on vans than on passenger cars. Stabilizer bars really work. Vans have a tendency to pitch forward and lean upon hard braking and/or cornering. The only apparatus counteracting this unfavorable action is the spring-and-shock setup, which is inadequate.

A stabilizer bar is actually a U-shaped bar that resists twisting or *torsion*. So, in the case of the front stabilizer, each end of the bar is attached

Fig. 23-6. For real improvement, the best thing you can add is a stabilizer or antisway bar. Its basic working principle is explained in the text.

to each side of the independent front suspension. The center of the bar is anchored on a forward cross member by clamps with rubber bushings which allow for a certain amount of twisting. The amount of resistance to twisting or *reactive torque* depends on the length of the arms and the diameter of the bar. When one control arm is forced upward independently of the other, a force is exerted by the bar to return it to its original attitude.

The job of the stabilizer bar is to keep the center of gravity from shifting as much as possible and keep the tires in even contact with the road. The bar helps counteract that feeling of rolling while cornering and also helps the driver maintain control in high winds and on bad roads.

The stabilizer bar does not, however, detract from the comfort and shock-absorbing ability of your vehicle. As long as both wheels are moving up and down at the same time, no reactive torque is applied by the bar.

The rear stabilizer bar usually has the arms attached to the chassis or leaf springs ahead of the axle housing while the center is attached by bushings and clamps to the housing itself. The rear bar also aids the front bar to prevent sway and improve handling.

Additional information on stabilizer or antisway bars, shocks, tires, and other suspension equipment is available in a booklet published by Addco Industries. The booklet can be obtained by writing Addco at 400 Watertower Road, Lake Park, FL 33403. The company, which has pioneered the manufacture of aftermarket antisway bars, lists kits for over 300 applications including all popular van models.

According to Addco, the most routinely asked question pertains to the correct weight of rear bar that should be added—standard or extra firm. The answer depends on load habitually carried in the van. If it runs empty most of the time, a standard rear bar in combination with a heavy front bar will provide excellent handling. If a load is frequently carried, the extra heavy rear bar should be used.

Correctly matched antisway bars are probably the one most important piece of customizing that can be done to a van. Wide tires, mural landscapes, way-out carpeting, and fish-eye windows are great, but they don't compare to the driving pleasure, added comfort, and increased safety of a first-class suspension.

Chapter 24

Installing Dual Batteries

If you run a lot of 12-volt accessories like a TV set, fancy interior lighting, etc., you have a choice. You can either take a chance on finding yourself stranded at some Truck-In with a dead battery, or you can install a dual battery setup that lets you run the "living quarters" battery flat dead without draining one ampere from the automotive battery.

To get the answer on how it's done, we called on AAA Trailer Supply at 8500 Sepulveda Blvd., Sepulveda, California. Manager Bill Wilson agreed to let us photograph the very next dual battery installation that came along.

The process itself is not very difficult, and with the excellent instructions furnished with the *Divi-Charge* isolator, a fair mechnic could make it a do-it-yourself project. The usual hand tools, including a ¼-inch drill and wire stripper, are all that are required.

Materials will include a new battery along with its mounting frame or bracket, the Divi-Charge, and a supply of electrical wire and connectors. Note that #8 wire is preferred, but there isn't always available a supply of connectors, or terminals, to be clamped onto #8; #10 is the absolute minimum wire to use. With the #8 you'll be putting maximum charge to your battery system any time your alternator is whirring away.

The installation process is shown in Figs. 24-1 through 24-14. Essentially, what happens after you've found a place to put the Divi-Charge and the battery is just hooking up the new components in a definite, prescribed electrical pathway. Your engine will charge both batteries, but when you use your interior accessories they will draw only on the secondary battery, leaving the primary battery charged to crank over your engine when you're ready to head for home.

Fig. 24-1. 1975 Ford E150 offers lots of under the hood room for dual battery installation (photo by Brad Barcus).

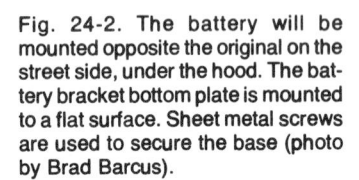

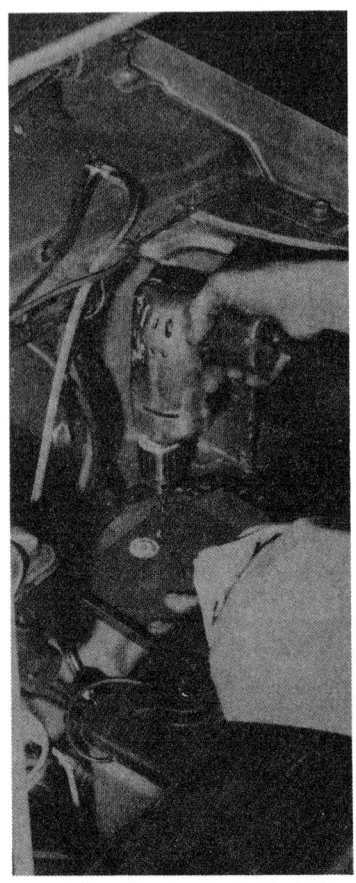

Fig. 24-2. The battery will be mounted opposite the original on the street side, under the hood. The battery bracket bottom plate is mounted to a flat surface. Sheet metal screws are used to secure the base (photo by Brad Barcus).

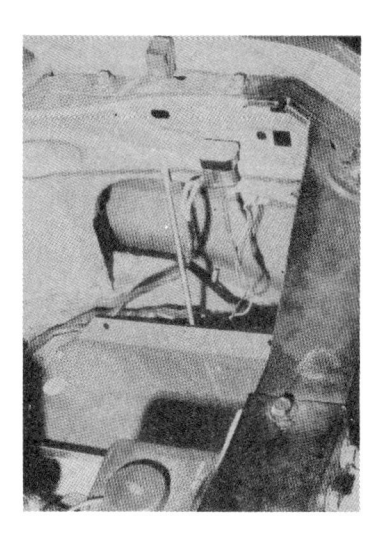

Fig. 24-3. Hold-down clamp rods are inserted (photo by Brad Barcus).

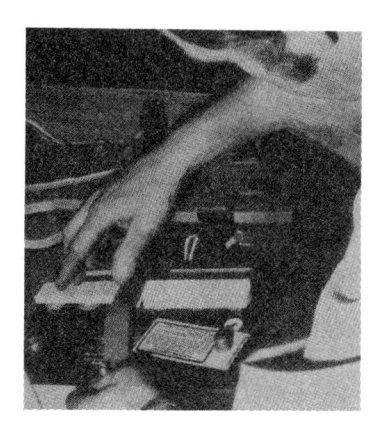

Fig. 24-4. Top securing plate is positioned and then tightened with nuts on upright rods (photo by Brad Barcus).

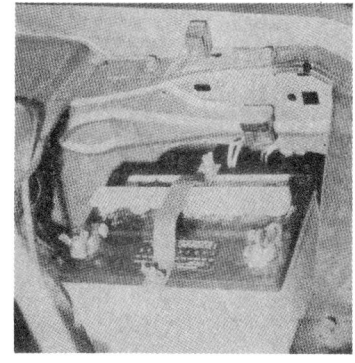

Fig. 24-5. Connectors are placed on battery terminals. Wire will be added later (photo by Brad Barcus).

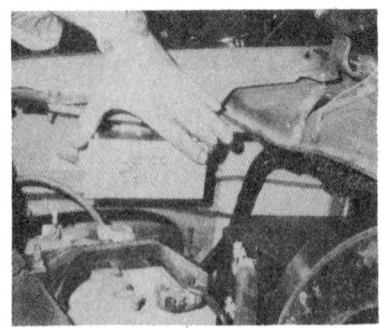

Fig. 24-6. Divi-Charge isolator is positioned on inner fender well wall near original battery. This is important for keeping wire length short (photo by Brad Barcus).

Fig. 24-7. Top is removed from Divi-Charge revealing terminal posts (photo by Brad Barcus).

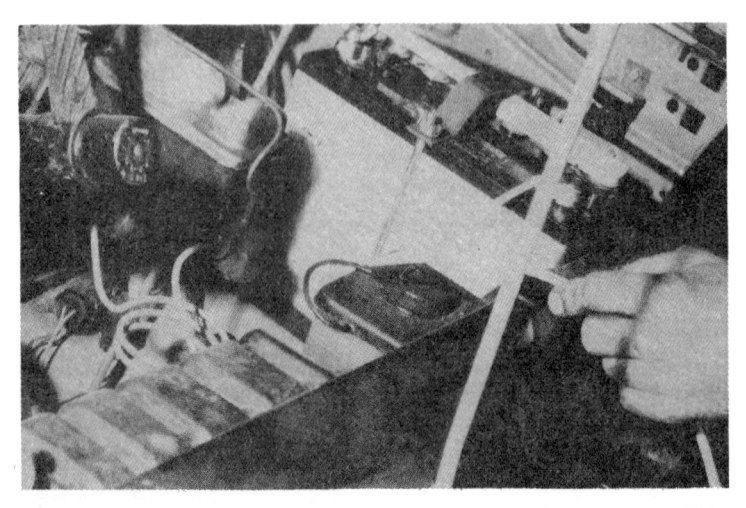

Fig. 24-8. Wire is now run from secondary (new) battery to ground at vehicle frame (photo by Brad Barcus).

Fig. 24-9. Another wire is run from the secondary battery to Divi-Charge. Routing is done carefully and neatly (photo by Brad Barcus).

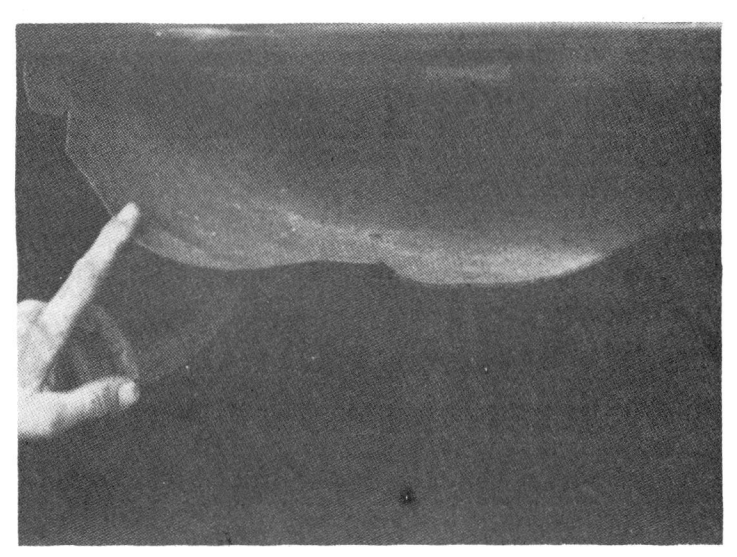

Fig. 24-10. Alternator in newer Ford vans is not easy to locate. Protective, neoprene shield which guards factory transmission oil cooling lines must be temporarily removed (photo by Brad Barcus).

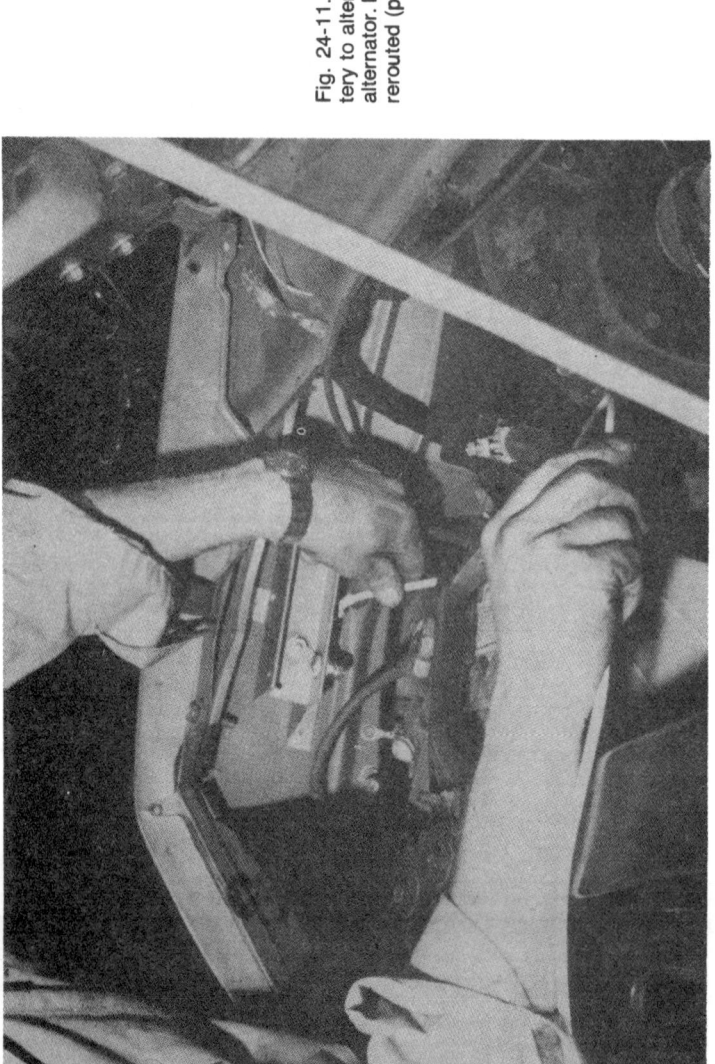

Fig. 24-11. Wire from primary battery to alternator is cut close to the alternator. It will be reconnected and rerouted (photo by Brad Barcus).

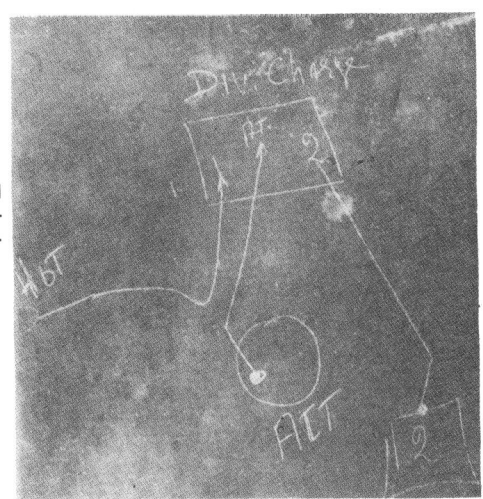

Fig. 24-12. Wire is fed from Divi-Charge to alternator (photo by Brad Barcus).

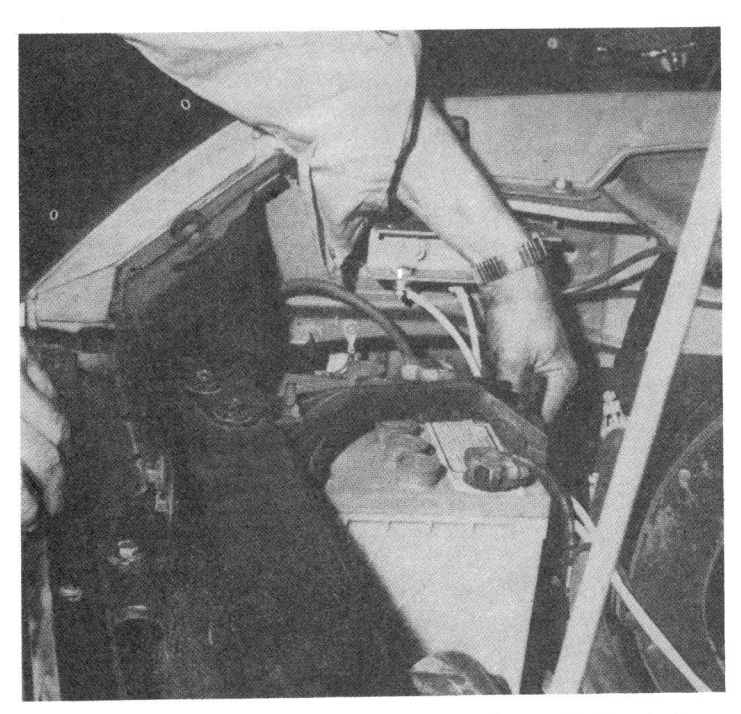

Fig. 24-13. Wire from secondary battery is connected to previously cut primary battery wire close to alternator. Battery end of cut wire is attached to post #1 of Divi-Charge (photo by Brad Barcus).

Fig. 24-14. Alternator end of cut wire goes to center position of Divi-Charge. From the #2 post on the Divi-Charge wire goes directly to the positive post of the auxiliary battery. A circuit breaker (not shown) is normally included in this line (photo by Brad Barcus).

Chapter 25

Installing an Auxiliary Fuel Tank

With the long, hot, and wonderful days of summer approaching, more and more vanners are anticipating the freedom of the open road. As anyone who drives long distances will attest, the fewer gas stops needed the better. The only way to accomplish that is to install an auxiliary fuel tank and/or a larger replacement tank. Most vans ride high enough off the ground for the installation of one or more tanks to be quite simple.

There are many manufacturers involved in the production of fuel tanks for vans, giving the prospective buyer a choice in size, construction, and function. Tanks may be bolted on or equipped with factory-type sheet metal bands. There are varying types of interior reinforcement and baffling used and differences in the metal itself.

Obviously, choosing the right fuel tank for your needs is not a decision to be taken lightly. It's wise to shop around.

The installation in this article was done by AAA Trailer Sales and Supplies, Inc., 8500 Sepulveda Bl., Sepulveda, California. See Figs. 25-1 through 25-12.

Fig. 25-1. Determine the distance from the side and from the end of the tank to the center of the filler neck. Drill 2¼-inch hole for filler. Lift tank, with filler neck through hole, using small jacks.

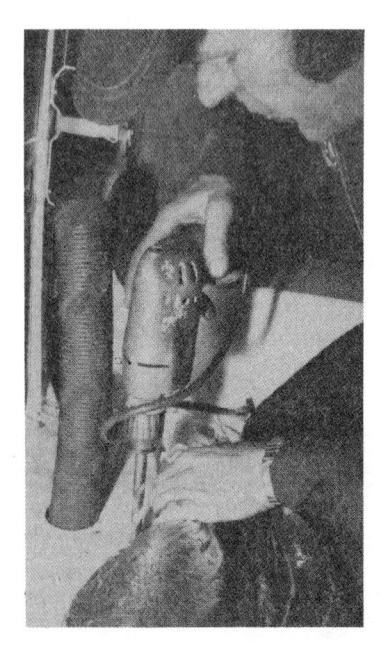

Fig. 25-2. Drill for mounting bolts. Either drill pilot holes from the bottom up with a long ¼-inch drill or mark holes with a long center punch. Remove the tank and enlarge holes to ½-inch.

Fig. 25-3. Place the tank back in position and drop mounting bolts from the top down through the floor of the van. Rubber grommet should be used to reduce vibration.

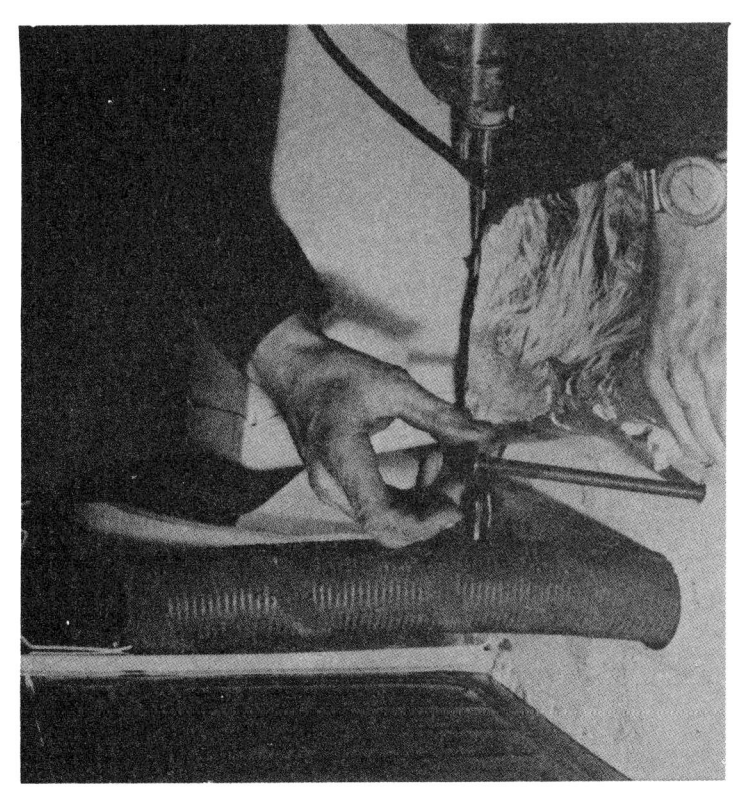

Fig. 25-4. Place the washer on bottom of the tank and double nut. Cut off excess bolt.

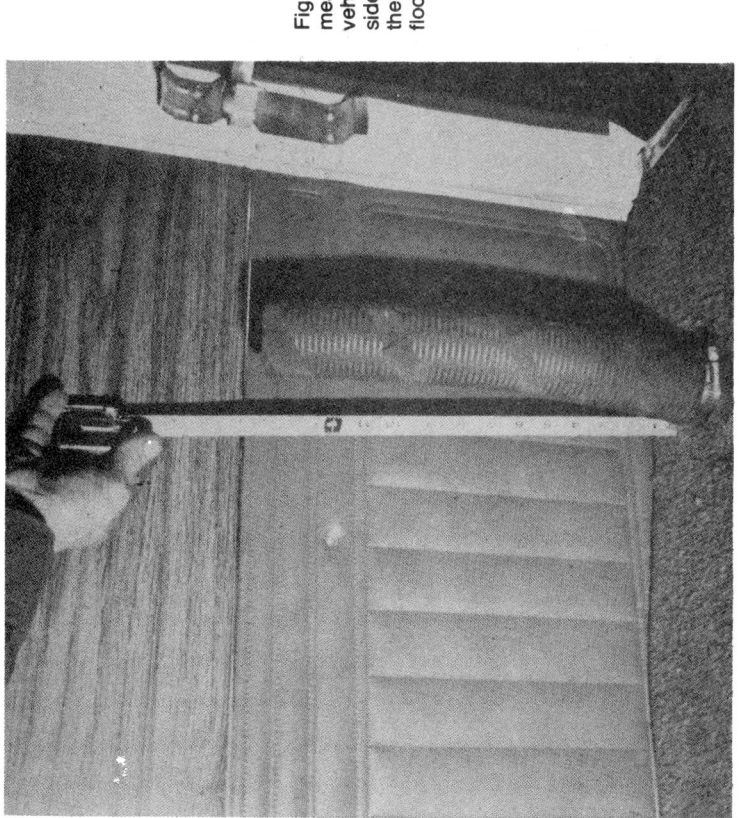

Fig. 25-5. After the tank is mounted, measure up from the floor inside the vehicle approximately 10" on the side of the vehicle. Stay in line with the filler neck extending up through the floor.

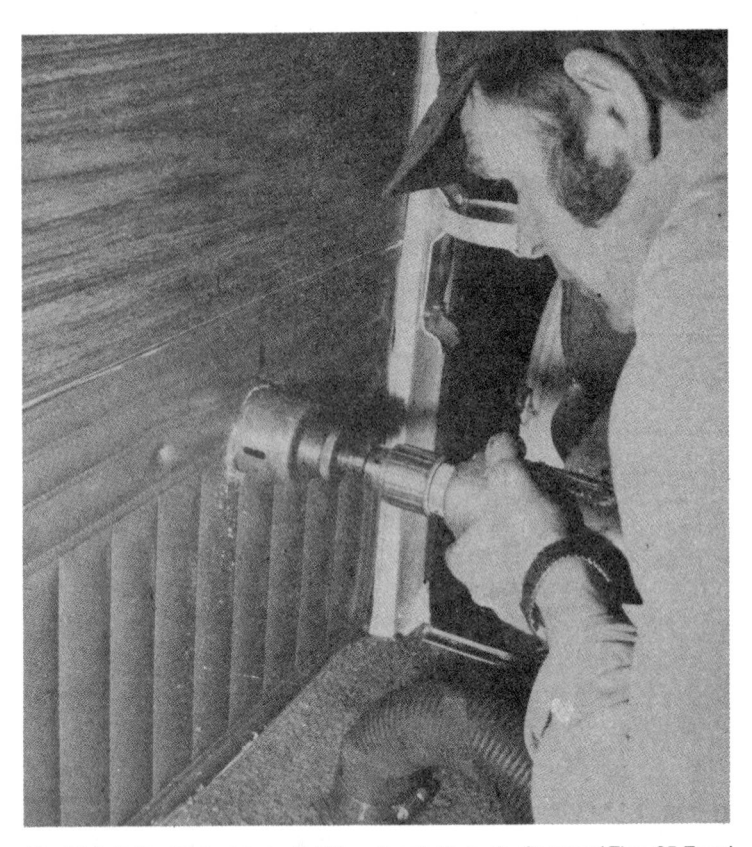

Fig. 25-6. Drill a 2½-inch hole. If drilling directly through, disregard Figs. 25-7 and 25-8.

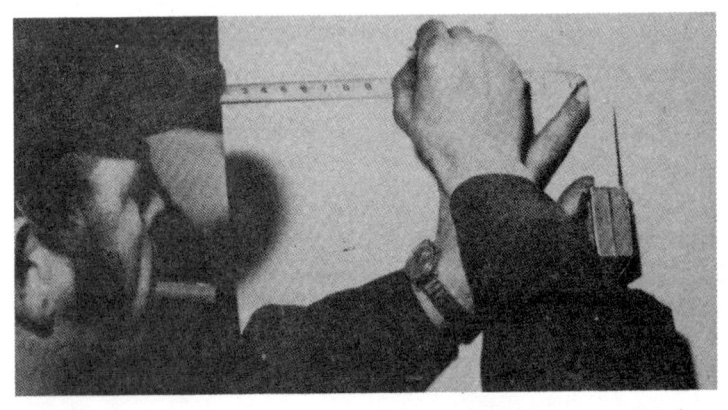

Fig. 25-7. On the outside of the vehicle, duplicate interior measurements from the front of the tank.

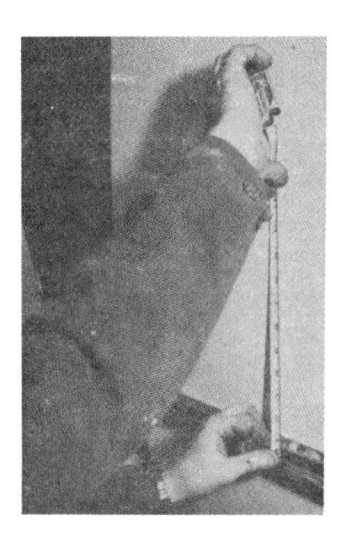

Fig. 25-8. Measure 10 inches up from where the floor meets the body.

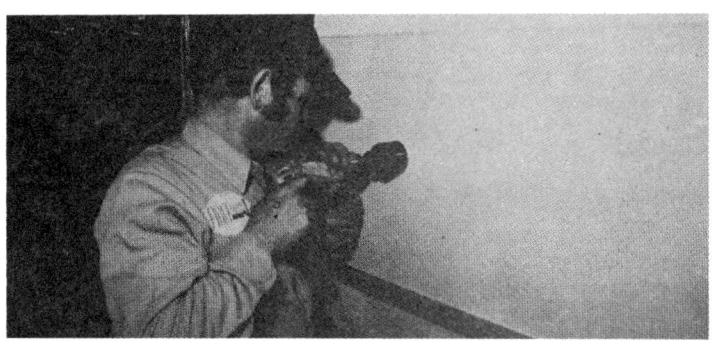

Fig. 25-9. Drill 2½-inch hole through the body wall.

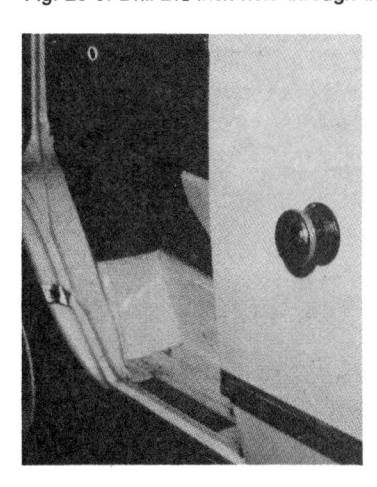

Fig. 25-10. Insert grommet and 7" filler neck through the hole, tilting slightly towards the floor of the vehicle.

Fig. 25-11. Fuel lines from main and auxiliary tanks are routed to an electric three-way fuel valve. Third line runs to a fuel filter, then on to the engine fuel pump. With an electric fuel valve, there's no fiddling with a manual valve when you want to change tanks.

Fig. 25-12. Switch for three-way fuel valve is located on the dash for easy access.

Chapter 26

Installing a Door Extender

Since none of us are happy with the original equipment wheels and tires on our vans, and as quickly as possible we go to the wider rubber, it goes without saying that almost as quickly, we need a *door extender* — that is, if we ever intend to open the side door again. This was exactly our problem after we installed our Cragar SS wheels with 10-inch rims at the rear and our Formula 1 Super Stock L60 tires on our van.

With the number of outstanding van converters in the San Fernando Valley, there were several we could have asked to help us with the installation of the extender. We settled on T&H Van Works Unlimited because, knowing Eddy Hice (the H of T&H), he would take the time to point out each step of the way and allow us to get plenty of photographs to show you how it's done (Figs. 26-1 through 26-26).

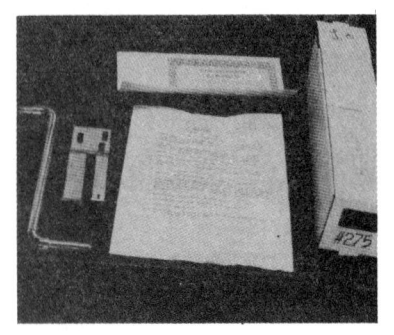

Fig. 26-1. The extender kit from L & M Products, 3200 E. 29th St., Long Beach, CA 90806. All the parts are the two pieces at the left. The instruction sheet is complete and comprehensive (photo by Brad Barcus).

Fig. 26-2. This is as far as the door would open before the extender was installed (photo by Brad Barcus).

Fig. 26-3. An important early step. Two jack stands are padded with shop rags. The door will rest here during most of the extender installation (photo by Brad Barcus).

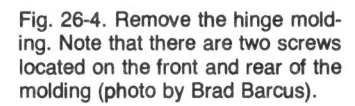

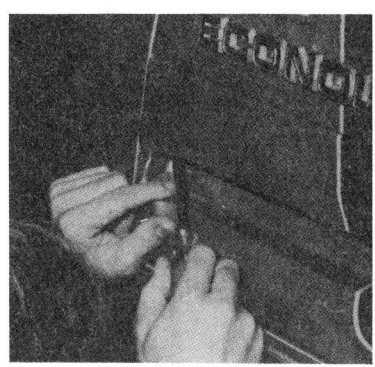

Fig. 26-4. Remove the hinge molding. Note that there are two screws located on the front and rear of the molding (photo by Brad Barcus).

Fig. 26-5. Eddy points out the slot in the top of the door molding which means it must be slid forward for removal (photo by Brad Barcus).

Fig. 26-6. Visually inspect the location of the door cams and mechanism before disassembly (photo by Brad Barcus).

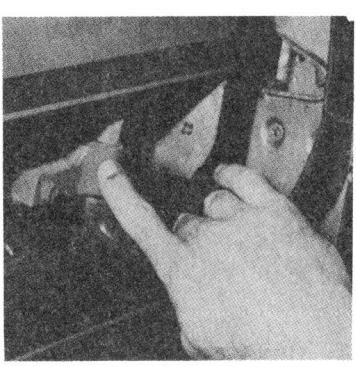

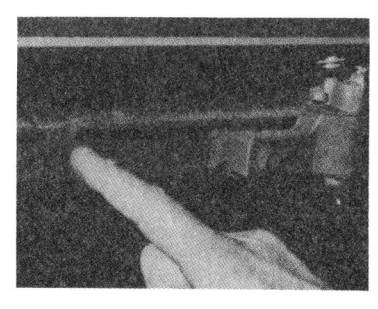

Fig. 26-7. Open the door approximately 12 inches until the carrier is aligned with the notch cut in the rail (photo by Brad Barcus).

211

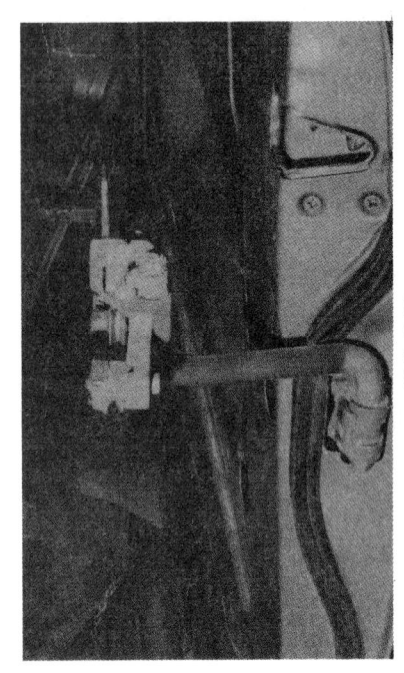

Fig. 26-8. Lift up and remove the door. Set the door on a jack stand or other support at the normal height (photo by Brad Barcus).

Fig. 26-9. Remove the outboard link nut and washer. Then remove the door link (photo by Brad Barcus).

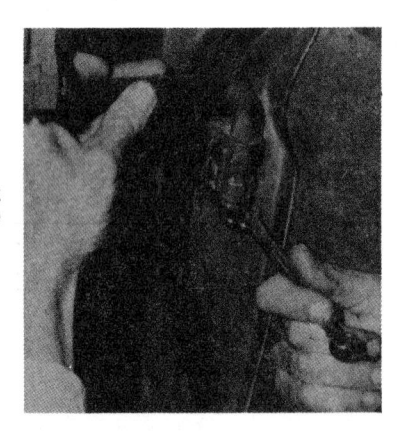

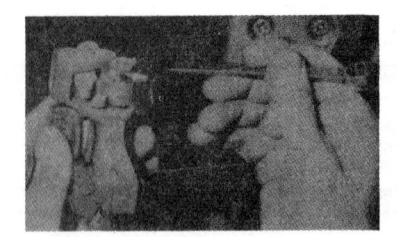

Fig. 26-10. Remove the inboard door link nut from the roller carrier (photo by Brad Barcus).

Fig. 26-11. Eddy Hice demonstrates the comparative length of the new and old links (photo by Brad Barcus).

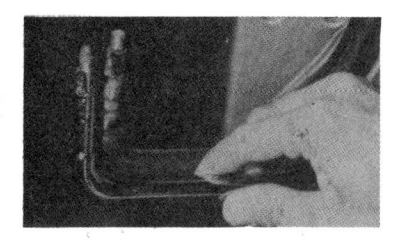

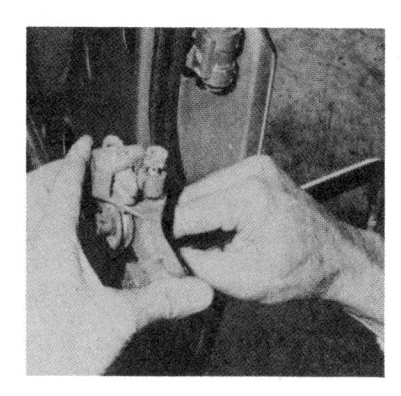

Fig. 26-12. Replace the stock link with the new link. The cams must be assembled exactly as the stock assembly to avoid damage to the new link (photo by Brad Barcus).

Fig. 26-13. Handle the washer and nut in this location with extreme care. Clumsy fingers could lose both inside the door (photo by Brad Barcus).

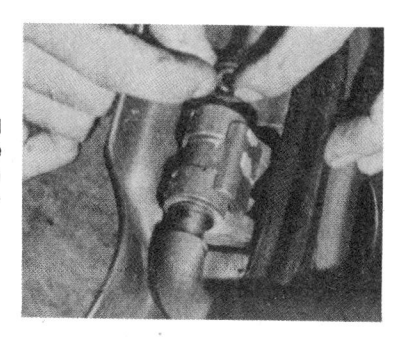

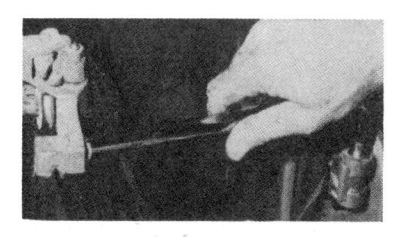

Fig. 26-14. Although the instructions don't mention it, a little juggling may be necessary to get the link alignment just right for it to drop into its slot (photo by Brad Barcus).

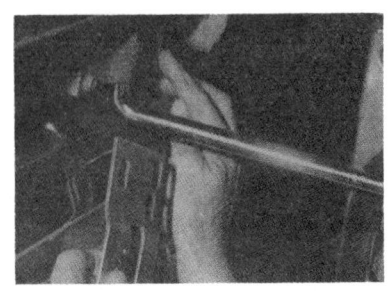

Fig. 26-15. Replace the door and hinge assembly on the track (photo by Brad Barcus).

Fig. 26-16. Remove the existing door hinge stop (photo by Brad Barcus).

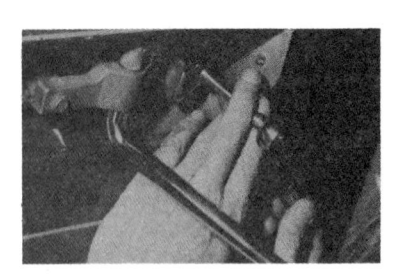

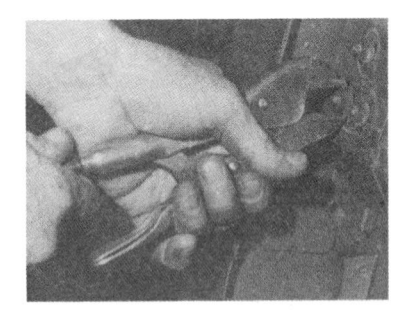

Fig. 26-17. Since we're showing how to make this a one man, do-it-yourself project, Eddy suggests using vise grips to hold the interior nuts (photo by Brad Barcus).

Fig. 26-18. Comparison of the old and new door hinge stops (photo by Brad Barcus).

Fig. 26-19. Replace the stock stop with a new stop (photo by Brad Barcus).

Fig. 26-20. Close the door carefully. Do not slam the door. We were lucky, or possibly due to Eddy's careful work the door lined up perfectly. The instructions are very complete in their recommendations should adjustment be required (photo by Brad Barcus).

Fig. 26-21. With the door closed, adjust the hinge stop (photo by Brad Barcus).

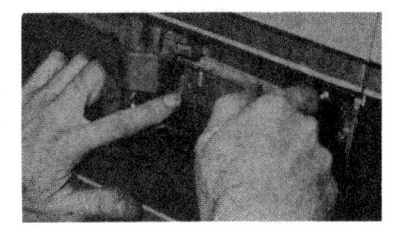

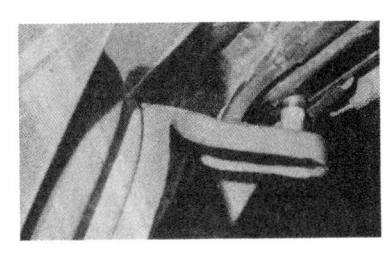

Fig. 26-22. We did have one problem—in no way a fault of the extender, but a possible minor design flaw, with the door fully open the top guide slid out of the track (photo by Brad Barcus).

Fig. 26-23. Being a perfectionist, Eddy Hice sought to create adjustment in the lower plate to prevent full opening (photo by Brad Barcus).

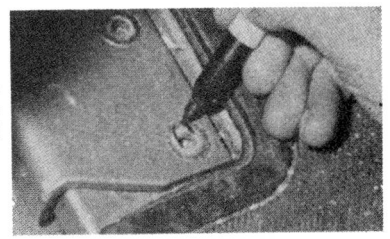

215

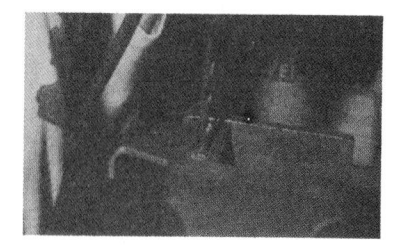

Fig. 26-24. The metal in the lower plate is extremely hard. One can dull several bits going this route (photo by Brad Barcus).

Fig. 26-25. The attempt was a failure as there just wasn't enough adjustment possible on the lower plate. So an easier solution was found. A sheet metal screw protruding at this point is used (photo by Brad Barcus).

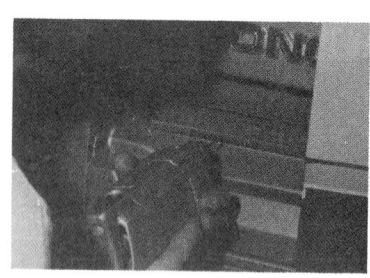

Fig. 26-26. New link in place permits door to swing past wide wheel and tire (photo by Brad Barcus).

Chapter 27

Changing a Roof Vent to a Roof Scoop

One of the most common add-ons found during the early van movement was the *roof vent*. These items were greatly needed to ease interior temperatures and provide ventilation for camping comfort.

Vents have been replaced with more attractive *roof scoops*. All has changed except those for owners who already had vents installed. The choice for these vanners until recently has been to leave well enough alone or remove the vent, make a larger opening in the roof, and install a full-size roof scoop. That amounts to a lot of work when you consider that the vent does the job adequately and the addition of a scoop is, for the most part, purely for cosmetic reasons.

Recent innovations from manufacturers have now given these van owners a third and more popular way to go. Several varieties of popular scoops already on the market have been introduced designed specifically for replacing standard, old-style vents. These scoops are the same size (square) as most vents and fit perfectly—inside and outside.

Replacing your vent with one of these special scoops is a very simple procedure. Your first step is to remove the screws or bolts that hold the unit in place, lift off the vent, and carefully scrape off the sealer from the roof along the edges of the cutout area (Figs. 27-1 through 27-3). Apply fresh caulking compound or sealer along the edges to make the scoop/roof interface water tight (Fig. 27-4).

All that remains in the installation procedure is to set the scoop carefully in place, make sure that the caulking seals properly, and bolt the unit securely onto the roof (Figs. 27-5 and 27-6). The inside "beauty ring" from the vent will snap into place in the scoop for a "finished" look on the interior (Fig. 27-7).

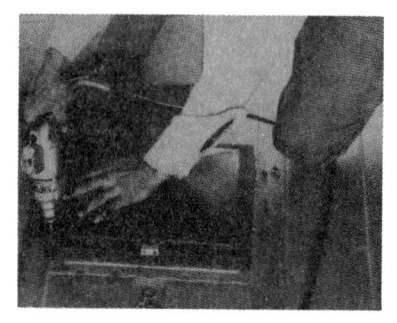

Fig. 27-1. First step in replacement is removal of the screws holding vent in place (photo by Ron Cogan).

Fig. 27-2. Lift off the vent. Depending on the type of caulking compound, it may be quite a tug (photo by Ron Cogan).

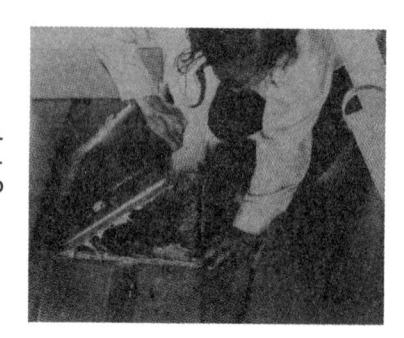

The final step to ensure that a proper installation has been completed is to check for water leakage. Simply close the door on the scoop and use a hose to spray water on the roof of the van. If there's a leak, you'll be the first to know.

Further information on these scoops can usually be obtained at local van and RV shops or from our advertisers. It's easy to update your truck and have the latest look with these slick scoops, so get out your tool kit and get on with it.

Fig. 27-3. With a putty knife or other scraper, remove all traces of old caulking (photo by Ron Cogan).

Fig. 27-4. Apply fresh caulking compound or sealer around all the edges to assure a tight fit when scoop is in place (photo by Ron Cogan).

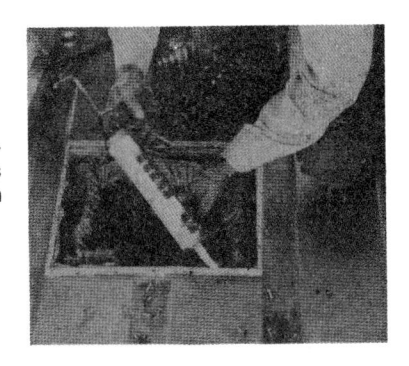

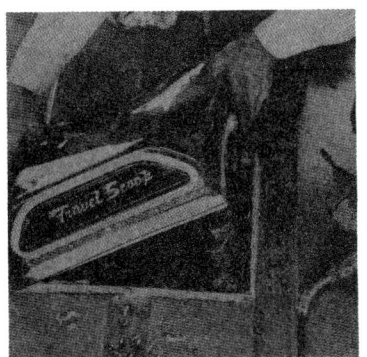

Fig. 27-5. Set the scoop into the freshly caulked hole (photo by Ron Cogan).

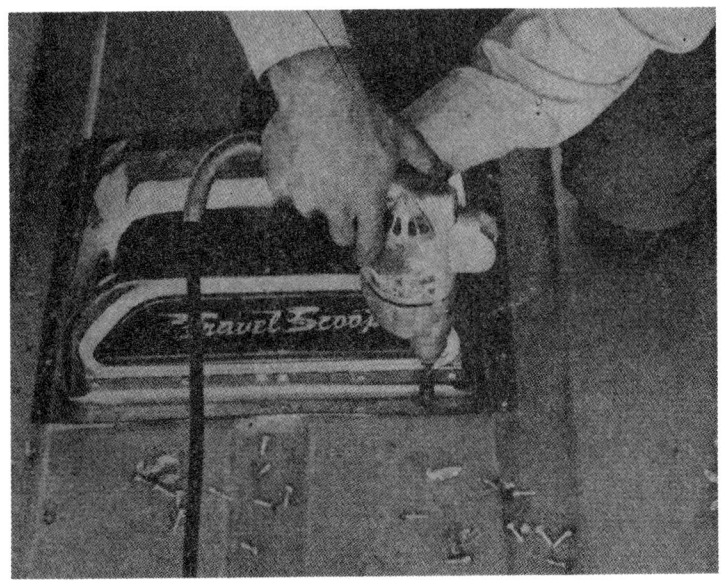

Fig. 27-6. Use fresh screws to anchor the scoop in place (photo by Ron Cogan).

Fig. 27-7. The new look. While the vent is adequate, the scoop looks fine (photo by Ron Cogan).

Chapter 28

Installing Flooring

There is nothing more basic to the creation of a custom interior than the flooring. You can't hardly start anything until you have a floor to put carpeting on and to build cabinets on. So that's the place that all of us must necessarily start.

There are so many really good van converters in Southern California that the choice can be difficult. We finally settled on Craig Smith and his Overland Enterprises, new address 14662 Titus Street, Van Nuys, CA 91405. Craig has moved into new, spacious, airy quarters in a recently completed industrial complex. Here we could watch each step as our interior developed and could photograph every operation.

PARTICLE BOARD AND SCREWS

The first thing you will need is two, 4 by 8-foot sheets of "particle board", ⅝ of an inch thick. This is for the short wheelbase van. Why not plywood? Particle board costs about half as much, is just as strong, and does a better job of insulation. Using particle board, which is available at lumber yards everywhere, you can do away with the 1-inch foam rubber under the floor. Tools required include one steel tape measure, saber saw, pencil, straightedge, air chisel, a ¼-inch drill with either a socket attachment for Tec screws or screwdriver attachment, one box of Tec screws, or one box of flathead self-tapping, sheet metal screws.

Whichever route you decide on, the Tec screws or the flathead sheet metal variety, we strongly recommend the motorized approach. Otherwise, you'll have to drill holes, first, then insert the screws. You'll have a mighty sore arm mighty soon. We mentioned the saber saw. Without it you'll be in deep trouble. You can get a pretty good one for around $15, and it will come in handy for several operations including your paneling installation.

Before you can proceed with your flooring, you'll have to remove the brackets that hold the spare. The best tool for this is an air chisel which you should be able to rent from your neighborhood U-Rent. The compressed air can be had at the service station you regularly patronize.

PROCEDURE

To get your flooring installation started, you have a choice of two ways to go. You can make a pattern out of old newspapers or butcher paper taped together, or you can go the careful measurement route directly onto the particle board. In either case, starting on the curb side, carefully and accurately scribe the wheel well area onto the board.

Remove the sheet of particle board from your interior onto a pair of sawhorses. Using the saber saw, carefully cut out the wheel well opening. Now you can reinsert the sheet into the van. If all is well, your flooring will neatly surround the wheel well. Moving forward, to the footwell opening inside the sliding or double doors, scribe on the underside of the flooring. This done, you can cut out the footwell, again using the saber saw.

Leaving this first sheet of particle board in place, bring in the second sheet overlapping the first. On the street side you'll have to carefully measure the intrusion of the fuel filler box as well as the wheel well.

After these two openings are cut out, you again have a choice. You can do as most of the commercial van converters do; measure down the center of the van and cut both sheets so that your seam is down the center. Or you can leave one large sheet intact. In our case we left the curb side and cut off a larger piece of the second sheet. For the do-it-yourselfer this makes more sense since it leaves you with a large piece of board that can be used for cabinet work later on. Now you are ready to drive the sheet metal screws

Fig. 28-1. There's nothing barer than the raw insides of a van. This is the "before" of a before and after flooring story (photo by Brad Barcus).

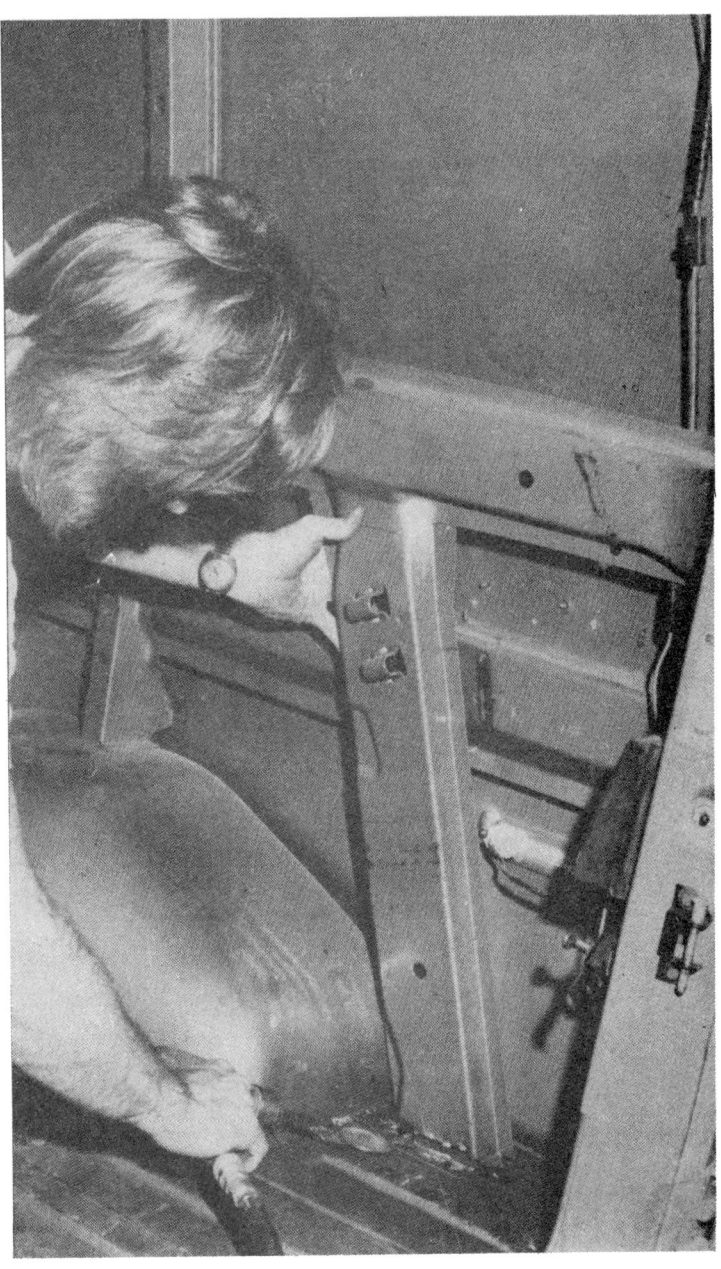

Fig. 28-2. Air chisel is used to break welds for removal of spare wheel bracket which would have prevented smooth flooring. Spare will wind up in the ottoman (photo by Brad Barcus).

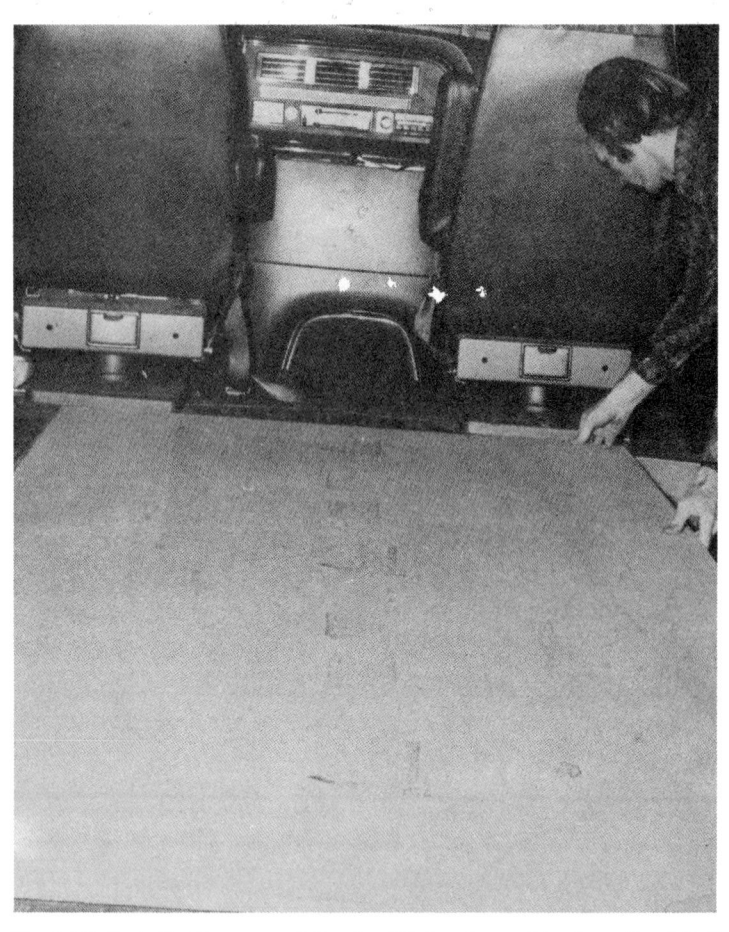

Fig. 28-3. Craig Smith, owner of Overland Enterprises, slides in an 8 × 4-foot sheet of particle board which is cheaper than plywood (photo by Brad Barcus).

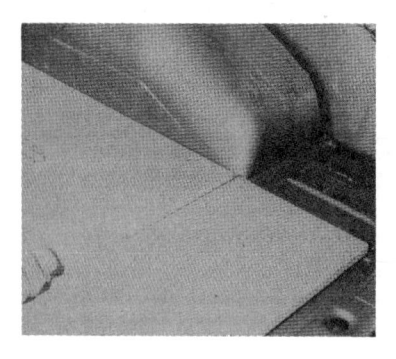

Fig. 28-4. Flooring must end about 5-inches from the rear doors to allow for closure. Measurement of wheel well depth must be accurate (photo by Brad Barcus).

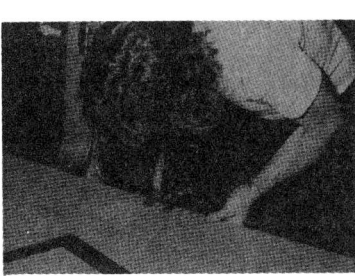

Fig. 28-5. David Proffer, one of Craig Smith's artisans, measures fore and aft dimensions of the wheel well (photo by Brad Barcus).

Fig. 28-6. Lines are drawn directly onto the board with corners curved. Saber saw is a virtual necessity and will come in handy for many jobs (photo by Brad Barcus).

right through the board and into the metal floor of the van. Set your screws a good 2 inches inboard to prevent edge splitting. Space the screws about 2 feet apart. Even with the help of the electric motor, your arm is going to know you've been busy. Be sure to check the location of the gas tank. Some vans have the tank mounted directly to the underside of the floor. By following Figs. 28-1 through 28-16, we think you'll be able to floor your van with no trouble at all.

Fig. 28-7. A good fit around the wheel well. Space to the rear will be occupied by insulation (photo by Brad Barcus).

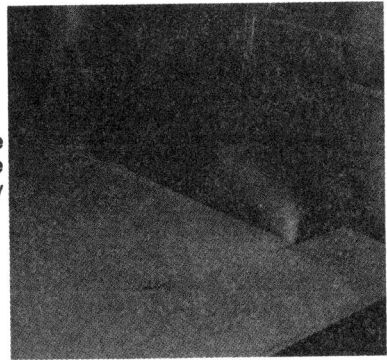

Fig. 28-8. Craig Smith traces footwell line on the underside of the particle board. Cut will be made slightly larger than the opening for carpet tuck-under (photo by Brad Barcus).

Fig. 28-9. Second saber saw cut has been made. Handle the sheet with care so that the narrow arm will not be broken (photo by Brad Barcus).

Fig. 28-10. From the looks of things, good progress is being made (photo by Brad Barcus).

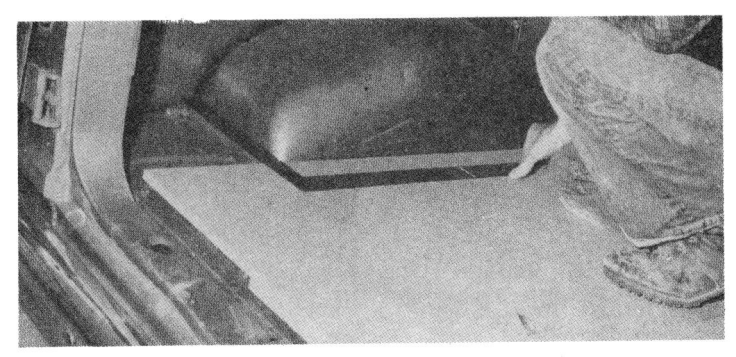

Fig. 28-11. Second sheet of particle board overlaps first. Two sheets must be perfectly lined up. Measurement of the street side wheel well is made (photo by Brad Barcus).

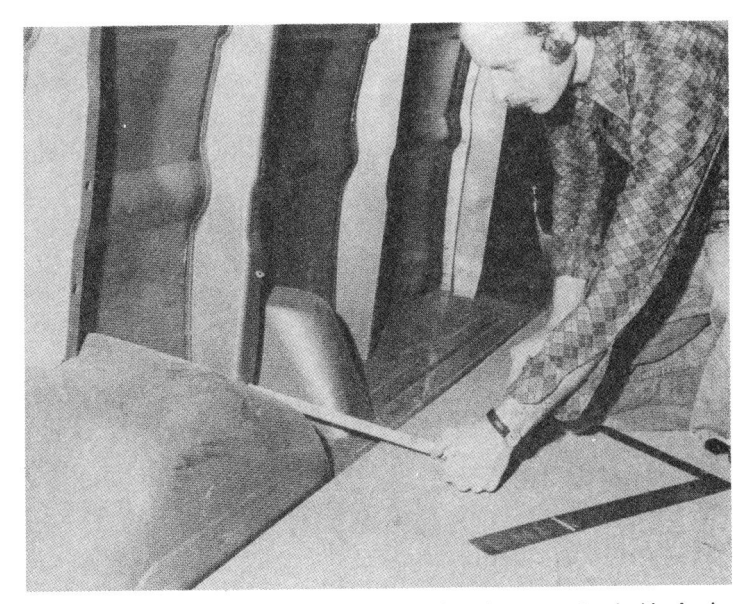

Fig. 28-12. On the street side there's the fuel filler box to contend with. Again, measurements must be precise (photo by Brad Barcus).

Fig. 28-13. Point at which the seam will be made is marked on the street side particle board sheet (photo by Brad Barcus).

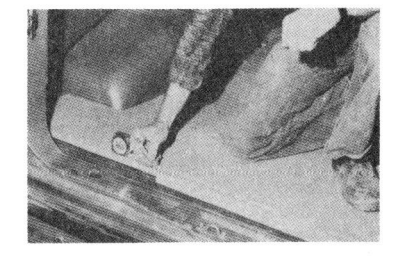

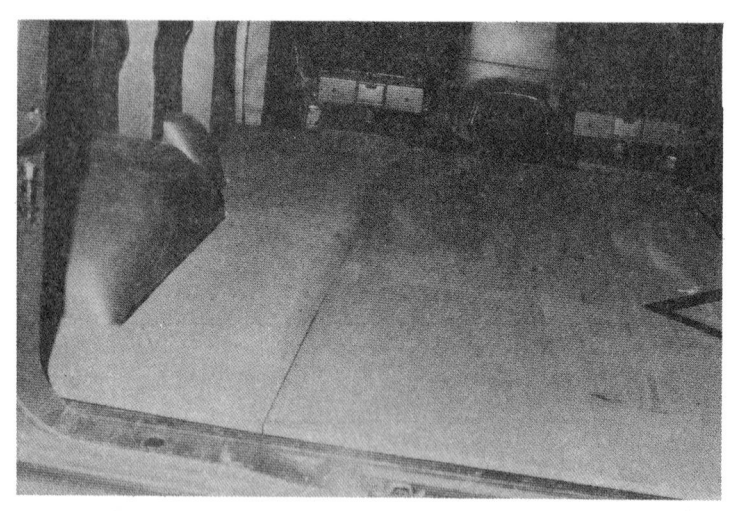

Fig. 28-14. The two pieces, seamed toward the street side, leave us a large piece for cabinet work (photo by Brad Barcus).

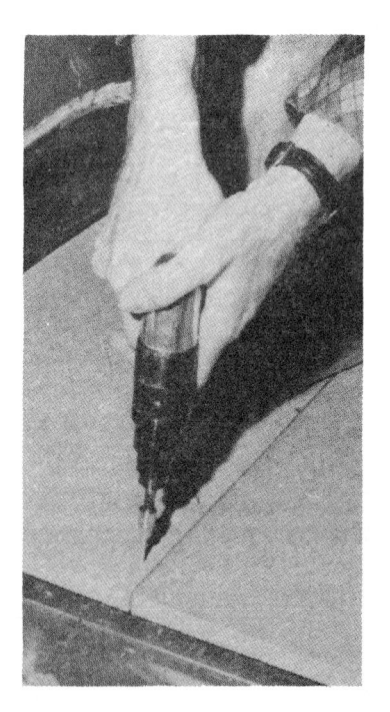

Fig. 28-15. With a bit of mechanized help from an air wrench, Tec screws (or flathead sheet metal) are drilled through the particle board directly into the metal van floor (photo by Brad Barcus).

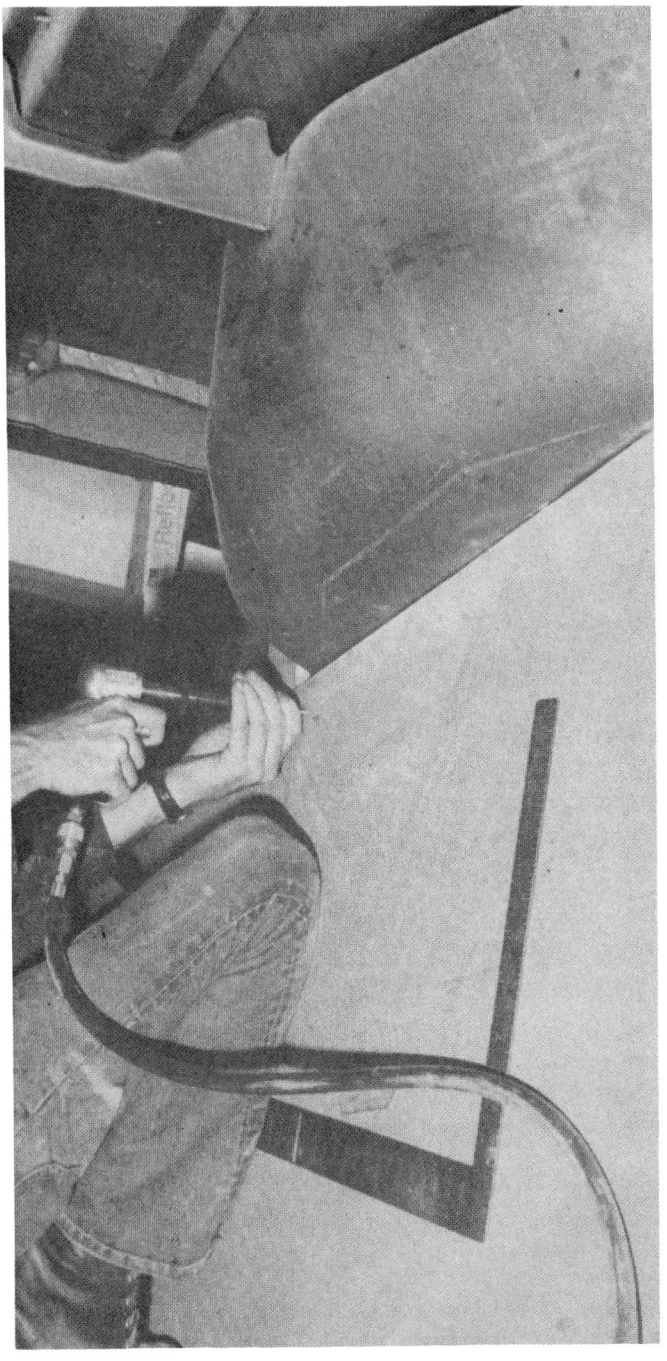

Fig. 28-16. Leave at least 2 inches from the edge when inserting screws. This is to prevent edge splitting and to permit carpet tuck-under (photo by Brad Barcus).

Chapter 29

Installing Headers for a Van

At the risk of oversimplification for the more sophisticated, we feel obliged to explain briefly what headers do. On a stock engine, the exhaust gases go from each cylinder into an exhaust manifold, a sort of collection chamber. From there they find their way out to the head pipe or front pipe then to a muffler.

FUNCTION OF HEADERS

In most stock installations at the factory the exhaust gases from both sides of the V-8 go to a common pipe and a single muffler. This is not a very efficient way of doing things, and the struggle of the exhaust gases to get out builds up back pressure which robs the engine of efficiency.

With headers, on the other hand, there is a tube from each exhaust port that carries off the gases from that port to a large diameter collector pipe. From there the gases can go to a dual muffler setup and out the rear or, as in the case of many vans, into any one of several designs of sidepipes.

We made arrangements to have our headers installed at the Hooker Headers factory in Ontario, a thriving city about 50 miles from Los Angeles. Working in the design department was Dave Eshelman, who campaigns an A sedan Camaro in IMSA and SCCA races.

INSTALLATION STEPS

The Hooker installation instructions are very detailed and to the point. Anyone with a good socket set and fundamental knowledge of the use of tools should have no trouble at all.

Since we were at the factory, there were a number of floor hoists available. The instructions point out that the van must be raised a minimum of 36 inches. Use a hoist or axle stands. A bumper jack should not be used.

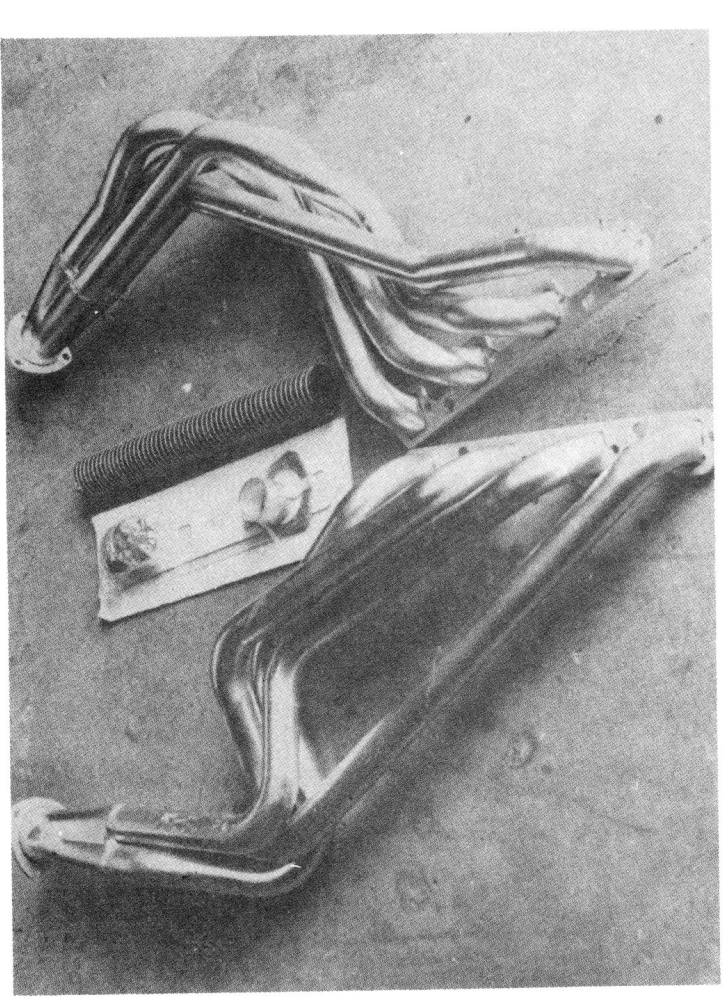

Fig. 29-1. Your header kit from Hooker will look like this when you get everything out of the box (photo by Jim Matthews).

Fig. 29-2. A first and very important step is to disconnect the battery (photo by Jim Matthews).

The first step is to disconnect the battery to prevent electrical system damage. It seems simple, but it's very important. On the right side the headpipe is disconnected from the stock exhaust manifold and pushed to one side. The spark plugs and the stock exhaust manifold are then removed. The header is then worked up from underneath the van, through the chassis, and into position. After the header gasket is in position, all the header bolts can be started with the most restricted one the best bet to start first. All bolts must be evenly tightened. Then the spark plugs are replaced. Starter wires should be checked for adequate clearance from the header. An illustration in the instructions gives a clear picture of how to install the heat stove.

On the left side, the procedure is almost identical, except that one stock bolt must be used in the stock header flange hole. It will also be used for mounting the dipstick tube. This is also illustrated on the instruction sheet.

After all bolts have been checked for even tightness, and spark plugs have been replaced, the headers may be hooked up to reducers and into a dual exhaust system or to the vanner's favorite sidepipes. (The factory calls them "sidemounts," but we doubt that it'll catch on.)

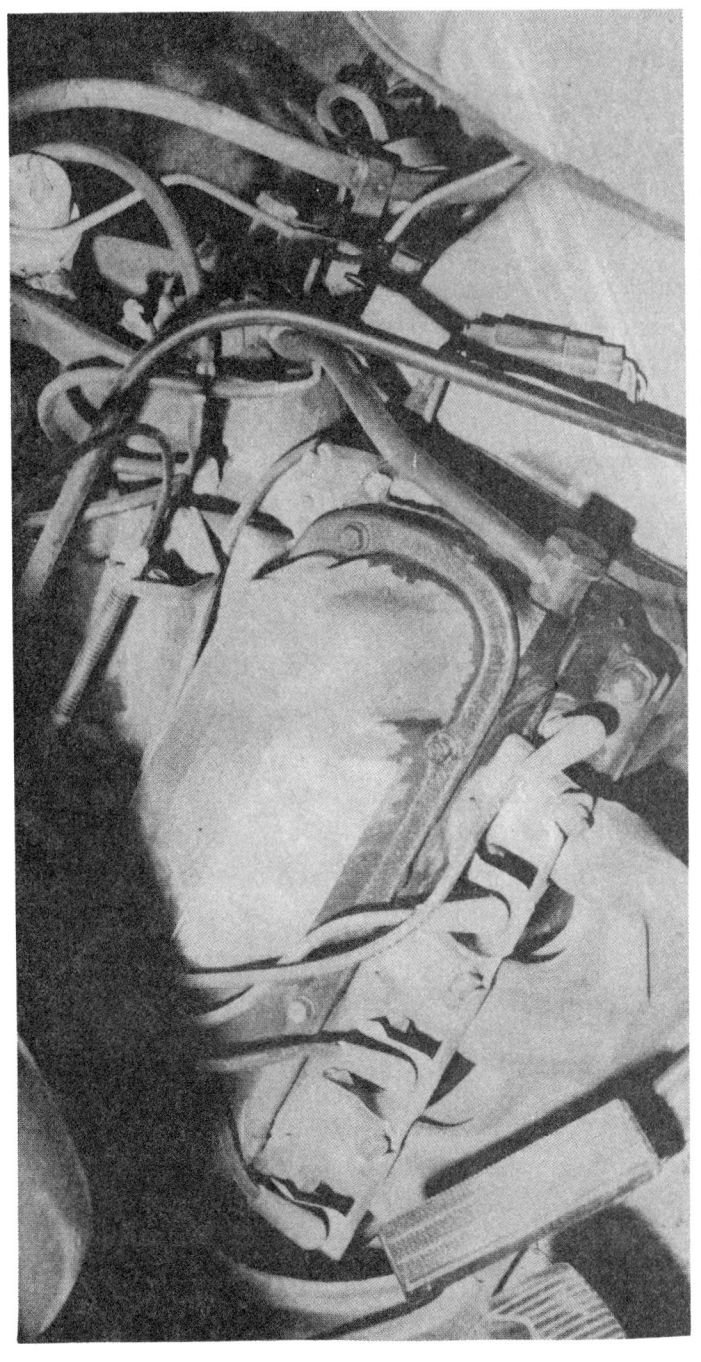

Fig. 29-3. The stock Ford manifold. Exhaust gases collect in the large chamber below the ports (photo by Jim Matthews).

Fig. 29-4. A difficult job for the camera's eye. Hooker mechanic is removing the spark plug heat shield (photo by Jim Matthews).

Fig. 29-5. Spark plug shield after removal. Exhaust manifold will be next (photo by Jim Matthews).

Fig. 29-6. The stock exhaust system, front pipe, muffler, and tail pipe headed for the scrap metal bin (photo by Jim Matthews).

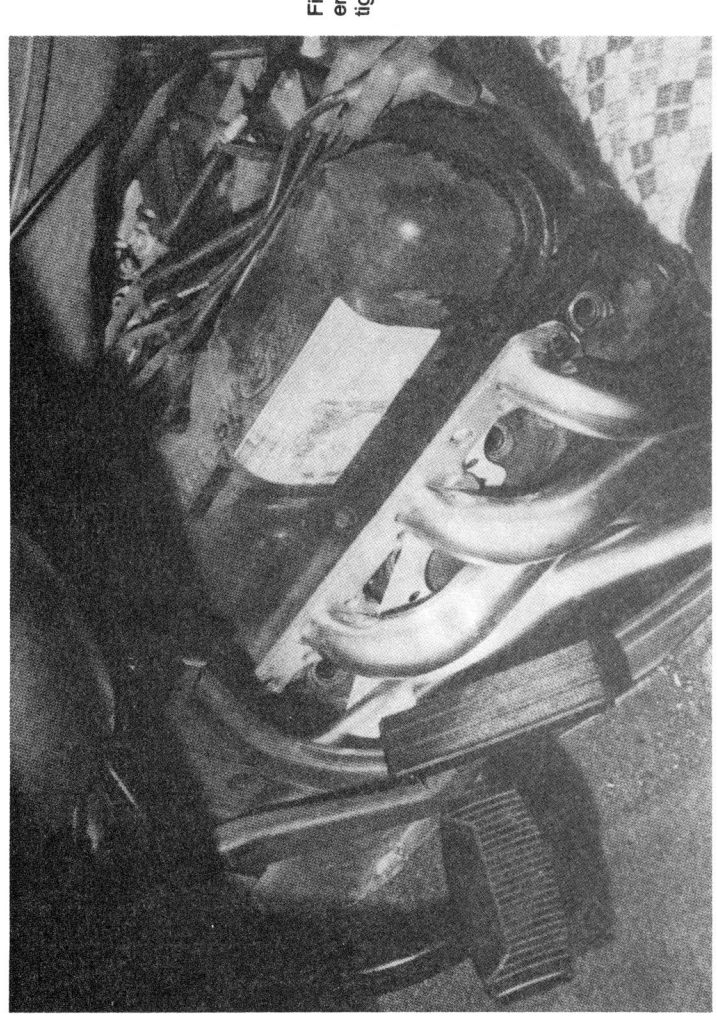

Fig. 29-7. From the inside the headers are almost ready to be securely tightened (photo by Jim Matthews).

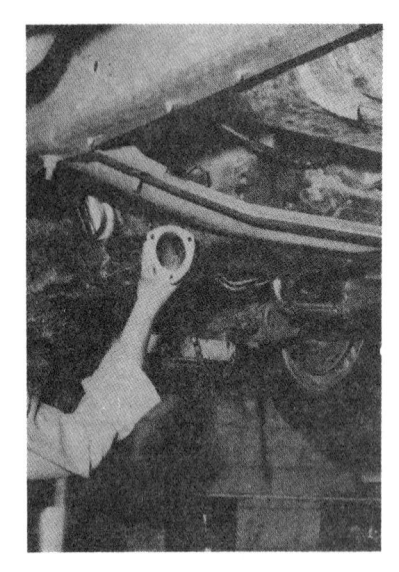

Fig. 29-8. From underneath the headers give a classy, race car look (photo by Jim Matthews).

Fig. 29-9. Reducers are bolted to the collector tube of the headers. Exhaust gas can now be routed to the dual muffler setup or to sidepipes (photo by Jim Matthews).

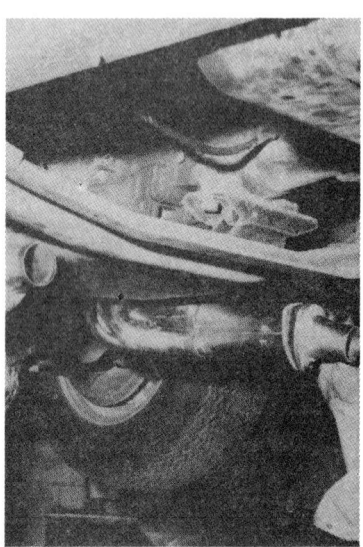

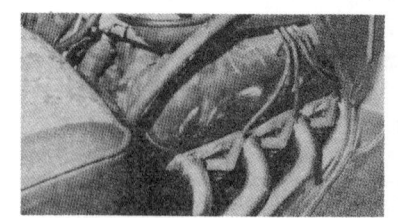

Fig. 29-10. Right side interior view just before the engine cover is replaced (photo by Jim Matthews).

Now we're hooked up to some kind of exhaust system (we went for sidepipes). We can hook up the battery connection, start the engine, and check for leaks. All brake lines, fuel lines, and electrical wires must have adequate clearance. If there isn't, lines should be rerouted. All bolts should be retightened after several days of driving. With Figs. 29-1 through 29-10 as a help, you should be able to install your own Hooker Headers. With a cold engine the job might take half a day. Incidentally, with the headers we're now getting two more miles to each gallon of gas.

Chapter 30

Hooking Up Sidepipes

There's hardly a custom van anywhere these days that doesn't sport a set of sidepipes or have a set planned for the near future. Sidepipes can be either functional or purely cosmetic. When they are functional, there's usually an increase in the exhaust decibel level which, for most of us, is fine. We like the increased sound level maybe because it makes us more noticeable.

HOOKER'S UNIVERSAL SIDEMOUNT EXHAUST SYSTEM

Since we were already at Hooker getting our headers installed, it seemed like the perfect time to get our sidepipes installed. Hooker had recently introduced their Universal sidemount exhaust system which has a real jazzy look. At the front of the pipe there are four tubes that look like the header is feeding right into the sidepipe. Three of them are cosmetic; however, only one comes from the collector to the sidepipe. Anyway, they looked great in the catalog, and that's the style we opted for.

The early stages of the sidepipe installation are a breeze and require little in the way of expertise. Later on the going gets tougher requiring knowledge of welding techniques. Tools required include a socket set, ¼-inch drill, center punch, heavy hammer, pipe cutter, and welding equipment.

Before starting your sidepipe installation, the van must be raised a minimum of 36 inches. If you can con your neighborhood service station into letting you use his floor hoist, great. Otherwise, get it onto the axle stands. No way should you trust a bumper jack. Those things are killers.

Hooker's installation instruction sheet is very detailed and easy to follow. We'll assume that you already have a dual exhaust system since it will more closely coincide with the photographs.

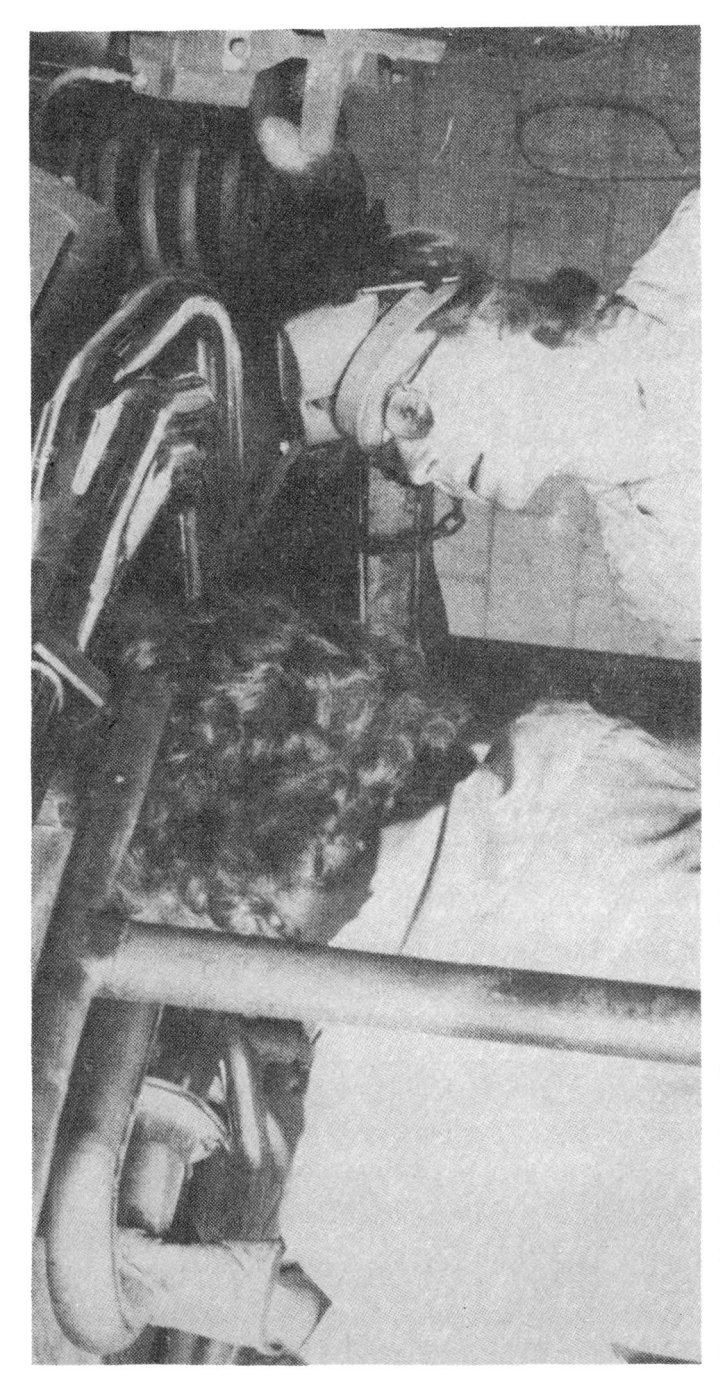

Fig. 30-1. Hooker sidepipes offer a new sound (photo by Jim Matthews).

Fig. 30-2. Hooker sidepipes can be functional or purely ornamental. Here they are seen without the slide-in mufflers (photo by Jim Matthews).

PROCEDURE

Step one is to disconnect the stock headpipes from the exhaust manifold or header. Place the new Universal sidemounts alongside the van and insert the simulated header section into the sidepipe. The instructions then call for you to insert all mounting hardware, hangers, rubber grommets, lock washers, flat washers, bolts, and nuts into the adjusting slots on the inner surface of the sidepipe.

Using props or a couple of friends, place the sidepipe in the desired position on the side of the van and level it up with the body line. Now you can determine the best location for the mounting hangers for your particular van. You may have to bend the hangers to get the ideal positioning.

Mark the desired hole location on the hangers. Rear hangers should have two holes. Now remove the hangers from the sidepipe and drill ⅜-inch holes at the marks. You can reattach the hangers to the sidepipes and mark the mounting hole locations on the inboard side of the body panels.

Since punched holes will hold self-tapping screws better than drilled holes, use a center punch and a heavy hammer to make the holes at the

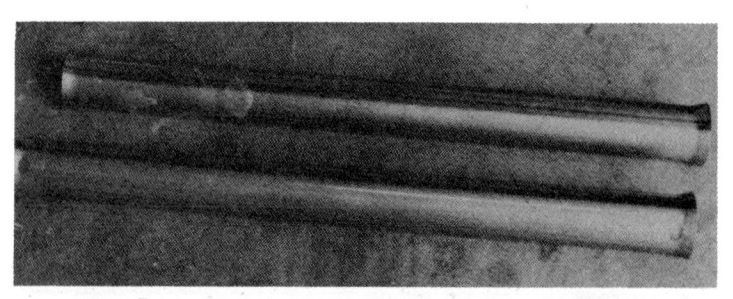

Fig. 30-3. Hooker mufflers to fit their sidepipes (photo by Jim Matthews).

Fig. 30-4. At Hooker we had the advantage of a supporting rack. You may have to enlist a friend or two. The pipe must be positioned for the hanger attachment (photo by Jim Matthews).

marks. Now you can attach the hangers to the body using the sheet metal screws that are provided with the Hooker Universal sidemount kit.

Refer to Figs. 30-1 through 30-15. Suffice it to say that if you're not an accomplished welder, you had better have a friend who is or trust this part of the job to your muffler shop. Hooker slip-in mufflers should be used with the sidepipes. They are the right size and give you a pleasant exhaust note.

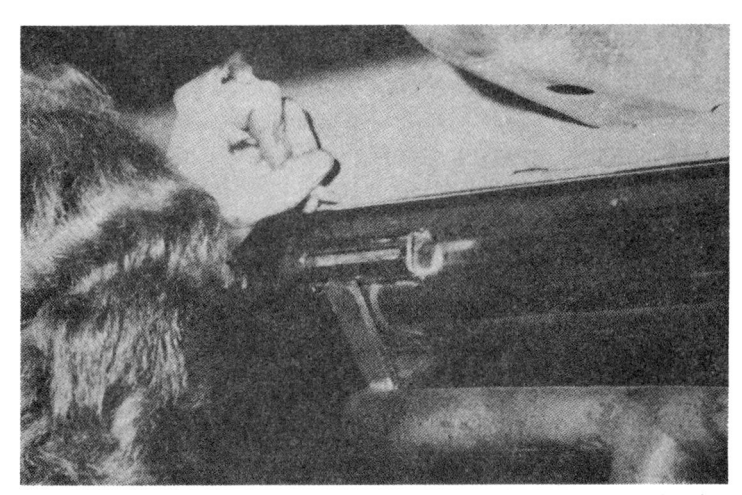

Fig. 30-5. With the correct location determined, the location for mounting bracket holes is marked in chalk (photo by Jim Matthews).

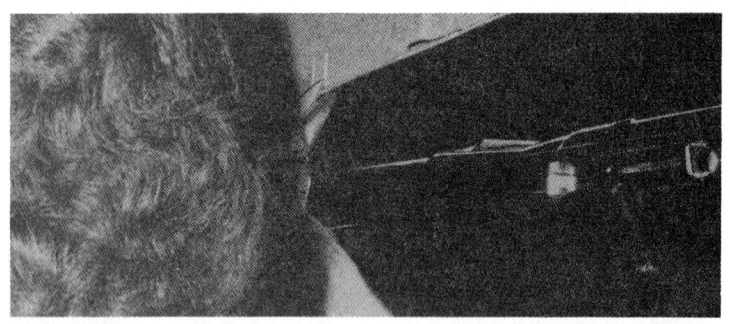

Fig. 30-6. Edge curl-under is straightened with the help of metal shears (photo by Jim Matthews).

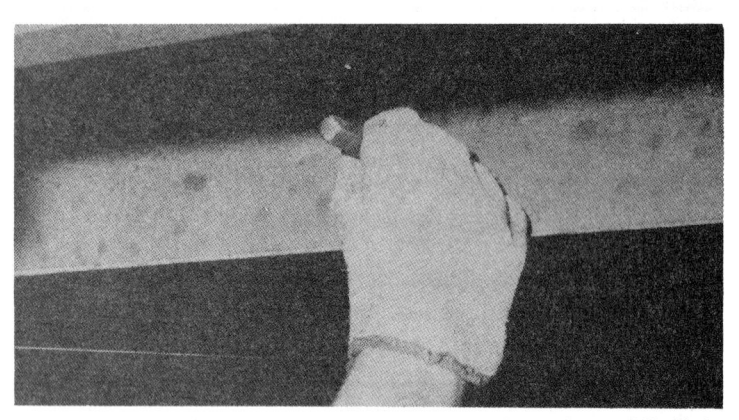

Fig. 30-7 A punched hole secures sheet metal screws better than a drilled hole (photo by Jim Matthews).

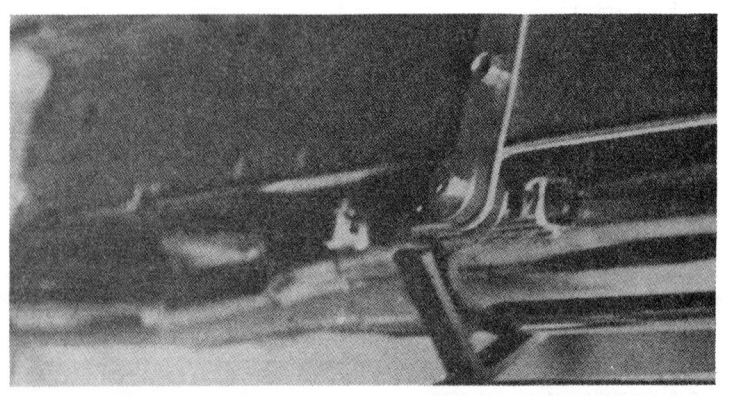

Fig. 30-8. Bolt with rubber, sound dampening washers, secures the hanger strap to the sidepipe. Strap is then bolted to body sheet metal (photo by Jim Matthews).

Fig. 30-9. Hooker muffler is slipped into the sidepipe (photo by Jim Matthews).

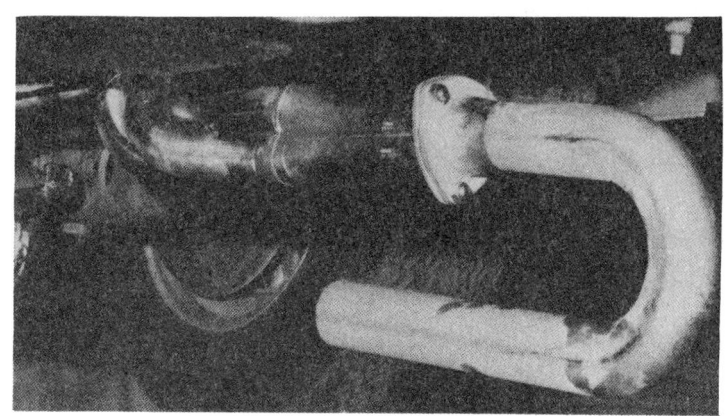

Fig. 30-10. For measurement only, exhaust tubing is inserted into the reducer (photo by Jim Matthews).

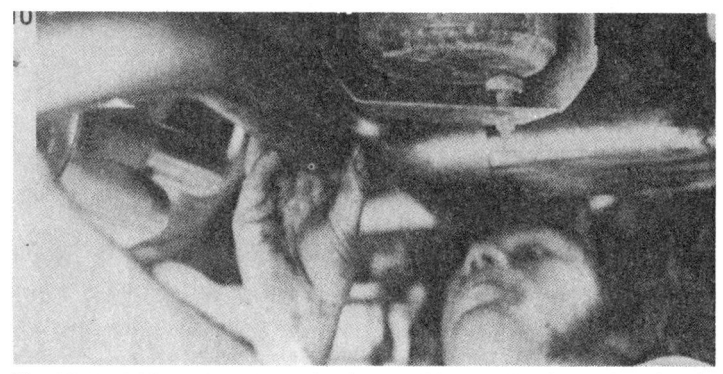

Fig. 30-11. Additional sections of exhaust tubing are lined up (photo by Jim Matthews).

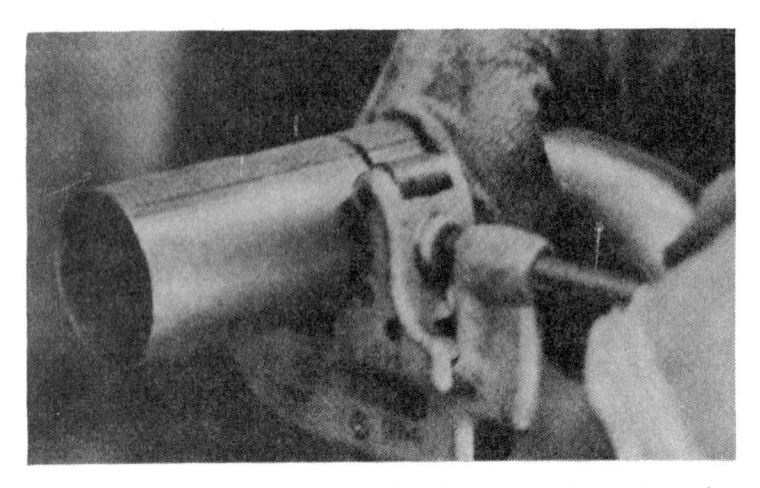

Fig. 30-12. Sections of tubing are shortened as required to match up other sections (photo by Jim Matthews).

Fig. 30-13. With all the exhaust tubing the correct length and shape, the sections are welded together (photo by Jim Matthews).

Fig. 30-14. The right side is finished. Procedure will be repeated on the left. Only one of the tubes in the simulated header section is functional (photo by Jim Matthews).

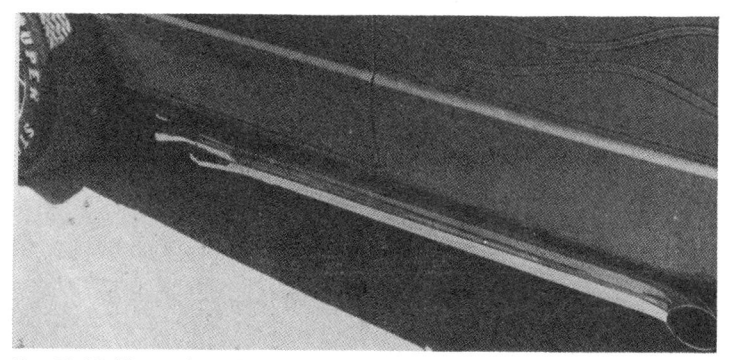

Fig. 30-15. The end result looks and sounds great (photo by Jim Matthews).

Chapter 31

Insulating a Van's Interior

Even if you live in the most ideal climate in the world, your van is going to become an oven if it sits in the direct sun for any length of time. A bare delivery van is also a fine echo chamber the way it comes from the factory. Everything, including a pebble tossed up from a rear tire, booms and resounds. You need insulation.

Protecting your interior from the elements of heat and cold as well as sound deadening is an easy do-it-yourself operation you can complete in one afternoon. For materials you'll need a roll or two of 1-inch foam rubber and a roll of 3½-inch paper backed fiberglass, the kind that's used in new home construction. Tools required will be a steel tape measure, razor knife, pencil, one quart industrial type glue, one 3 or 4-inch wide brush, and a screwdriver.

Your first step will be to remove the modesty shield over the interior of the upper, side door mechanism and the sheet metal, trim pieces over both passenger and driver's doors. Also remove the headliner in the driving compartment. With these pieces out of the way, you are now ready to go to work.

FOAM RUBBER

If we had been prepared to go ahead with our interior conversion, chances are we'd have done the ceiling in the same fiberglass that covers the wall. Since we weren't ready, Craig Smith, whose Overland Enterprises was doing the work, suggested we didn't want bits of fiberglass down our neck. The stuff itches like crazy. We agreed that foam rubber would be far and away the best bet on the ceiling.

Carefully measure the distance from the roof center beam to the outside edge in the cab section of the van. Be sure that your tape measure extends down into the slot at the outer edges under the roof. Now you are ready to cut your first piece of foam rubber. If you make a mistake it's not the end of the world. You'll find a place to use your mistake later on. Once cut, hold the piece of insulation up into the section it is to occupy. You'll quickly see whether you cut your first section too small.

This next step could have been done earlier. Be sure that your seats or anything else that could be damaged by a glop of glue are well covered either with plastic or other liquid proof material.

With the foam rubber cut to the right size, it's time to get out the screwdriver again and open the glue. With your brush, spread the glue evenly over the section to which you're about to apply foam rubber. Press the foam up into place working from the center line end to the outer, tucking the material down into the recess. With the experience of the first piece of foam, you're now ready to repeat the same procedure on sections of the ceiling in the "living" area. Here you will use longer sections of foam. Take your time and cut your foam a little generously. After the entire ceiling is insulated, replace the metal trim and headliner removed earlier.

Fig. 31-1. Before starting your insulation project, remove metal trim from over the side door mechanism and cab doors (photo by Brad Barcus).

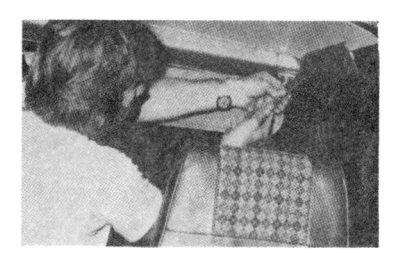

Fig. 31-2. Headliner in cab must be removed. It will be replaced after insulating (photo by Brad Barcus).

Fig. 31-3. Seats and other areas that might suffer from glue spots are covered with liquid proof material (photo by Brad Barcus).

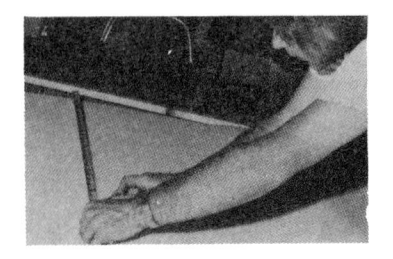

Fig. 31-4. Having measured the ceiling in the cab area, the first cut is made on the foam rubber. Insulation is laid on van flooring as a clean surface (photo by Brad Barcus).

Fig. 31-5. Commercial van converters like Overland Enterprises use enormous amounts of glue. You should only need a quart (photo by Brad Barcus).

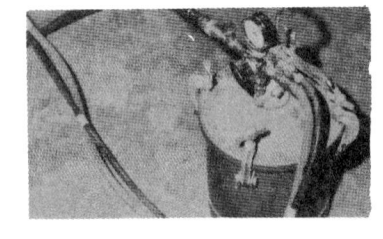

Fig. 31-6. For Craig Smith's operation, an air compressor spray gun is used to apply glue (photo by Brad Barcus).

FIBERGLASS

Now you're an old hand and you're ready for the walls. Here we use the 3½-inch paper backed fiberglass. The procedure is very much the same, requiring careful measurement of the area to be covered. Using this type of material, the fiberglass side is pressed against the glue, with the paper facing into the living area. It will be necessary, with some of the insulation panels around wheel wells and gas filler, to cut the fiberglass into angular shapes.

Since we weren't going to get started on our paneling and cabinet work for a few days, we felt it wise to secure the wall insulation. Strips of pine were screwed to the wall uprights to hold everything in place. See Figs. 31-1 through 31-16.

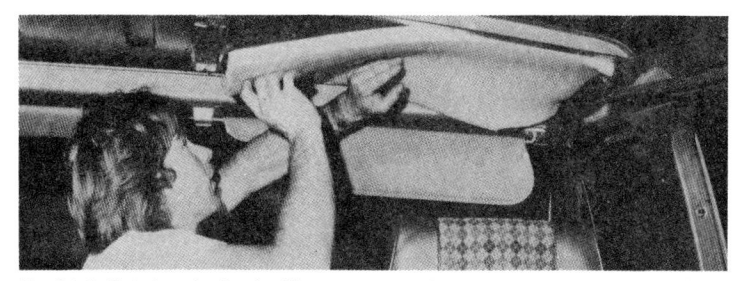

Fig. 31-7. Cut piece is checked for accuracy before gluing in place (photo by Brad Barcus).

Fig. 31-8. Glue is blown onto ceiling panel and applied in even strokes (photo by Brad Barcus).

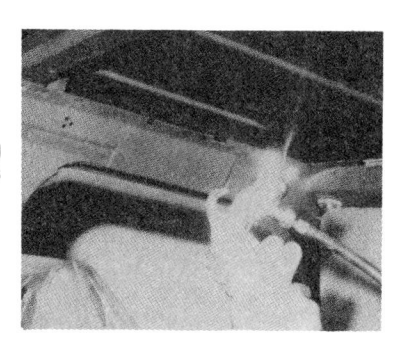

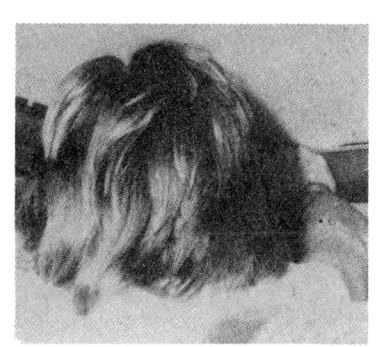

Fig. 31-9. Edges must be tucked down into recesses at outer wall perimeter (photo by Brad Barcus).

Fig. 31-10. With the cab section finished, we're ready for longer strips for the "living area" (photo by Brad Barcus).

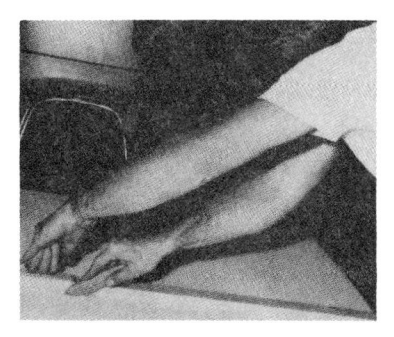

Fig. 31-11. Here the center is placed first against the ceiling and material pressed in position working outward (photo by Brad Barcus).

Fig. 31-12. With the ceiling insulated we'll move on to the next step (photo by Brad Barcus).

Fig. 31-13. In many areas the width between upright supports is exactly right for the fiberglass insulation (photo by Brad Barcus).

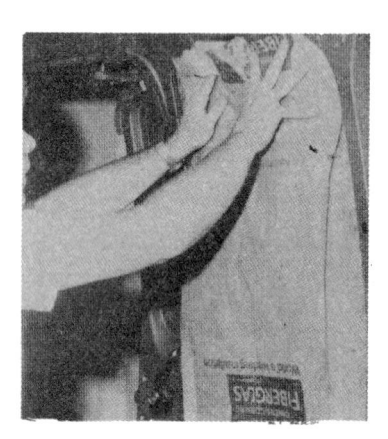

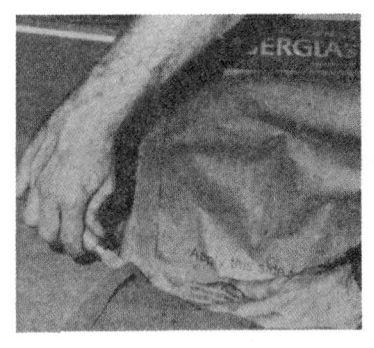

Fig. 31-14. Working around wheel well obstructions, insulation must be cut in angular shapes (photo by Brad Barcus).

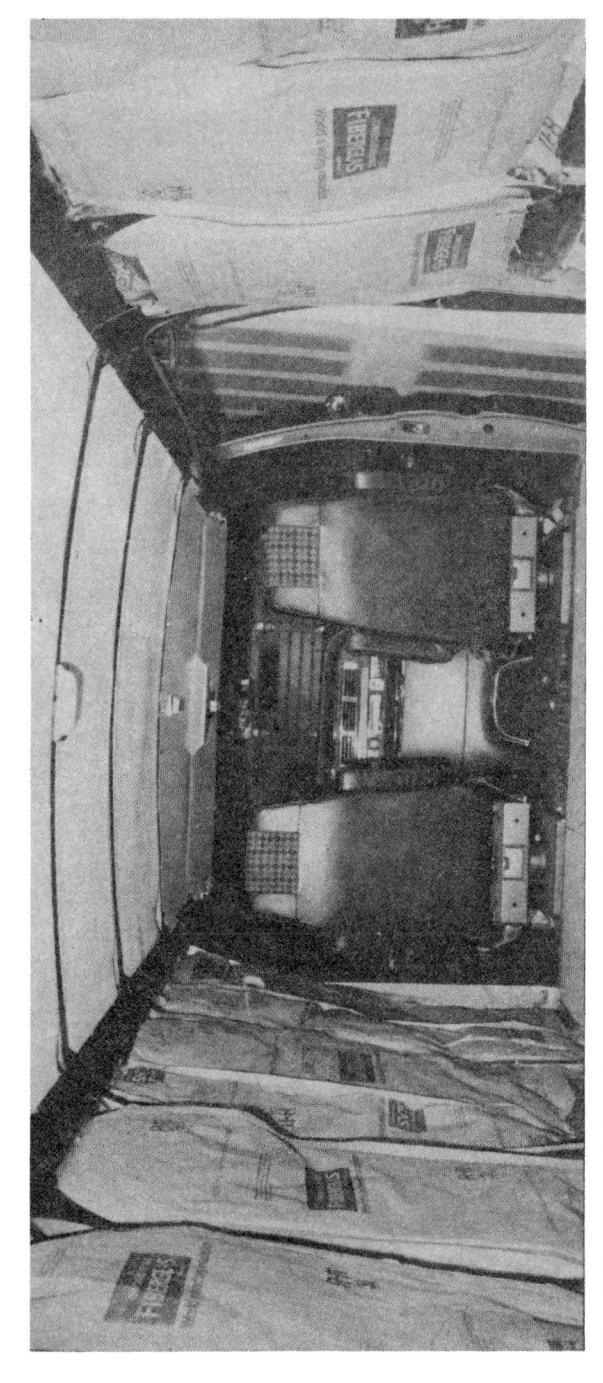

Fig. 31-15. Wide angle lens shows us the interior, fully insulated (photo by Brad Barcus).

Fig. 31-16. Since we're not quite ready for paneling, strips of pine hold fiberglass in place (photo by Brad Barcus).

Chapter 32

Installing a Sunroof

A sunroof is one of the best ways to keep hot air from accumulating in your van during a sunny summer day. It also looks good. If your van isn't equipped with automotive air-conditioning, it is a fine source of fresh air and can let the sunshine in.

We had been impressed with the quality of the products of the Stretch Forming Corporation when we did a story on the multitude of windows and port holes they produce, so we decided to use their sunroof on our van. We probably could have done the installation ourselves, but it gets very awkward to do the installation and the photography too. Since Craig Smith and his excellent Overland Enterprises of Van Nuys were already involved in our interior, we asked if he'd do the sunroof installation. He agreed.

Tools required to do a real professional job include: ¼-inch drill with ⅝-inch drill bit, phillips head screwdriver, tape measure, saber saw with metal cutting blades, thin and wide masking tape, caulking, wax and grease remover, air chisel, and a center punch.

After opening the box containing your sunroof, make sure the instruction sheet is handy. You'll be referring to it frequently. Next, check to see whether your instructions mention a template. Often an outline of the sunroof will be printed on the box and is designed to be used as a template. If so, cut it out and you're in clover. No template was called for in our kit. With Craig Smith looking in on the operation now and then, Jim Eck got on with the work at hand.

Step number one was locating the sunroof in the position it would occupy. This was just ahead of the cross support over the cockpit. The frame was then secured in position with masking tape. The masking tape was then applied all around the frame as a guide for the saber saw cuts to be

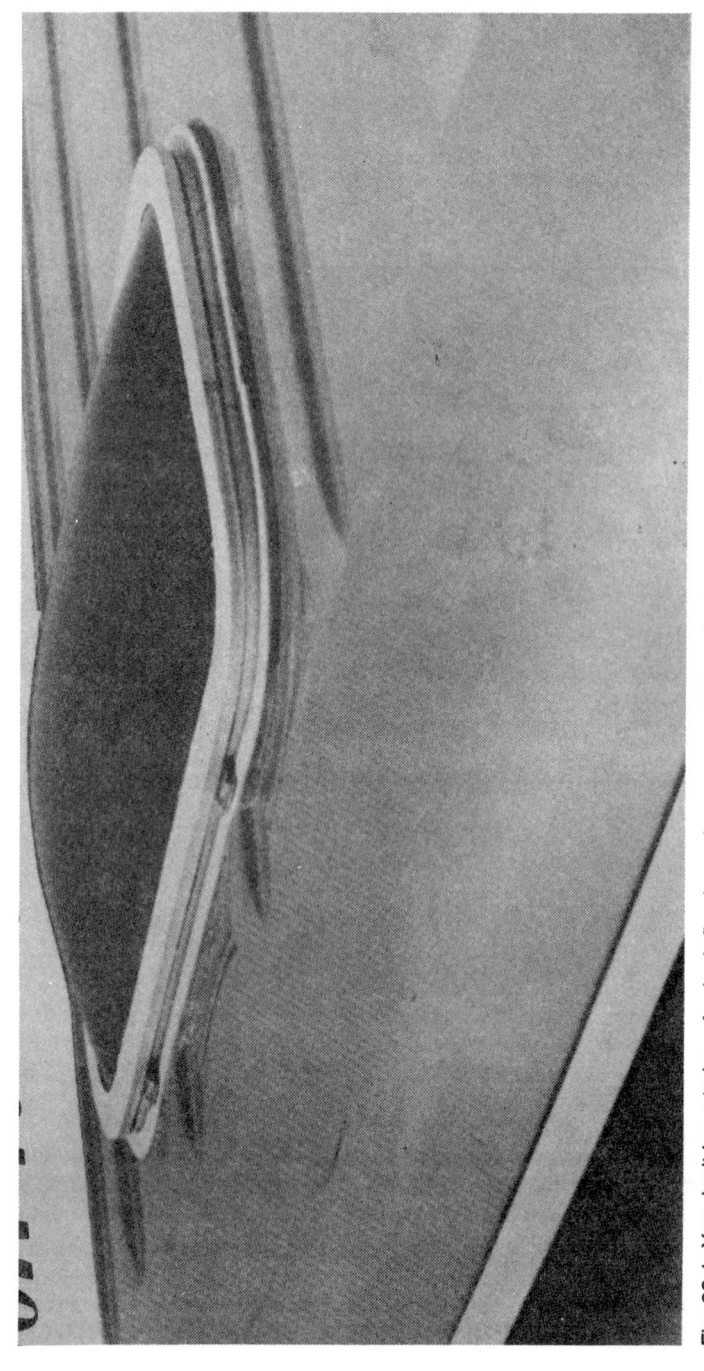

Fig. 32-1. You don't have to be a fresh air fiend to enjoy a sun roof (photo by Jim Matthews).

Fig. 32-2. Your sunroof looks like this when you open the box. Some boxes have templates printed on the cover (photo by Jim Matthews).

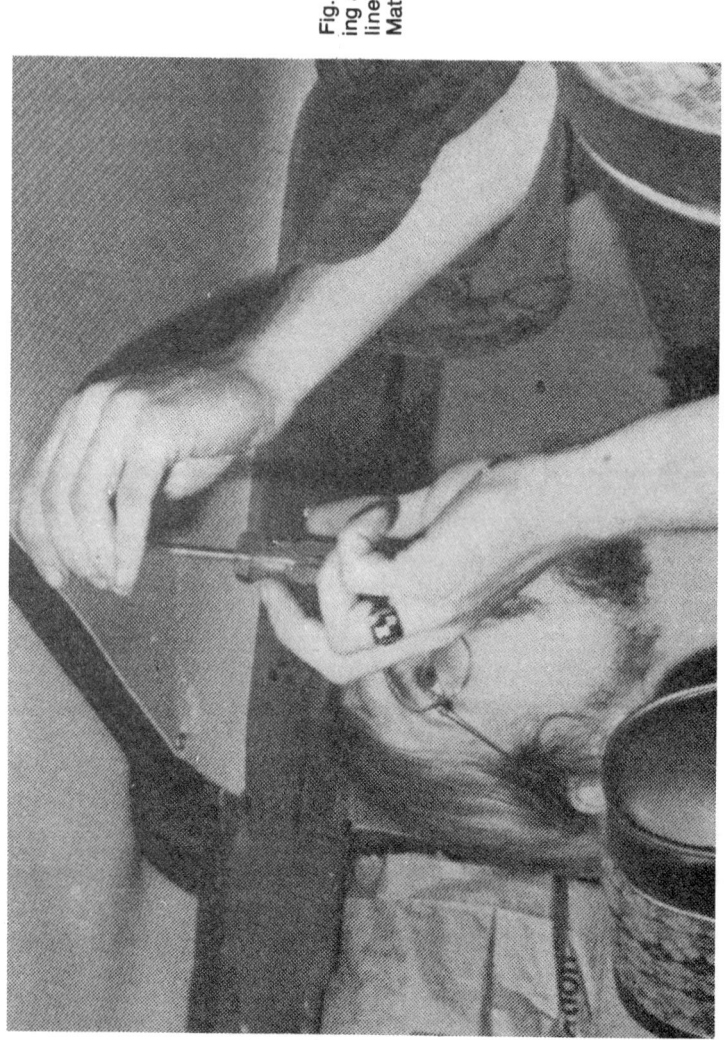

Fig. 32-3. In order to disconnect wiring and facilitate marking the headliner is removed (photo by Jim Matthews).

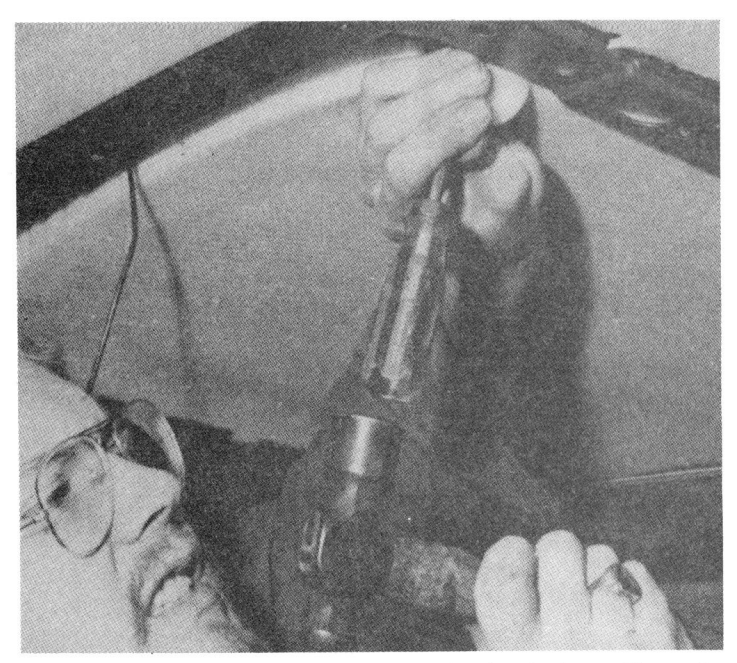

Fig. 32-4. A center punch is used to make a tiny dent in the roof for center alignment. Each side of the longitudinal braces is marked (photo by Jim Matthews).

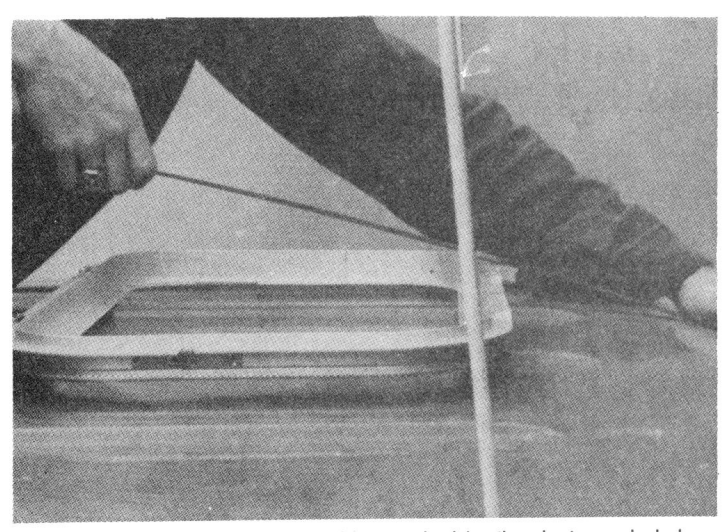

Fig. 32-5. On the roof, with the guides marked by the dents made below, measurements are carefully made for locating the sunroof frame (photo by Jim Matthews).

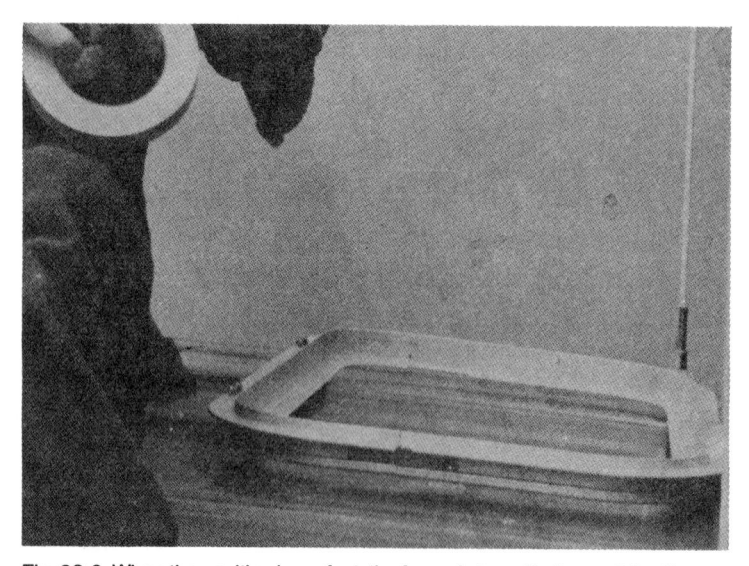

Fig. 32-6. When the position is perfect, the frame is taped to the roof. It will serve as a template (photo by Jim Matthews).

made. When the outline was established, 2-inch masking tape was placed outside the line to protect the roof from scratches.

Time now to go below into the cockpit, remove the headliner, and with the air chisel remove the longitudinal brace. If you can rent or borrow an air

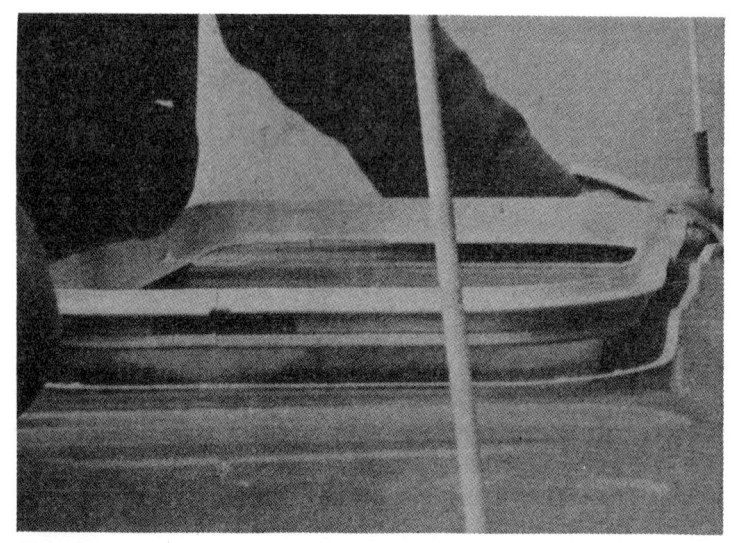

Fig. 32-7. Using thin masking tape and the "eye ball" method, the outline of the frame is made on the roof (photo by Jim Matthews).

Fig. 32-8. A surrounding, 2-inch wide (minimum) area of masking tape will protect the roof from scratches in the event a tool slips (photo by Jim Matthews).

chisel, your service station can provide compressed air.

From here on it's a matter of cutting and fitting. Our sunroof installation was photographed every step of the way (Figs. 32-1 through 32-26). With patience and courage (cutting a big hole in your roof is pretty scary) and following instructions, you should be able to install a sunroof yourself.

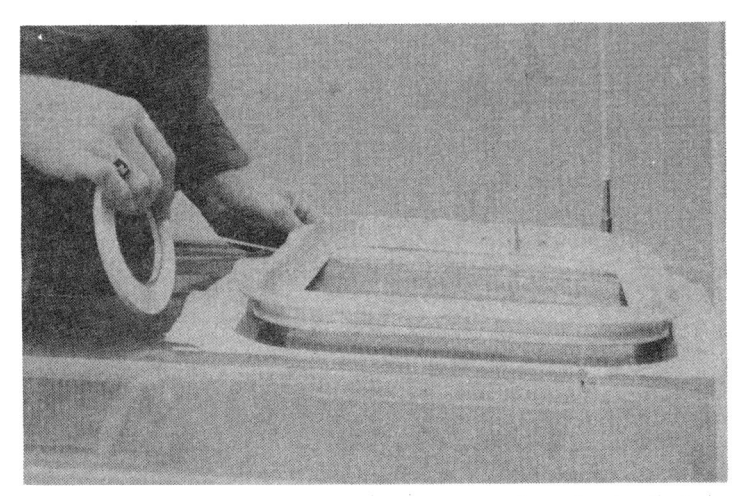

Fig. 32-9. An additional strip of narrower tape is placed, overlapping the inner edge of the original thin strip. This will allow the cut to be made within the masking tape (photo by Jim Matthews).

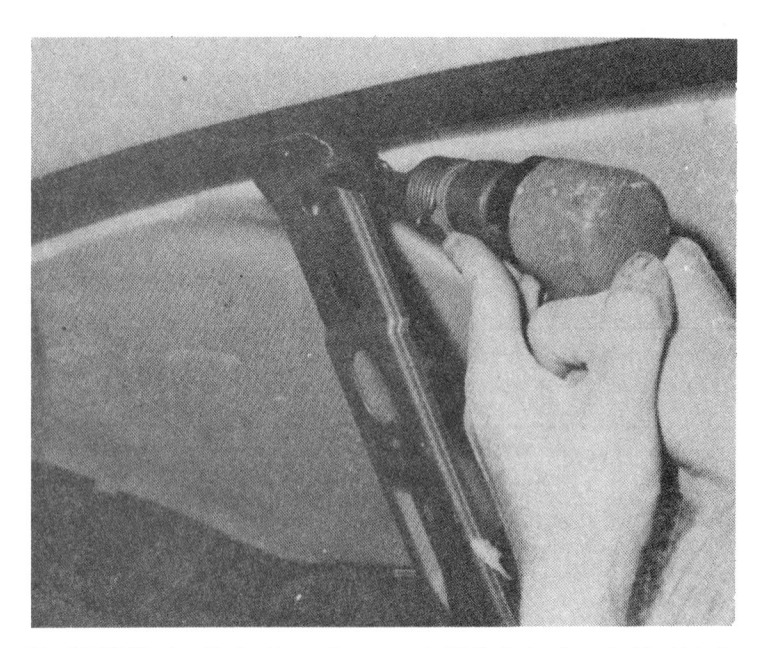

Fig. 32-10. The longitudinal brace is removed with the help of an air chisel (photo by Jim Matthews).

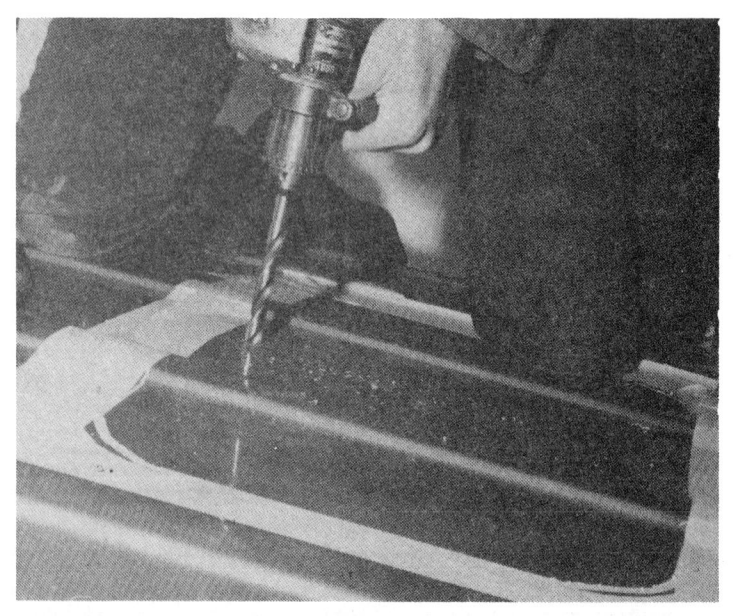

Fig. 32-11. Electric drill with ⅝-inch bit makes a hole as a starting point for the saber saw (photo by Jim Matthews).

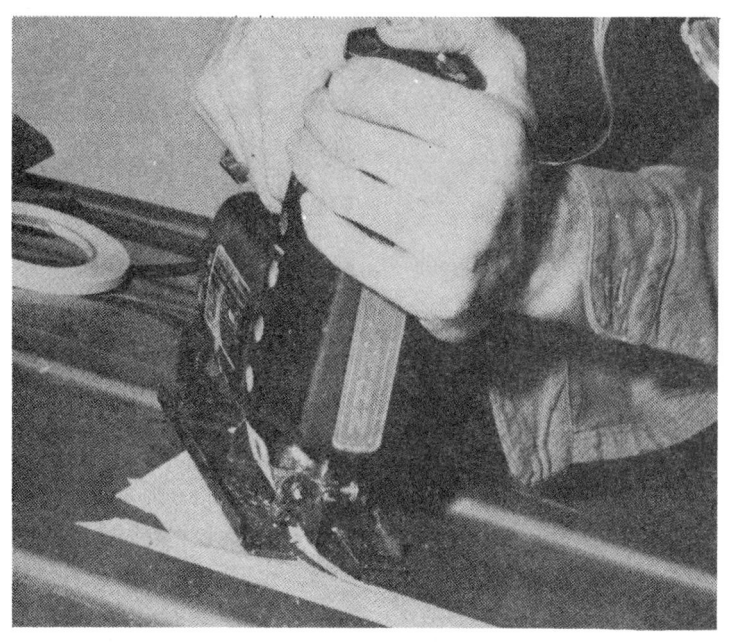

Fig. 32-12. Saber saw is a must. It will cut around corners and be handy for many future jobs (photo by Jim Matthews).

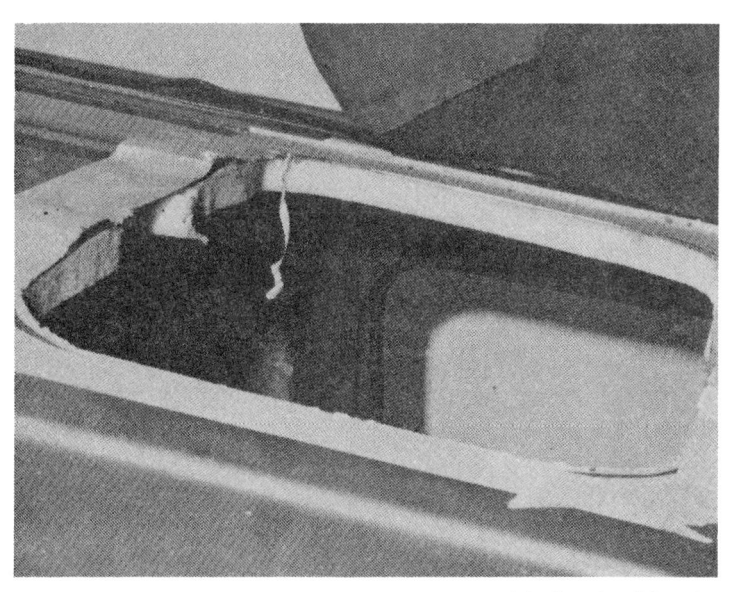

Fig. 32-13. It's a little scary to see that big hole in the roof the first time (photo by Jim Matthews).

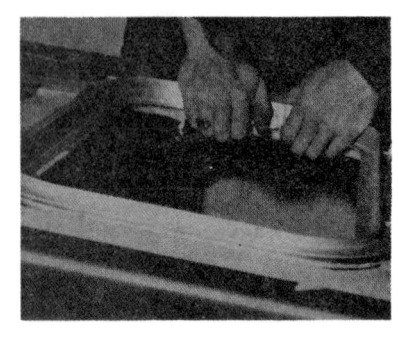

Fig. 32-14. Frame is fitted into the hole. Often a little additional trimming is necessary. Fit should be tight (photo by Jim Matthews).

Fig. 32-15. Headliner has been cut at the same time the steel roof section was cut (photo by Jim Matthews).

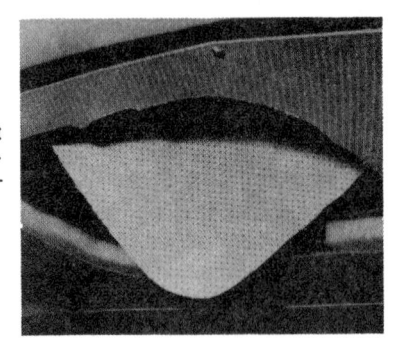

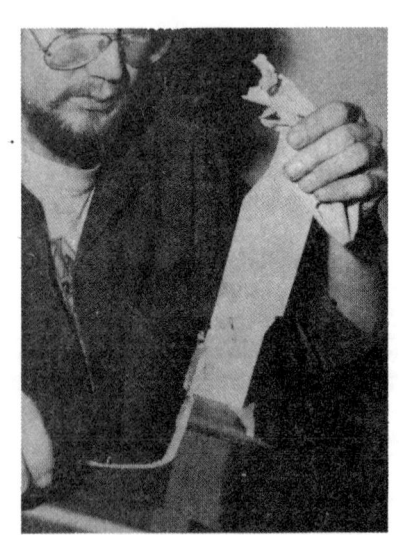

Fig. 32-16. All the masking tape may now be removed from the roof (photo by Jim Matthews).

Fig. 32-17. Caulking, which comes in large rolls, is applied around roof opening (photo by Jim Matthews).

Fig. 32-18. Caulking is also applied to the frame, making a double thickness (photo by Jim Matthews).

Fig. 32-19. With the frame in position, the caulking is pressed into the groove (photo by Jim Matthews).

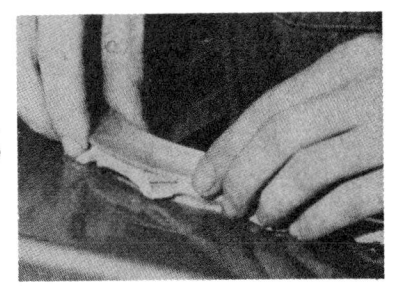

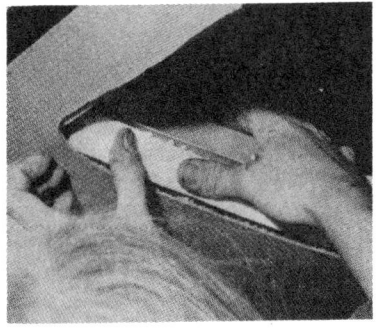

Fig. 32-20. Styrofoam pieces are pushed in place to give inner and outer frames a "bite," something to pull down on. Our kit did not contain the foam plastic. Overland Enterprises had extra pieces (photo by Jim Matthews).

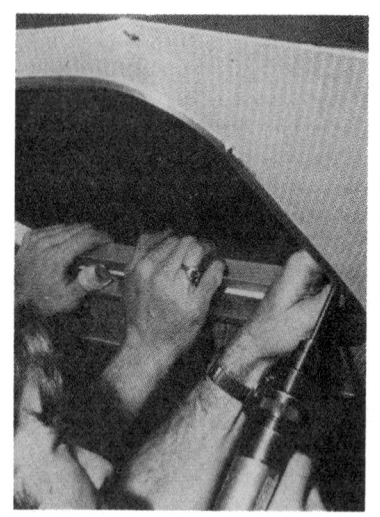

Fig. 32-21. An extra helping hand is brought in to tighten the self-tapping sheet metal screws and see that both frames remained aligned (photo by Jim Matthews).

Fig. 32-22. The view from below with inner and outer frames joined (photo by Jim Matthews).

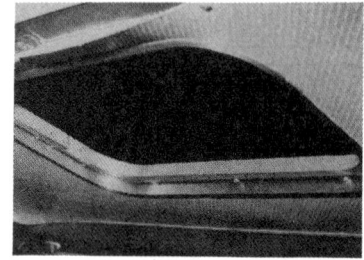

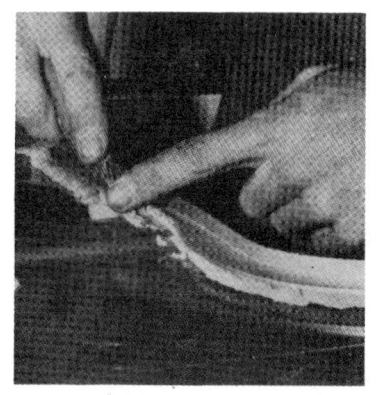

Fig. 32-23. Caulking will have been pressed out of the groove. As much as possible should be forced back, then trimmed (photo by Jim Matthews).

Fig. 32-24. Caulking material leaves sticky residue. Wax and grease cleaner removes gumminess and smooths edges for a finished look (photo by Jim Matthews).

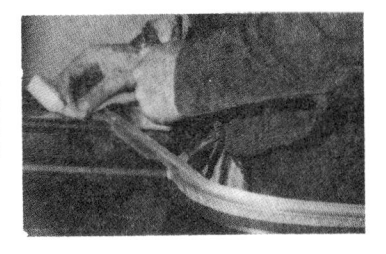

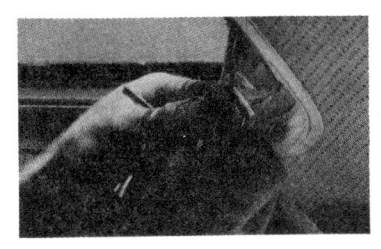

Fig. 32-25. Crank mechanism is installed from below after plastic "glass" portion has been hinged, up top (photo by Jim Matthews).

Fig. 32-26. The finished result. We have sun, light, and fresh air plus an exit for heat on a sunny day (photo by Jim Matthews).

Chapter 33

Installing Flares and Spoiler

While we were at Hooker Headers getting our van outfitted with sidepipes and headers, we were much impressed with the fiberglass shop and the flares and spoilers being made. When it came time to make our next major improvement in the rig's appearance (and legality), we made another visit to Hooker. Scott, who did most of the header installation, was joined by Tim, who does a lot of the flare installations.

Since this was to be a two-man installation procedure, our photo story is going to be a little jumpy. We moved from front to rear as various stages of the operation progressed. Nevertheless, the procedure is very similar, from front fender to rear. In our case, we had the flares and spoiler sent to our office. From there they were taken to World of Difference where Leon Killebrew sprayed them with paint of the exact matching color as the existing fenders. Hooker recommends the necessary holes be drilled before painting, but since Hooker experts would be doing the installing we weren't too worried about chips or scratches.

Before you get started, these are the tools, you'll need: ¼-inch drill, 3/16, 1/8, and 1/4 drill bits: pop rivet gun, three C-clamps or three vise grips, socket set, ice pick or stiff wire scribe, scissors, and a center punch.

The ideal method of installation is to borrow the hoist at your nearby friendly service station. If he's too busy, use jack stands (axle stands). Never do this kind of a job using a bumper jack.

The Hooker installation instructions are very complete and easy to follow. Rather than a narrative description of the step-by-step procedure. Figures 33-1 through 33-19 make the installation much easier to follow.

When you have your spoiler installed, you must immediately adopt a whole new style of defensive driving. Steep driveways that formerly could be taken with ease now present an expensive and formidable obstacle. At all

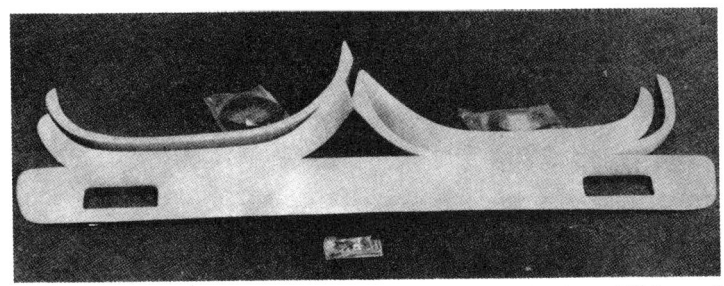

Fig. 33-1. This is the way the flares and spoiler looked before Leon Killebrew at World of Difference painted them (photo by Brad Barcus).

times you must remember that your ground clearance at the front has been reduced by about 6 inches.

We find ourselves in an admirable position from which to offer this advice. Our new spoiler wasn't on the van four days until we fell victim to a hazard in the form of an upright pipe in a parking lot. The pipe had anchored a wooden end strip, long gone. Unfortunately the pipe was also the color of the pavement. A day at Bruno's Corvette, fiberglass specialists in North Hollywood, California, made it as good as new, but we still had to go back to World of Difference and have Leon Killebrew spray it the matching color. So we learned the lesson we are passing on to you the hard way.

Fig. 33-2. At Hooker for the installation, we first removed all four wheels (photo by Brad Barcus).

Fig. 33-3. A number of C-clamps will be employed. This is about the right size (photo by Brad Barcus).

267

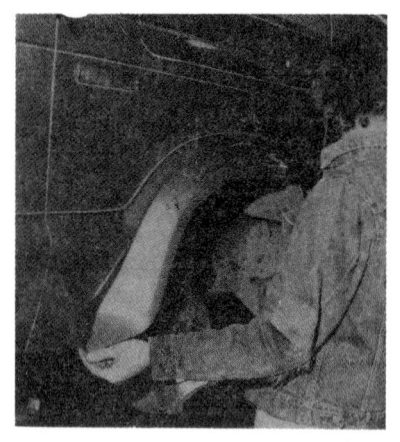

Fig. 33-4. The flare is positioned at the wheel well opening (photo by Brad Barcus).

Fig. 33-5. It is clamped in position using only the inner lip of the flare (photo by Brad Barcus).

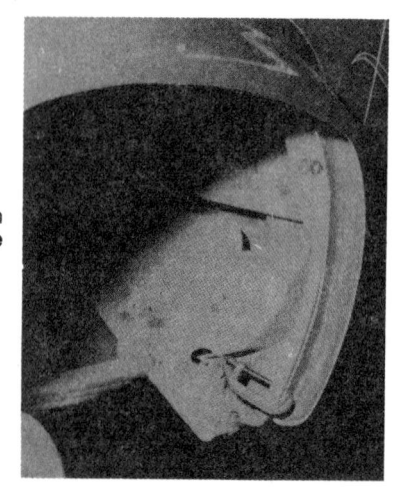

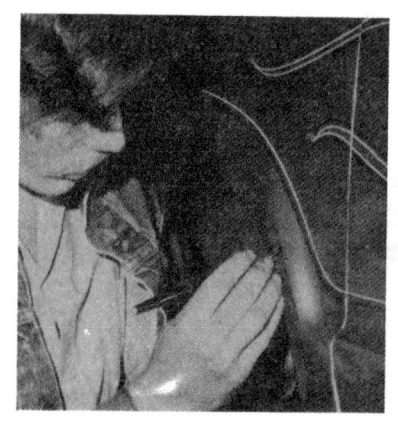

Fig. 33-6. Seven evenly spaced points are marked on the rear fender, nine on the front (photo by Brad Barcus).

Fig. 33-7. A center punch is used to facilitate drill starting (photo by Brad Barcus).

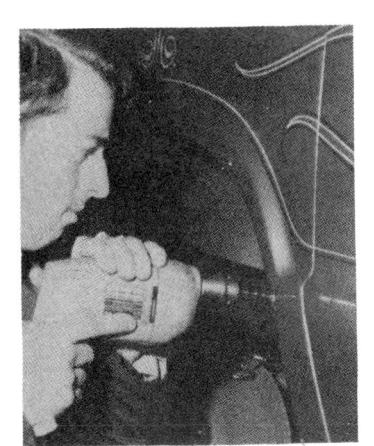

Fig. 33-8. Check the instructions carefully. Not all the holes are drilled the same size (photo by Brad Barcus).

Fig. 33-9. The flare is again cleaned in position after holes are drilled (photo by Brad Barcus).

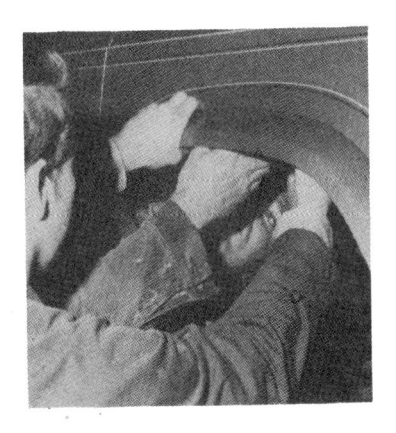

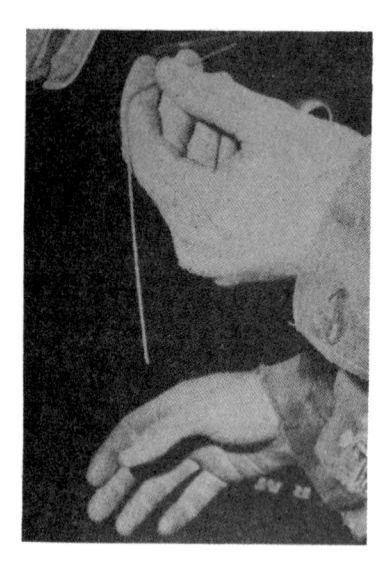

Fig. 33-10. An ice pick or stiff wire scribe is used to mark through the fender onto the flare (photo by Brad Barcus).

Fig. 33-11. Flares are removed, drilled at marked locations, then bolted loosely in position. Molding must be "V" notched to follow contour of fender and flare (photo by Brad Barcus).

Fig. 33-12. Molding is pressed between flare and fender making sure height is the same at all points. Then final tightening can occur. Each end of the flare is pop riveted (photo by Brad Barcus).

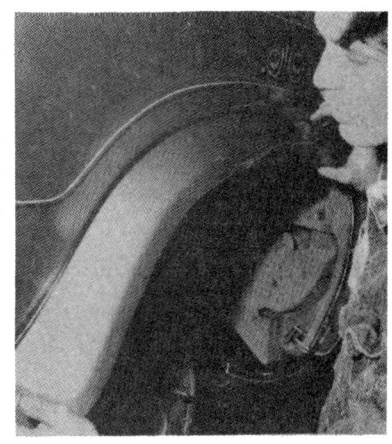

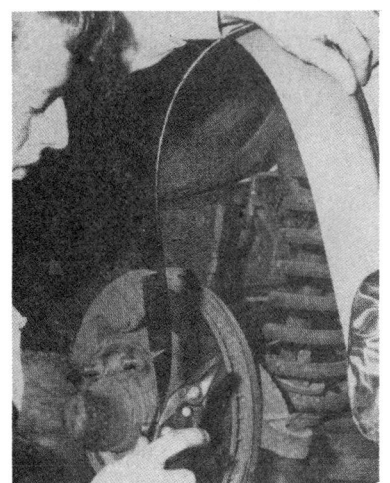

Fig. 33-13. Often additional "V" notches must be made if molding buckles (photo by Brad Barcus).

Fig. 33-14. The flare neatly covers the tire. There are no more problems with dirt on the body (photo by Brad Barcus).

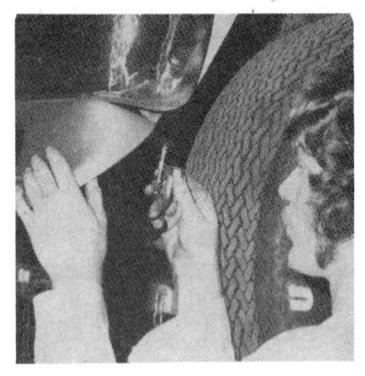

Fig. 33-15. Spoiler installation begins with the same C-clamps securing the spoiler to the front bumper (photo by Brad Barcus).

Fig. 33-16. The instructions call for seven, evenly spaced points to be marked for drilling. These are the nuts and bolts that will secure the spoiler to the bumper (photo by Brad Barcus).

Fig. 33-17. Holes must be centered in the lip of the spoiler to prevent cracking (photo by Brad Barcus).

Fig. 33-18. Drill bit size here is ¼-inch. Tim wears protective glasses during all metal drilling (photo by Brad Barcus).

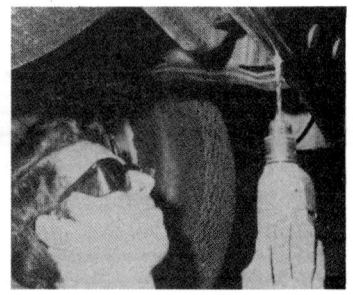

272

Fig. 33-19. Out in the daylight we present an image far removed from a delivery van (photo by Brad Barcus).

Chapter 34

Installing Maserati Air Horns

Did you ever wish you had a set of those powerful horns the big diesel 18 wheelers have? Ever want to move people out of the way in a hurry? Now you can, at a very modest cost and without the big compressor and tank the truckers have to have. The answer is a compact set of Maserati air horns imported and distributed by Vilem B. Haan of Los Angeles. The trick to the set is a small electric compressor and a very small but high pressure tank.

MOUNTING THE HORNS

The installation itself is not difficult. The complete and detailed instructions supplied with the air horn kit are given in five languages: English, German, French, Spanish, and Italian. Mounting the horns themselves is largely a question of finding a good location, under the hood or elsewhere concealed by the body, for the horns, the compressor, and the relay. There is some wiring involved, but this is covered in six schematic diagrams to fit all applications and either negative or positive ground.

Tools required for the job will be: small socket set, vise grip wrench, electric drill with ¼-inch bit, wire stripping tool, knife, screwdriver, and an in-line fuse.

Step number one is to mount the horns on the bracket supplied. Once this is accomplished, you can go looking for a place to locate them. The horns are only about 6 inches long, so a great deal of room is not required. Once you've found your spot, you can hold the bracket in place with the vise grips while you mark the spot to drill your holes.

With the trumpets mounted, you'll want to have a spot nearby staked out for the compressor. This unit should be mounted vertically.

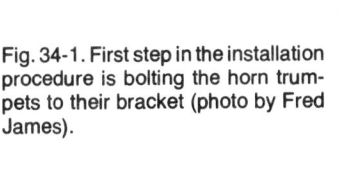

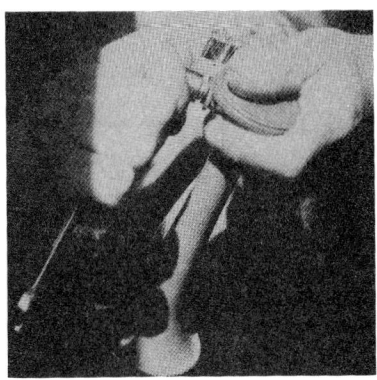

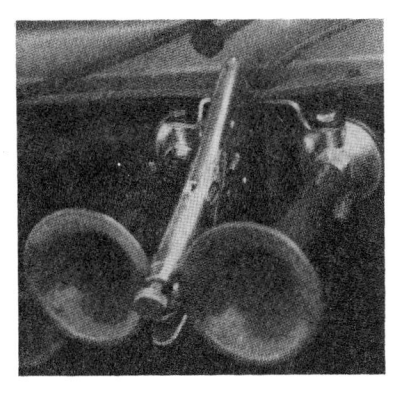

Fig. 34-1. First step in the installation procedure is bolting the horn trumpets to their bracket (photo by Fred James).

Fig. 34-2. Vise grip wrench holds horn assembly in position for marking holes (photo by Fred James).

PLASTIC AIR HOSES AND RELAY

Plastic air hoses are supplied with the kit along with a "Y." A little eyeball measuring will get you the right length from each horn to the "Y" and from the "Y" to the compressor. Hose lengths should be short so that the horns will respond the moment the horn button is actuated.

Fig. 34-3. Electric drill with ¼-inch bit makes holes for mounting brackets (photo by Fred James).

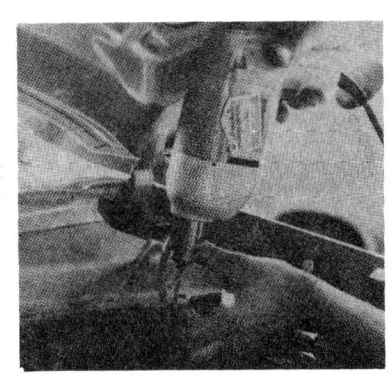

Fig. 34-4. We tried mounting them above the rail, but the hood wouldn't close. Horns should point slightly downward in the ideal position (photo by Fred James).

Fig. 34-5. Plastic tubing is supplied with the kit. Single tube goes from compressor to "Y" where tubing is carried to each horn. Tubing lengths should be short (photo by Fred James).

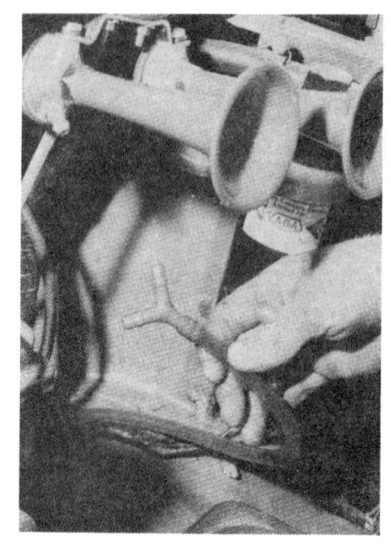

Fig. 34-6. Compressor is mounted vertically, here located on the firewall. All components should be as far as possible from heat sources (photo by Fred James).

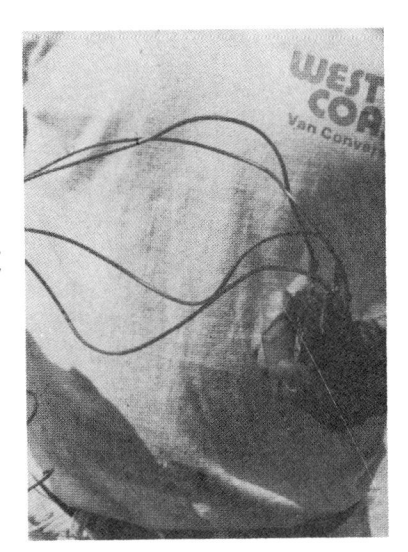

Fig. 34-7. Dan, of West Coast, has the relay wiring figured out (photo by Fred James).

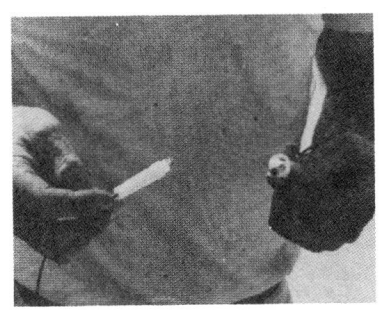

Fig. 34-8. Although the kit calls for a fuse, none is supplied (photo by Fred James).

The relay is where wiring expertise comes in. We had Dan, the electrical wizard at West Coast Van Conversion, do the installation. A few minutes of study with the complete wiring diagram and schematic was all he needed to hook everything up right.

Fig. 34-9. Relay unit secured to an inside surface. Kit warns to keep the relay out of the splash areas (photo by Fred James).

Fig. 34-10. The complete installation ready to blast through traffic or startle marauding dogs (photo by Fred James).

There are several ways you can go with the horn set up. You can have your stock horn sound in unison with the air horns, the air horns alone, with the stock horn bypassed or, with an auxiliary switch, have the air horn on a separate control. The wiring diagram gives you all of them.

One thing you'll quickly notice is the horns are loud. They are also piercing. They have that European high pitched blast—an unexpected side effect we learned by accident. We happened on a pair of dogs terrorizing a trash barrel. One blast of the air horns, and they dashed away. It must be an audio frequency they just can't stand.

We're very pleased with our Maserati air horns. We don't have a bit of trouble now moving traffic out of our way. See Figs 34-1 through 34-10.

Chapter 35

Installing a Roof Rack and Ladder

A roof rack and a ladder to reach it by are a very handy combination. The rack is dandy for strapping down all the extra things you find so useful, and the roof itself becomes a great spot for sun bathing when a ladder is available.

On one of our visits to Recreational Vans Incorporated (RVI) we spotted a van being built to special order for one of those "cost is no object" types. One of the things that caught our eye about the rig was a new style roof rack and ladder.

The ladder reminds one of the kind most often seen on expensive yachts. The steps are mahogany, the rails of both the roof rack and the ladder come to tapered points, and all the metal is hard chromed. The whole set looks expensive, and we'll get to that later.

A phone call to Tom Farmer, the merchandising man, assured us that we would be able to obtain one of these handsome sets, but not at any price could we have immediate delivery. The factory was already back ordered, and it had only been manufacturing for a few weeks.

Actually, the wait wasn't all that long and we were soon making a call to our handy neighbor West Coast Vans. Could they install a new style roof rack and ladder? They could.

The set comes complete with all mounting hardware and excellent instruction sheets. The logical way to go is to install the ladder first to give yourself an easy way to the roof for the rack installation. For tools you'll need: felt tip pen, electric drill, 9/64-inch bit, screwdriver bit or large screwdriver, and caulking compound.

279

MOUNTING THE LADDER

The ladder comes completely assembled, all you have to do is mount it. The initial step is a two-person job, one to hold the ladder in place, the other to mark the location of the first sheet metal screw using a center punch and hammer. Be sure of your location. If you're not, use a felt tip pen or a pencil. With the first hole location marked the rest is clear sailing. Each sheet metal screw tip should receive caulking compound to ensure a watertight installation. Henry, of West Coast Vans, placed a small strip of masking tape over each of the ladder's mounting pads as a precaution against scratching the van's paint.

After the initial sheet metal screw is loosely in position, align the ladder with either the center line or some other vertical line and position of one of the holes in the bottom pad of the ladder. Check the ladder alignment, and then the remaining 9/64-inch holes can be drilled. When all the screws have been driven in, the job is complete.

ROOF RACK

The roof rack takes a little more time primarily because there are more measurements to be made and more holes to be drilled. The short, straight, end rail is positioned first, and here it's a good idea to use a felt tip

Fig. 35-1. The rack is fully assembled when you buy it. All hardware and instructions are provided (photo by Brad Barcus).

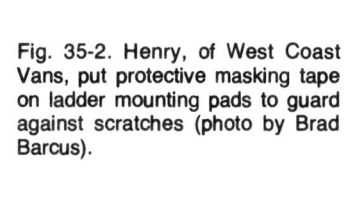

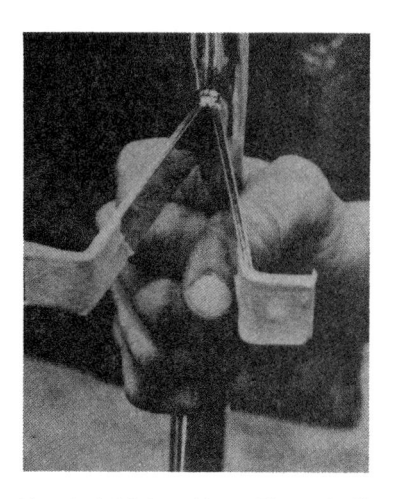

Fig. 35-2. Henry, of West Coast Vans, put protective masking tape on ladder mounting pads to guard against scratches (photo by Brad Barcus).

pen rather than the center punch in making the initial markings. The end rail is usually located 5 to 6 inches from the rear of the van with care being taken to position the end rail centered in relation to the center line of the van. Once you're sure of the location you can drill your 9/64-inch holes and secure the rail, again using caulking compound on the sheet metal screws.

The side rails are next aligned with the already installed end rail with equal spacing on both sides. Before drilling your holes, check the center line alignment of both rails.

The instructions carry a special note for late model Dodge and Chevy vans. A spacer pad and longer sheet metal screw (provided) are required under one rack foot on each side.

The instructions also point out that the excellent chrome should be given the care it deserves. Polish regularly with a quality chrome polish. The wood of the ladder is high grade mahogany and, the instructions say, will withstand normal wear. The wood may bleach from the sun which will not affect the mahogany. If original color is desired, the steps may be

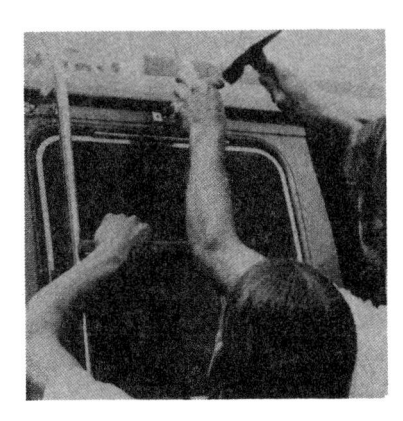

Fig. 35-3. This is the only two-person stage of the mounting operation. One holds the ladder in position; the other marks the drilling spot with a center punch (photo by Brad Barcus).

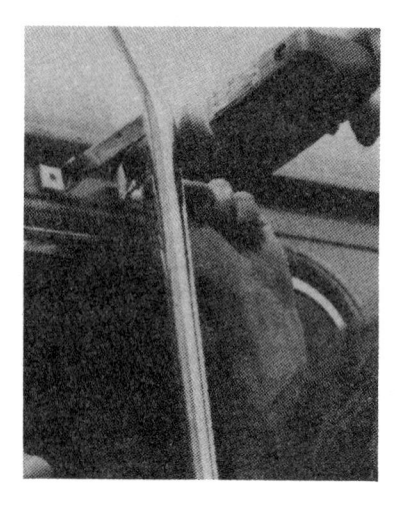

Fig. 35-4. First sheet metal screw is inserted using screwdriver bit on the electric drill (photo by Brad Barcus).

restained with a medium walnut wood stain. No varnish is needed. We use an oily furniture polish on ours.

Now we promised a word on the cost. For all it's sharp appearance, the set carries a suggested retail price of $139.95, but we don't have a merchandising name for them. They'll be marketed by TGF Sales, 3152 Newell Drive, Riverside, CA 92507. The Manufacturer is J-M Industries of Los Alamitos, California. See Figs. 35-1 through 35-14.

Fig. 35-5. After alignment is checked, position for the sheet metal screw is marked on the lower pad (photo by Brad Barcus).

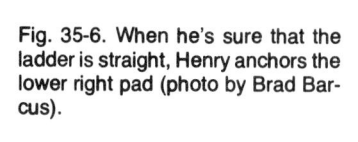

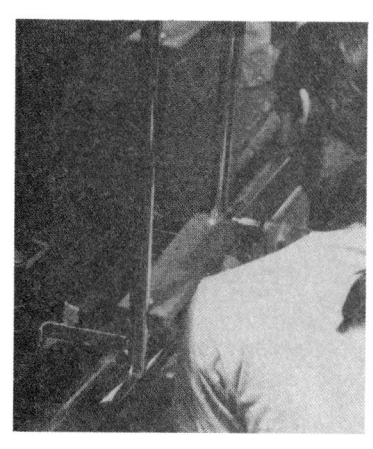

Fig. 35-6. When he's sure that the ladder is straight, Henry anchors the lower right pad (photo by Brad Barcus).

Fig. 35-7. Balance of screws are cinched down after each has received a dab of caulking compound to ensure waterproofing installation.

Fig. 35-8. Climbing up the newly installed ladder, Henry takes all rack parts to the roof. A short, straight, end piece will be mounted first (photo by Brad Barcus).

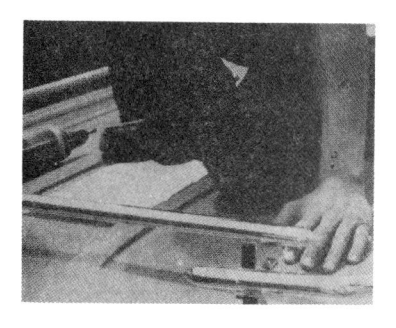

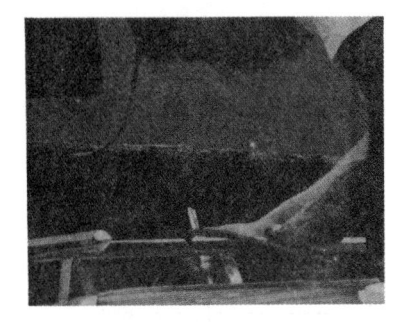

Fig. 35-9. With the position for the end piece determined, side rail locations are checked (photo by Brad Barcus).

Fig. 35-10. End rail is bolted to the roof using sheet metal screws (photo by Brad Barcus).

Fig. 35-11. Each of the screws used in the installation receives a small coating of caulking compound (photo by Brad Barcus).

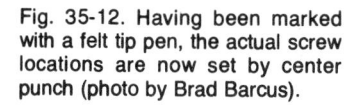

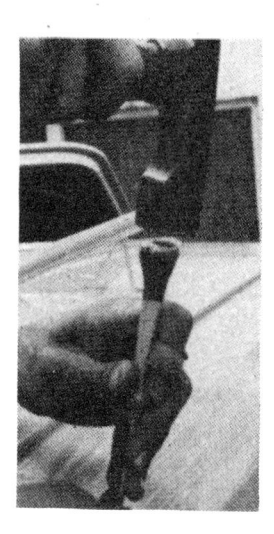

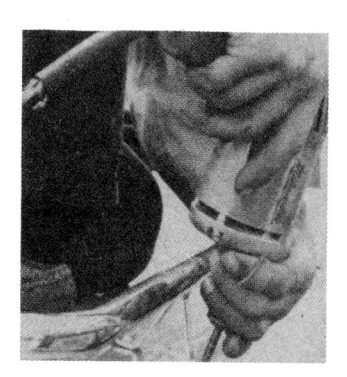

Fig. 35-12. Having been marked with a felt tip pen, the actual screw locations are now set by center punch (photo by Brad Barcus).

Fig. 35-13. From here on out, it's a question of cinching down 12 sheet metal screws (photo by Brad Barcus).

Fig. 35-14. The finished job: a rich yachting look with mahogany steps and hard chrome finish (photo by Brad Barcus).

Index

a

Acetylene torch	100
Adapter	89
Addco Industries	192
Air chisel	222
Air cleaner	177
Air filter, Filtron	19
Air horns, Masarati	274
mounting	274
Air hoses, plastic	275
Alternator	199
AMC Jeepster	176
Analyzer, exhaust gas	86
Antisway bars	192

B

Baja conversion kit	30
Baja 500	16
Ball joints	188
Bass, Don	177
Batteries, dual	193
Blazer	5, 20, 100
facelifting	152
Bolts, hex	187
Bono, Sonny	174
Bottom dead center	42
Brackets	152
Bronco	20

Bronco power-steering unit	1
Brush guard	100
Hickey	19
Bumper guard	100
Bumper jack	230
Bumpers, Datsun	114

C

C-clamp	157
Cab protection, GMC Sierra	169
Cabinet work	248
California Highway Patrol	124
Cam, Crower Baja	2
off-road	43
RV	47
Sig Erson RV-10-H cam	42
Camaro Z-28 engine	13
Cam lobe	41
base circle	41
clearance ramps	41
flanks	42
heel	41
nose	41

Camshafts	10, 38
Capacitive discharge units	116
Carburetors, Impco	177
Catalog, Hayden Cooler	91
Caulking compound	105
CB radio	123
Cement, contact	25
Center punch	257
Cepek, Dick	16
Chain-drive conversion	10
Chain saw	133
Channel bar	165
Cibie driving lights	19
Clifford Computerized Preprogrammed Locks	128
Cloyes roller chain	57
Coat hanger	75
Commando Jeep	168
Compression ratio	8
Compressor	274
CompuSensor ignition system	116
Contact cement	25
Conversion, chain-drive	10
Courier	1
four-wheel-drive mini-truck	30
liquid petroleum gas (LPG)	174
Converter	180
Coolers, engine oil	88
Hayden	96
Rapid Cool	96
Slim Line	96
Space Saver	96
Cooper, Spike	176
Courier	1
conversion	1
modifications	3
C-P Auto Products	19
Cragar SS wheels	209
Crankshaft	41
Crower Baja cam	2

D

Dana/Spicer front driveshaft	32
Dana transfer case	32
Datsun	30
Datsun bumpers	114
Desert Dynamics side-door extender	16
Dipstick	81
Distributor breaker-point	115
LED-type	116
Divi-Charge isolator	193
Dog house	19
Door extender	209
Dome light	28
Driveshaft, Dana/Spicer front	32
Driving lights, Cibie	19

E

Edelbrock Torker manifold	2
Electric drill	275
Electric window installation	67
Engine, assembly	13
Camero Z-28	13
internal combustion	115
preparation	13
small-block Chevy	5
V-8	1
Eshelman, Dave	230
Exhaust manifold	81
Exhaust pipes	81
installation	84

F

Fay step bumper	19
Fenders, fiberglass	4

Fiberglass	246
Filter, spin-on	89
Filtron air filter	19
Firestone tires	3
Flanges	78
Flares	270
installing	266
Flooring installation	221
Flywheel	6
Foam rubber	246
Formula 1 Super Stock L60 tires	209
Four-wheel-drive mini-truck conversions	30
Freon	112
Fuel Lock, Gora	125
Fuel tank, auxiliary	201

G

Gabriel shocks	1
Gaskets	82
Gas shocks, KYB	32
Gear ratio	7
Gears	6
Glue	248
GMC Sierra cab protection	169
GMC Sierra pickup	168
GMC Sierra suspension	168
Goodyear Wranglers	169
Gora Fuel Lock	125
Grille guard	100
Grommets, rubber	240
Guard, brush	100
bumper	100
grille	100
Gun, pop rivet	266

H

Haan, Vilem	67
Hardware	152
Harmonic damper	55
Hayden Cooler	96
Hayden Cooler catalog	91
Headers	8, 230
function	230
installation	230
Headlights	153
Headliner	25
Heating, oil	91
Heco steering stabilizer	16
Hex bolts	187
Hice, Eddy	209
Hickey brush guard	19
Hickey skid plates	19
Hole saw	139
Hood realignment	104
Hood Stiff'Ners	102
Hooker Headers	266
Hub, Warn	171
Hurst shift kit	2

I

Ice pick	266
Ignition system	115
CompuSensor	115
Impco carburetors	176
Intake manifolds	10
Edelbrock Streetmaster	11
Holly Street Dominator	11
Ionization voltage	183

J

Jacobs, Chris	123
Jacobs Electrical Products	122
Jacobs Stop Action System	124
Jeep	20
Jeepster, AMC	176
J-hook	186
J-M Industries	282

K

Kal Kustom kit	23
KC Daylighters	4
K-C rocker switches	22
Key lock	126
Killebrew, Leon	267
Kit	
Baja conversion	30
Kal Kustom	23
Trans-Go	143
KYB gas shocks	32
KYB shocks	19

L

Ladder	279
mounting	280
Leaf spring	189
Lift	
cam	42
Lifters	45
Light, dome	28
Lines	
brake	237
fuel	237
Liquid petroleum gas (LPG)	174
Liquid petroleum gas conversion	174
advantages	179
disadvantages	184
Locking hubs	171
removing	171
replacing	171
Warn	32
Lug wrench	33

M

Mahogany	281
Manifold	
Edelbrock Torker	2
exhaust	81
intake	10
Marchal quartz iodides	169
Maserati air horns	274
Masking tape	253
Mazda	30
Mercury Tool and Engineering Company	143
MIG welder	31
Molding	271
Montague, Bill	110
Moody, Gary	174
Mufflers	
low-restriction	80
slip-in	241

N

National Off-Road Racing Association	16
Nelis, Greg	23
Neoprene	197
Nitrogen	113
Nut, rocker stud	47

O

Off-Road Chassis Engineering	110
Oil cooler	
function of	89
installation of	89
Perma-Cool	89
Oil filter	89
Oil heating	91
O-rings	171
Overlap	43

P

Particle board	221
Pearlman, Ed	16
Pellandini, Rene	67
Pickup, GMC	
four-wheel-drive	50
Pine	248
Pipe cutter	238

Pipes, exhaust	81
Piston, floating	113
Pitman arm	1
Plyacell	112
Plywood	221
Power-steering unit, Bronco	1
Propane	175
Pump	
air conditioning	50
power steering	50
smog	50
Push rods	41
PVT plastics	152

Q

Quadravan	16
transformation	16
Quartz iodides, Marchal	169

R

Racks, rigid	185
Radiator	94
Raiser blocks	168
Rapid Cool cooler	96
Ratchet	147
Ratio	
compression	8
gear	7
Recreational Vans Incorporated	279
Relay	277
Rigid racks	185
Rocker arms	41
Rocker panel	166
Rocker switches, K-C	22
Roll bar	4
Roller chain, Cloyes	57
Roof rack	279
side rails	281
Roof scoop	217
Roof vent	217
Rough Country shocks	168
Rucker, Johnnie	89
Ruff Rider Grille	152
Running boards	157
EZ-Sider	157

S

Saber saw	221
Santana, Johnny	78
Scoop, roof	217
Scout	20
Screwdriver	274
Phillips head	157
spin tight	147
Screws	
hex-head	90
self-tapping	240
sheet metal	221, 281
Tec	221
Seat belts	16
Superior Industries	18
Seats	16
Security systems	123
Shift kit, Hurst	2
Shock absorbers	10, 189
hydraulic	110
telescopic	111
Shocks	
Armstrong	190
Dutch Koni	190
Gabriel	1, 190
KYB	19
monotube	112
M/T	109
OEM	107
performance	107
Rough Country	168
twin-tube	111
Side-door extender, Desert Dynamics	16
Sidemounts	232
Universal	240

Sidepipes, hooking up	238
Sig Erson RV-10-H cam	42
Skid plates, Hickey	19
Slim Line cooler	96
Smith, Craig	253
Smittybilt	19
Socket set	266
Space Saver cooler	96
Spark plugs	81
Specialty Equipment Manufacturers Association	67
Spirit level	157
Spoiler, installing	266
Springs	47
Stabilizer bars	191
Steering stabilizer, Heco	16
Step bumper, Fay	19
Stephan Wood Products	185
Stereo, 8-track	4
Stop Action system, Jacobs	124
Straightedge	221
Stretch Forming Corporation	253
Suburbans	102
Sunroof	253
installation	253
Superior Industries seat belts	18
Suspension, GMC Sierra	168
rear	188
Sweeney, Tim	168
Swinging step	165

T

Tab-lock washers	171
Tappets	41
Techne Electronics Ungo Box	133
Template	253
Tetrafluoroethylene	114
Timing figures	42
Tires	
Firestone	
Formula 1 Super	3
Stock L60	209
Top dead center	42
Torch, acetylene	100
Torque, reactive	192
Torque output	6
Torsion	191
Toyota	30
Transfer case, Dana	32
Trans-Go kit	143
Transmission, automatic	6
Trippedi, Mike	152

U

Ungo Box, Techne Electronics	136
Unistop Stop Hit	136
Universal sidemounts	240
U.S. Army	185

V

Valve	
exhaust	38
intake	38
Valve train	38
Van interior, insulating	246
Vehicle theft	123
V-8 engine	1
Vent, roof	217
Vilen B. Haan Inc.	136
Vise grips	157
Voltage ionization	183

W

Wagoneer	174
Warn hub	171
Warn locking hubs	32
Washers	
flat	240

lock	240	Wire stripper	75
tab-lock	171	World War II	185
Welder, MIG	31	Wrench	
West Coast Van		box	157
Conversions	67	lug	33
West Coast Vans	157	open end	157
Wheel wells	248		
Wheels, Cragar SS	209	**Y**	
Wilson, Bill	193	Yellow Pages	101
Windows, electric	67	Younger, Gil	143